The
New Vegetarian

*Clockwise from top left: Mixed fruit salad,
Terrine rose on a bed of cous cous, Lettuce and
egg mould with Jajiki, (see pages 125, 163, 123,
162 and 190).*

The
New Vegetarian

Cooking with Style the Vegetarian Way

Colin Spencer

Foreword by Wolfgang Puck

VIKING

A GAIA ORIGINAL

Editorial Research	Patricia Burgess Miren Lopategui
Design	Sara Mathews
Illustrations	Alison Wisenfeld

Photography
  Backgrounds
  Glossary
	David Johnson
	Tim Stevens
	Philip Dowell

Stylist	Kit Johnson
Home economist	Berit Vinegrad
Nutritionist	Michèle Sadler
Direction	Joss Pearson Lucy Lidell
Production	David Pearson

VIKING
Viking Penguin Inc.
40 West 23rd Street,
New York, New York 10010, U.S.A.

First American Edition
Published in 1986

Title, Design, Illustrations and Concept
copyright © Gaia Books Ltd., 1986
Copyright © Colin Spencer, 1986
All rights reserved

The copyrights to the recipes contributed by guest
cooks are owned by the individual authors.

Library of Congress Cataloging in Publication Data
Spencer, Colin.
    The new vegetarian.
    Includes index.
    1. Vegetarian cookery. I. Title.
TX837.S6883 1986   641.5′636   85-41097

ISBN 0-670-81271-4

Printed in Italy by Mondadori, Verona
Set in Great Britain by Marlin Graphics Ltd.,
Orpington, Kent
Reproduction by Anglia Reproductions Ltd.,
Witham, Essex.

Author's acknowledgements

Because this book attempts to explore a new kind of
vegetarian cooking, it is, I believe, even more in debt
to the mentors who have influenced me in the past.
There are always the nameless cooks across the world
who have astonished and pleased one with an
original combination of foods and flavours. But one is
most grateful when intelligence and food meet in a
crisp evaluation and a telling phrase. No one can
write about food without a debt of gratitude to
Elizabeth David. But there are also now other cooks
and writers who have looked at vegetables in a fresh
light – Madhur Jaffrey, David Scott, Arto der
Harounian and Josceline Dimbleby, to name a few. I
am also thankful to Patrick Rance – the doyen of
cheese – for his information on vegetable rennet.
    In conclusion, I must also thank the team at Gaia
who ate and complained until dishes and recipes
were recreated, and my editors, Trish Burgess, Miren
Lopategui and Mindy Werner who were
indefatigable in taming my excesses and leading a
comma back home.

Publisher's acknowledgements

Gaia Books would like to thank John, Alan, Ken, Paul
and Barry at Marlin Graphics, Mike, Steve and
Malcolm at Anglia Repro, Lesley Gilbert for word
processing, Paul Holloway for design assistance,
Andy and Ruth for photography assistance, and
Norma Macmillan for checking Americanization.

Foreword

Growing up in Austria, I remember the wonderful taste of fresh vegetables picked first thing in the morning, simply sautéed and served with a soft-boiled egg and a little butter. This fills my memory as one of the most delicious meals I have ever had, as good as any I have eaten in fine restaurants.

Today, vegetables have moved from the shadows of the dinner plate and are elevated to the starring role as exciting appetizers and main courses. Centuries ago, the ancient Indian, Chinese and Middle Eastern cultures understood the benefits of vegetables, and prepared many lavish feasts focusing mainly on vegetables, herbs and spices.

My kitchen is no longer in the countryside, alongside rows of corn and beans, but a nearby family of farmers grows vegetables with the same careful tending of those country farmers. Vegetables and salads grown in a garden with close attention are best, since they are always fresh and picked at the peak of their flavour. My special passion for baby vegetables is due to their intensity of flavour and tastes which are enhanced by simple cooking with fresh herbs.

This beautiful and informative book offers so many interesting recipes, that I'm convinced it will enlarge your culinary horizon.

Wolfgang Puck

Top to bottom: Stir-fried beans and tofu with umeboshi plums, Clear celestial soup and Mixed steamed vegetables (see pages 242 and 112)

Contents

The Happy Vegetarian

Twelve years ago, in the context of a world awakening to famine, I made the decision to stop eating meat. It was an ethical choice that I felt comfortable with.

My friends took a dim view. They regarded the step as, at best, cranky, and at worst, evidence that I had taken leave of my senses. How would I, a gourmet, survive? It was useless for me to protest that I could dine on truffles and champagne, and take my pick of the world's many vegetarian cuisines. Useless to point out that choosing to 'live lightly off the land' did not mean I intended to forget haute cuisine, insult my guests' digestion and become a bore. My critics gloomily presaged a regime of brown rice, soggy nut rissoles, leaden puddings and a morbid trend into malnutrition, sandals and the spouting of revolutionary verses.

There is thus a pleasant irony for me in the health boom today, and the now fashionable status of low meat diets and whole foods. But I take a genuine delight in the popularity of the new vegetarianism - that elegant usurper of Cuisine Minceur and Cuisine Nouvelle, the Cuisine Verte which I hope I have helped to create. Long may it flourish and grow! There is no menu more lively, more enlightening, more a celebration of life itself.

Even today, however, new vegetarians may find their friends looking askance, and feel themselves unwelcome at a dinner party or in a restaurant. So in case you too are accused of brown rice, sandals, and spouting verses, I lay out for you here all the cogent facts with which you can reply.

First and foremost, vegetarian food is delicious - varied, tasty, digestible and full of fresh delights - menus are creative, and dishes rarely go wrong. It is the meat-eater's menu whch is more often narrow, unappetizing, and occasionally inedible - the leathery steak, dire stew, and foulest of battery-fed fowls. How often have you sat in a restaurant, assessing the prospects for a good meal, and wished you could eat only the hors d'oeuvres and the desserts? Those mushrooms in garlic, or artichoke hearts in batter, followed by that enticing crème brûlée or fresh strawberries and lychees? Who wants that doubtful fish, smothered in sauce, with all the little bones to fidget with? Or that massive steak, which is probably tough, and will certainly give you heartburn? Rather the crisp, exotic salad, dark bread with exciting cheeses and delicately flavoured vegetable pâtés and terrines.

Many cultures of the world are largely vegetarian, and provide a rich resource of recipes - from the Mediterranean dishes to the African, from Mexican chillies to Indian curries, from Chinese delicacies to Jamaican snacks. Indeed, the vegetarian tradition in cuisine is as old as civilization and has an honourable record. Outside Western society, a predominantly meat diet has been eaten mainly from necessity, not from choice - by people who cannot grow crops or gather plant foods - the ice and desert dwellers, and nomadic hunters.

The practically minded may like to point out that vegetarian living is inexpensive - a feast of delicacies for the plant eater can cost no more than a dull everyday meal for the carnivore. Vegetarian foods also keep well; even without a freezer, vegetarians need never get home from work and find nothing to cook because they could not get to the shops that day. If tired with mundane routine, the vegetarian need not even cook at all - bread, fruit, nuts, seeds, cheese and fresh vegetable crudités are fine uncooked - a raw steak is a different matter.

There are even those who argue that vegetarianism must be better because it is 'natural' - the foods are natural, and the diet is natural to us, because humans as a species were originally vegetarian (an argument spelled out further in Chapter 1).

All these arguments are of primary importance to our palate and our purse, and our pleasure in life. But there are more serious matters to consider. George Bernard Shaw once said, 'Vegetarianism strikes at the root of all evil'. His words seem prophetic now, as the arguments mount up and the consequences of an overcrowded, ill-managed human society become apparent.

First of all the more important reasons for vegetarianism is the one I began with myself - the world food situation. A vegetarian diet exhibits compassion for the poor of the world. The steak or hamburger on your table comes from beef cattle, which need either land for ranching or grain for factory rearing, and usually both. Land taken for ranching is usually the best, which means small farmers are pushed on to poor land, and into hunger. Grain fed to cattle also requires land to grow it, which means less land to grow food for people, and also means more small farmers pushed on to marginal farms. In a hungry world, meat production is an efficient way of feeding people; an acre of soya beans will feed a person for five years; the same acre put to barley to feed cattle will give only enough beef to feed a person for four months.

The second argument is Gaian - that is, it concerns the state of the living planet of which we are part, the life system dubbed Gaia (after the Greek earth goddess) by the modern ecological movement. A vegetarian diet exhibits compassion for the planet and its natural and wild places. Meat ranching, and the millions of acres of feed crops, take land that was once forest, more every year. And the small farmers who are pushed off their traditional lands must eke out a living from forest or arid lands, and destroy these lands too in the process. World wide, nearly forty per cent of the grain we grow feeds cattle - and the pressure this land demand puts on the planet's soils and animal life is unnecessary. If we fed some of this grain to people, we could grow less, ranch less meat, let the land rest, and still feed all of us in comfort.

The third argument concerns health. A vegetarian diet exhibits compassion for ourselves. There is increasing evidence that vegetarians are healthier than meat-eaters, and live longer. Their diet is naturally lower in saturated fats, refined foods, and additives, the villains of many of the diseases of civilization.

Fortunately, I live in the country. I can grow my own food, and taste the pleasures of red potatoes in their skins, cooked straight from the soil; of sun-picked tomatoes and fresh rained asparagus. I can toss up a salad of wild sorrel, and even occasionally gather field mushrooms.

This good fortune and the romanticism about the natural world and about good food that goes with it, I would like to share with every hardened city dweller or diehard carnivore. Most of all, I am glad to encourage the enthusiasm of the growing band of new vegetarians, for vegetarianism is a movement which has changed society and will continue to do so.

CHAPTER 1

A New Diet

All over the Western world a very real, radical change in our eating habits is occurring. More and more people are taking a positive interest in a good diet – fresh foods, uncontaminated by artificial substances, whole, and low in animal fats. Many are turning to vegetarianism, many more cutting out or reducing meat, fowl or fish. The movement towards this new diet is growing all the time, in an astonishing and exciting shift of perspective, fuelled by the revelation that our health is determined above all by the type and quality of the foods we consume.

We are what we eat. Now that this truism has become an accepted concept, it seems remarkable that such a simple idea did not have universal credence long ago. But what is a healthy diet? And is the vegetarian diet, *per se,* better than any other?

It has been known for some time that a highly processed, meat-rich diet is a contributory factor in more than twenty of the graver diseases of civilization, and the evidence keeps on accumulating. Medical opinion urgently advises a correction to this trend. We should eat less saturated fat, sugar and protein, and avoid processed foods which are far too high in additives. We should eat more starchy and unrefined foods, with more fibre from fruit and vegetables.

A vegetarian diet takes you naturally along this road. But it is not enough simply to give up meat and carry on as before. If you replace the meat protein with cheese and eggs, you will still be getting too much fat and cholesterol. If you are too busy to obtain fresh ingredients, you may still be buying and consuming worthless or harmful processed foods.

There are three essential criteria of a good diet. It should be natural – whole, unrefined, fresh, additive-free. It should be nutritious – balanced in protein, fat and carbohydrate content, varied in supply of vitamin and mineral sources. And it should suit you. No one can legislate for differences in dietary needs and the likes of the individual.

In the last few years there has been such a wealth of information on good and bad foods and dietary recommendations that you could understandably feel confused. We are all too likely, at the moment, to drive people to the health stores in such a state of worry as to give them coronaries through anxiety.

This chapter makes it easy for you. In the first place, stop worrying and relax, put your feet up, have a cuddle and stroke flesh. It is the nearest you will get to it in this book, for we here present you with a happy, healthy vegetarian future. Even as I write, new evidence is heralded that vegetarianism is the life for us all.

*Clockwise from top left: Carrots en papillote,
Peanut sauce, Baked apple, Glazed pineapple, Ful
medames with marbled eggs, Assorted vegetables
cooked en papillote (see pages 194,
201, 152 and 58)*

Changing over

The experience of changing to a vegetarian diet will vary from person to person. There are many shades of green that fall short of real vegetarianism – eating less meat, or no red meat on grounds of health or concern for the environment; refusing battery-farmed fowl or eggs or beef, or any foods one knows to be cruelly produced; simply eating less food altogether, and most commonly, eating mainly vegetable foods with the occasional return to meat. The true vegetarian, by contrast, eats no meat, fish or poultry, and some cut out animal foods altogether.

The decision to become vegetarian may be deliberate and planned; but there are many people who find that they have started to give up meat quite naturally, without fully realizing the implications. One day they wake up to the fact that they never order it in restaurants, hardly ever buy it, perhaps have only eaten it once or twice in the last few months, and don't much miss it. They may begin to question why, and might consider changing for good to the vegetarian diet on ethical or health grounds, or from personal taste. Strong ethical reasons for changing over do help while the urge to eat meat is still there. But once the new diet is familiar, most people stay with it because they prefer it, feel better, and find their eating patterns changing. In general the change is likely to have only positive effects – on your health, your self-esteem, and your cuisine.

If you are actually going to make a conscious decision to change your diet, however, it's best to do it gradually. Plunging headlong into a regime of beans and garlic is likely to upset both your digestion and your friends. You can, for example, have alternate weeks of meat-eating and vegetarian food for a couple of months before leaving out the meat weeks altogether. Or you can simply start by eliminating red meat one month, white meat and chicken the next month, and finally fish and seafood. Dropping dairy foods and eggs should be handled even more slowly, as you must then attend carefully to the new protein sources needed in your diet (see page 25). In any of these cases I would suggest that you consciously widen your diet at the same time, and give yourself plenty of vegetarian treats. Experiment with new foods and don't be put off by unexpected flavours and textures.

Tastes are fickle, the product of our established attitudes. Change those attitudes, and you will be in control of your diet. To me, meat-eating is a form of cannibalism which doesn't appeal. If I were starving, however, I dare say I might eat my neighbour – but then my attitude would supposedly have been changed by biological necessity.

● **Lacto-ovo vegetarian** *The most common form of vegetarianism; includes milk, eggs and all dairy products.*
● **Lacto-vegetarian** *Milk and dairy products are eaten, but eggs are omitted.*
● **Vegan** *The ultimate ethical diet; avoids all animal foods, including eggs and dairy produce. Consists of vegetables, grains, nuts, seeds, seaweeds, fresh and dried fruit.*
● **Fructarian** *Variation of vegan diet. Contains only foods that can be picked while leaving the parent plant to flourish. This includes fruits, nuts and some vegetables.*

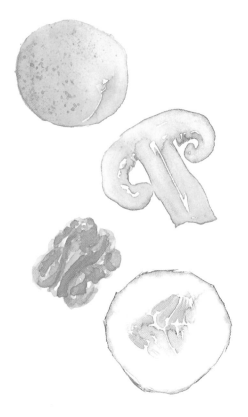

Other diets

The range of alternative diets now promoted in our health-conscious society is astonishing. Some have a whole philosophy behind them, some are primarily therapeutic, many are slimming diets. Some are vegetarian, some not. Here is a selection.

Philosophic

● **Yogic** *Basically vegetarian, natural foods. Yoga divides foods into 3 types. **Sattvic**, or pure, foods bring calm and serenity; they include cereals, wholewheat bread, fruit, vegetables, nuts and seeds. **Rajasic**, or stimulating, foods bring restlessness and discontent; they include spicy, bitter, sour, dry or salty foods, coffee, tea, fish, eggs and chocolate. **Tamasic**, or bad foods bring inertia, anger and greed; they include meat, alcohol, tobacco, onions, garlic, and all fermented foods.*

● **Macrobiotic** *Grains and natural whole foods; includes some meats at the lowest levels. There are 10 levels in all, the purest and highest being just brown rice. Drink, drugs and tobacco are forbidden. Macrobiotics is a life philosophy based on complementing interdependent opposites, yin and yang. Yin foods are acid; yang foods are alkaline. Diet is thus seen as the main tool for achieving harmony with the world around us.*

Health-based

● **Raw energy** *Raw vegetables and fruit. Works on the principle that only these foods supply full nutrition.*

● **Biogenic** *Uncombined, high-water content natural foods; includes meat. Avoids mixing concentrated proteins and starches. Designed to achieve biochemical balance.*

● **Naturopathic** *Advocates fasting to cleanse the system and a diet high in raw and unprocessed foods.*

Slimming

Whatever the system or regime, all slimming diets work by recommending a lower intake of calories.

● **F-plan** *The best known. High-fibre, unrefined foods, includes meat. High-fibre foods, being bulky but less calorific, help weight loss.*

● **Scarsdale and Cambridge diets** *Medically approved weight loss diets, include some high-calorie foods.*

Curative

● **Bristol diet** *Natural foods, containing no chemicals, low fat, low salt; devised at Bristol Cancer Prevention Centre.*

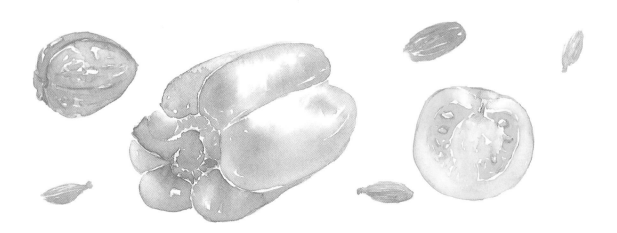

Eating naturally

You could be happily vegetarian and following a balanced diet, yet still be eating unhealthily – simply because you are consuming too many over-processed, refined foods. Ours is a busy, pressurized society, one placing a high premium on convenience and speed in all fields of everyday life, and most of all in how we eat and prepare our food. Packaged foods, take-aways and TV dinners are our answer. Yet in creating these convenience foods, we have often sadly ignored that we are losing valuable nutrients in the process. White flour, for instance, has lost up to eighty per cent of its vitamins and minerals in refining. Worse still, we are adding chemicals without regard to their combined effects on our health.

Nutritionists and health experts, though they dispute the details, tend to agree on the fundamentals of a wholesome diet. First and foremost, the food we eat should be as near the natural state as possible. Foods should be fresh (or frozen) and unrefined, and 'whole' – that is, containing as much as possible the whole of the original plant with its fibre and nutrients intact. They should be free of unnecessary chemicals in preparation, in preserving and storage, and preferably during the growing period too. We should also cut down on sugar, salt, and stimulants like tea and coffee. Lastly, if we wish to live long, we should eat less altogether, and more lightly at each sitting – following the natural needs of our bodies.

Eating naturally makes good sense. It is quite obvious that the more raw fruit and vegetables one can eat in a diet, as soon after picking as possible, the better the intake of vitamins, minerals and fibre will be. And if you are taking your sugar in the form of apples, you would have to eat twenty large sweet ones to consume the equivalent of 100g/4oz of refined sugar – an empty food in any case (see page 17). From my experience, flavour is also hugely improved the less time the vegetable has between being plucked and cooked. Indeed, some vegetables like sweetcorn and globe artichokes are so radically transformed when home grown that there seems little similarity between them and the commercial equivalent. Another controversial issue is that of pesticides. There is increasing evidence that some poisonous residues remain on the food. Organically grown vegetables are preferable, and of superior quality.

We should be more selective over which manufactured food we eat. Be discriminating, read labels, check food for freshness, search out organic and wholefood suppliers, eat more raw foods generally, and prepare meals from unrefined ingredients. Your menu will improve as well as your health.

The digestive clock
- *Regular meals are not a biological necessity.*
- *It is important to establish eating patterns that your body becomes used to.*
- *Missing a meal you usually eat adversely affects your system.*
- *If you prefer to eat several small meals rather than one or two large ones, be careful not to snack on cakes and biscuits/cookies that are high in fats.*

Fasting
- *Fasting cleanses and revitalizes the system.*
- *Fasting means drinking lots of juice, water or other fluids. You may also eat fruit if you wish.*
- *Do not fast for more than 36 hours.*
- *You should rest while fasting and eat lightly when you first break the fast.*
- *If fasting is out of the question for you, keep to your normal diet and try drinking a glass of warm, slightly salted water first thing in the morning.*

Natural eating patterns

What you eat is important. But when you eat it, and how much, is important too. Natural foods are generally valuable to all of us, but natural eating patterns vary from individual to individual. Try to recognize your own needs and patterns. Never eat when you are already full – try eating slowly, as this gives your stomach more time to signal its satiety before you have had too much. Our bodies have different needs at different times of day and year. Most of us respond to this quite naturally – we tend to eat the bulkier carbohydrate foods we need for warmth and energy during the winter months, turning to lighter foods and salads in hot weather.

Our eating patterns during the day vary according to lifestyle, where we live (in Mediterranean countries, for instance, lunch is often the largest meal; in England it is usually the lightest), and simple personal preference. Some people are incapable of doing anything until they've had a hearty breakfast; others will pass out at the mere thought of it. Such is life. Similarly, some people feel better on a number of small meals a day, at whatever time they feel like it; others need the routine of three regular meals a day. There are no hard and fast rules – except to work out what your body feels well on, and stick to it.

If you are following a diet that is natural in content, and natural in pattern for you, you should be thoroughly healthy, and have no weight problems. If you do let rip on the occasional feast, it doesn't matter. You may even like to try the occasional fast as a counterbalance. Provided you are healthy, a short, 24-36 hour fast on water and juice cleanses the body and can clear the mind too.

Processed and refined foods

● *There is almost always some loss of nutrients during processing, no matter which method is used. During canning, vitamin C, thiamin and folic acid will be removed; in drying, as much as half the vitamin C content may be lost.*

● *All processed foods – particularly snack foods – tend to be high in fat, salt and sugar. Be on the lookout particularly for so-called 'bran' cereals or mueslis that are commercially produced, as they will be high in sugar. Make your own.*

● *Many chemical additives in processed foods have been found to be harmful to health (see page 21).*

● *When flour is refined, the bran (containing fibre) and germ (containing polyunsaturated fats, vitamin E, thiamin, riboflavin, B_6 and protein) is removed, leaving only the endosperm, or starchy part of the grain. Up to eighty per cent of essential nutrients can be lost.*

● *During refining, rice is stripped of protein, B vitamins and minerals. It actually has less than half the vitamin B_6 content of brown rice.*

Cross section of a wheat grain

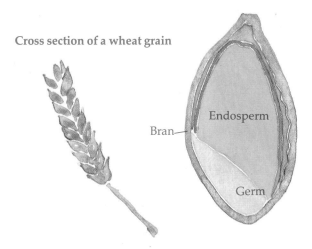

Bran

Endosperm

Germ

During refining the bran and germ, containing vitamins, protein and fibre, are removed, leaving only the starchy endosperm. Up to 80% of nutrients can be lost in this process.

High fibre

Fibre is the new magic word in nutrition, and with good reason. A menu high in dietary fibre is now believed to reduce the risk of diabetes, cancer of the bowel and possibly heart disease. It keeps the digestion healthy, combats weight gain and, because fibre will adsorb some chemicals, may also be a safety buffer against food toxins. And, of course, a fibre-rich diet automatically contains much unrefined food, with greater nutritional content, and is low in saturated fats (see page 28).

Fibre is present in many foods, and is not, one substance but many; it includes all those parts of our food which cannot be broken down by our digestive enzymes, especially the cellulose of carbohydrates (see page 26).

Perhaps the greatest benefit of fibre is that it bulks out in the intestines, taking with it any toxins that may have accumulated in the lower intestine, thus reducing the risk of disease and constipation. Moreover, the bulkier food satisfies our appetites without building up calories.

Facts
● *Fibre in food encourages bulk and rapid removal of wastes from the intestine. It relieves constipation and protects against bowel disease.*
● *High-fibre foods are additionally good for you because they are low in fats and high in vitamins and minerals.*
● *High-fibre foods are filling and satisfying.*
● *Diets that contain a lot of cereal fibre may interfere with the absorption of certain minerals (e.g. calcium and iron), though this is only likely to matter in diets for the very young and elderly, who may do better to get fibre mainly from fruit and vegetables.*

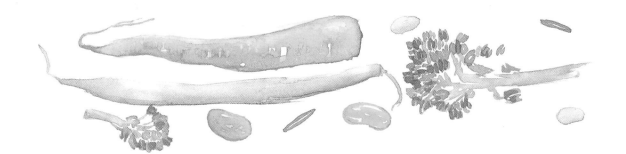

To get the most from fibre:
1 Increase the fibre intake of your diet gradually, over a period of two or three months, so that your system gets used to it.
2 Eat potatoes with their skins on (unless they're green).
3 Eat homemade muesli (see page 97) rather than shop-bought. The latter will probably contain sugar.
4 Eat plenty of wholegrain pastas and cereals, fruit and vegetables.
5 Avoid refined breads and flours. Eat wholewheat bread and use wholewheat flour for cooking.
6 Eat more legumes (beans, grains and nuts) – add them to soups and stews.
7 The outer leaves of vegetables are a richer source of fibre than the inner leaves. Don't throw them away, but chop them up finely and add them to soups and stews.
8 Eat foods that are naturally rich in fibre rather than adding bran to foods, which you may find unpalatable.

Low sugar

Try to avoid sugar. It is an 'empty' food, and a main contributory factor in obesity, which can lead to heart disease. It is also linked with diabetes and, of course, causes dental caries.

Excess sugar is bad for you. There is little difference between the white, refined sugars and the brown – demerara, soft brown and raw cane have a tiny amount of minerals, but nutritionally that will make no difference to the diet. Honey, syrup and molasses are little better either.

The only exception is fructose, or fruit sugar. Although actually sweeter than ordinary sugar (sucrose), fructose is absorbed much more slowly by the body, and so doesn't affect blood sugar levels quite so sharply. And since it is so much sweeter, you can use less.

Eating refined sugars in isolation from other foods causes a rapid rise in the blood sugar level, which falls again, and causes hunger – even a craving – for sweet things. Like all addictions, it is best to give it up entirely. Certainly it is sensible never to introduce children to a sweet tooth, or offer sweet dishes as a 'treat' – and sugar should be banned from baby foods.

However, balance in the diet is the most significant point. For the sake of your teeth and your waistline, try not to over-indulge. There are a few recipes in this book which contain sugar, but you can omit it, or use fruit juice or another substitute, to taste.

To cut down on sugar:
- *Cut out sugar in hot drinks. For cold drinks, drink mineral water or unsweetened fruit juice rather than fizzy drinks. Drink dry wine or cider rather than sweet.*
- *Use less sugar than stated in recipes. Cut by at least half to begin with, and steadily reduce further.*
- *Buy sugar-free or low-sugar jams.*
- *Check all labels on processed foods, as these are often high in sugar. Ingredients are listed in order, according to the amounts used. A surprising number of savoury foods contain sugar. Examples are tomato ketchup, baked beans, soups, sauces, pickles and canned vegetables.*
- *If you feel like a snack, eat savoury sandwiches, such as wholewheat bread with alfalfa sprouts, rather than biscuits/cookies.*
- *Try some of the substitutes shown here.*

Useful sugar substitutes
- Fructose has recently become available in powdered and syrup forms; it is also present in fruit juice and fresh and dried fruit.
- Honey, molasses and maple syrup are slightly more nutritious than sugar.
- Try spices for sweeteners in desserts (e.g. cinammon, cloves).
- Use dried fruit, or dried fruit purées, or fruit juice concentrates in cakes.
- Use fruit juice instead of milk and sugar on cereals.
- Try having yoghurt, fresh, stewed or dried fruit, or low-fat cheese for dessert.

Reduce intake of
- Processed foods where sugar is featured
- Cyclamates (They contain substances that are thought to cause cancer.)
- Ready-made biscuits/cookies, cakes and pastries, sweets/candy and ice cream

Low salt

There are a lot of stubborn myths about salt. For years we have had the idea that we need plenty of it in our diets, and in particular, that we should take salt tablets in hot climates. There is a grain of truth in this. Salt is sodium chloride; when we sweat we do excrete salt, and lose sodium; excessive sodium loss, if not replaced, could produce muscle cramps and dehydration. But this is a rare danger, to bodies unused to hot climates and exposed to bursts of heat. Acclimatization takes about a month.

The truth is that salt is necessary, but only in minute amounts (about 200 mg a day), and we can easily get this much from whole, fresh foods. We currently consume ten to twelve times more than we need.

For the last fifty years or so, it has been believed that salt (or more specifically, sodium) may be a contributory factor in high blood pressure. But the picture is still far from clear. It is now thought that it may be an incorrect balance between salt and other minerals in the body which is to blame.

The message so far then is: salt may or may not be the criminal, but it will do no harm to cut down on it in cooking. In the recipes I have merely put 'season to taste', and left it to you to decide.

To cut down on salt:
- *Add less salt than the amount stated in recipes. (Start by cutting in half.) Preferably, leave it out altogether.*
- *Don't add salt at the table.*
- *Eat high-potassium foods as potassium seems to counteract the effect of sodium. Good sources of potassium are: fresh fruit and vegetables, fruit juice and dried fruit, particularly prunes.*
- *Try one of the substitutes shown here whenever possible.*

Useful salt substitutes
- Any tasty flavouring with herbs or spices can replace salt, but try especially lemon juice, herb salt, gomasio (see page 61), garlic or peppers.
- Use miso, shoyu or tamari to flavour soups and sauces. (They do contain sodium, but are so concentrated that they need only be used in small amounts; unlike salt, they also have other useful nutrients.)
- Try low-sodium salt (half potassium, half sodium) to start with. It is useful as a transition before giving up salt altogether.
- To flavour bread try grated orange rind instead of salt.

Reduce intake of
- All foods that are high in sodium. (Don't be fooled into thinking that these will automatically taste salty; if you only avoid foods that taste salty you may actually be choosing to eat foods that contain even more sodium than the ones you have shunned. Examples of deceptive high-sodium foods are breakfast cereals, biscuits/cookies and cheese.)
- Margarine, butter, spreads, yeast extracts (though these are high in vitamin B_{12}), salted crackers, sauces, canned vegetables, soups and pickles.
- All processed foods or foods with additives, as many are sodium-based.

*Here is a selection of foods that may be used in
place of sugar and salt to give flavour. Many are
described in the Glossary (see pages 59–93).*

The additives problem

There is nothing new about food additives. The pollution of food to make it convenient or enticing has happened throughout history. And for food to travel well or keep during winter months, it has to be preserved. Sulphur dioxide, that ubiquitous present day preserver, has been used since the ancient Greeks, spices such as cloves, cinnamon and pepper since even earlier.

But the scale of food additives today is wholly different. As well as preservatives, there are stabilizers, emulsifiers, colourants, anti-oxidants, flavour enhancers and artificial sweeteners. Many of the common additives are now known to cause health problems from allergic responses to stomach upsets and skin rashes, and some may be positively harmful, even carcinogenic. Most of all, our present anxiety is with the chemical cocktail created when we eat a range of processed foods and the different additives intermingle in our bodies. There is no way of telling what the effects of this may be.

Legislation on food labelling helps. But sadly this does not extend to meat and fish. Factory-farmed animals are fed an unpleasant package of antibiotics, additives and growth hormones.

However, things are looking up; we are reaching a time when the consumer's voice is making itself heard and food manufacturers are responding positively, if slowly.

Food irradiation
A new method of preserving food is now being considered for widespread use, which involves bombarding it with gamma radiation to destroy bacteria. The process leaves no radioactive particles in the food, and may be an alternative to chemical additives – though it is more likely to be used in conjunction with them.

It is not, however, the panacea some consider it could be. Food can still be contaminated after irradiation, and not all the bacteria may be killed. The process also depletes nutrients in some foods – the B vitamins in rice and fish, vitamin C in fruit and potatoes.

The other real anxiety is the siting of irradiation plants and safety for workers. Before governments legislate on this new process, public debate is needed.

To protect yourself
● Read all labels carefully.

● When shopping, keep with you a list of E numbers and/or additive names and the hazards they represent.

● Search out stores which sell additive-free, preservative-free lines.

● Cook and eat fresh, organically grown foods wherever possible.

● Buy 'free range' eggs.

● Wash all fruit and vegetables, especially those imported from countries where pesticide controls are weak.

Reduce the intake of
● Highly processed foods. Never buy any where ingredients are not listed.

● Factory-farmed foods.

● Foods labelled simply as 'containing preservative'.

● Foods with the hazardous additives listed opposite.

● Bottled and canned drinks other than natural mineral water and fruit juices.

Identifying additives

Not all additives are undesirable. Many are natural products and there is no documented evidence that the proper use of them is harmful to the majority of the population. More people get food poisoning from badly preserved food than suffer ill-effects from additives, so it is important to keep them in perspective. However, constant research work in this field continues to uncover new information, and the list of additives known to provoke or exacerbate certain conditions in some people continues to grow. Given the painstaking nature of this research, there can often be a considerable time lapse between the discovery of harmful side effects and the eventual ban on the additive. Those particularly criticized are tartrazine, for its possible link with hyperactivity in children, and sodium nitrates and nitrites, implicated in cancer of the stomach.

Note: The legislation on food labelling varies from country to country. In the USA both the name of the chemical, and its functions, must be listed. In the UK and other EEC countries, additives are given the code 'E' followed by a number. There is no EEC legislation that all additives must be mentioned.

E100s are generally colours
E200-282 are mainly preservatives and acids
E300-341 are mainly antioxidants and acid regulators
E400s include emulsifiers, stabilizers, thickeners, anti-caking agents, release agents and bulking agents.

Caution
In those who suffer from hyperactivity, asthma and aspirin sensitivity, the following additives are believed to exacerbate the condition. Those asterisked are suspected, but unproven, carcinogens.

E102 (Tartrazine)
Used in soft drinks, desserts, cakes, biscuits/cookies, confectionery, canned and packet convenience foods.

E123 (Amaranth) *
Sometimes used in burgers and blackcurrant drinks. Banned in USA.

E150 (Caramel) *
Used in soft drinks, gravy mix, brown bread, cakes, biscuits/cookies, marmalade, malt vinegar and beef products.

E250 (Sodium nitrite) *
Although valuable in preventing botulism in canned meats, nitrites have shown carcinogenic properties in tests on animals. They are used in bacon, sausages and frozen pizza.

E251 (Sodium nitrate) *
Similar to E250. Found in pressed meats, bacon, cheese and frozen pizza.

Useful
It is a mistake to treat all additives with suspicion. Some, such as those listed below, are commonly used in the home, and some are nutrients.

E101 (Riboflavin or Vitamin B2)
Used mainly in processed cheeses.

E170 (Calcium carbonate)
Used in bread, cakes, biscuits/cookies, ice cream and confectionery.

E260 (Acetic acid or vinegar)
Used in pickles, cheese, sauces and creamed horseradish.

E300 (Ascorbic acid or Vitamin C)
Used in soft drinks, powdered milk, butter, beer and some potato products.

E336 (Cream of tartar)
Used in packet desserts, such as lemon meringue pie.

E406 (Agar agar)
Used in ice cream and for glazing meats.

E410 (Carob gum)
Used in some jellies/jellos, canned pie fillings and bottled salad dressings.

A balanced diet

It is often considered that vegetarians restrict themselves in not eating fish or meat. But the truth is that today's vegetarians are generally open to a range of foods and a variety of ingredients the average carnivore cannot imagine. Meat-eaters, in fact, usually eat the more restrictive diet. Moreover it can lead to those very dietary deficiencies of which vegetarianism is unjustly suspected.

Food is survival. It gives us the energy and raw materials to keep body and soul together – to build flesh, repair ills, walk, talk, dance, make love, think and be. Getting the right balance and variety in the diet is essential to well-being and vitality.

There are five classes of food essential to a healthy diet: proteins, carbohydrates, fats, vitamins and minerals. The first three supply energy, measured in calories (though in varying amounts – weight for weight, fats supply twice as many calories as proteins or carbohydrates). All five supply essential nutrients, for the daily work of the body.

The following pages give you the vital statistics of the five essential foods, with practical pointers on how to make the best of each type, and what to avoid. The recipes in Chapter 4 are coded for protein content and suitability for vegans, and for those with extra dietary needs further help is given in Chapter 6. Should all this advice confuse you however, there are a few much simpler rules to follow.

Try to eat as many different foods as possible. Most whole, natural foods contain all five elements in varying proportions, so if your diet is high in these, you need not worry too much. Eat more small meals, fewer large ones, to get the most out of your diet and if you are a vegan, especially, mix complementary protein foods (see page 25) in your menus. We naturally eat such combinations anyway. Don't totally rely on dairy foods and eggs for your protein, as they are high in fats and cholesterol (see page 28); seek varied vegetable protein sources as well. Experiment with everything from raw vegetables and exotic fruits to seaweeds, from miso to nuts and grains. Make interesting breads, gorgeous salads and delicious stuffings. The wider your diet, the better.

What you drink

Recommended intake is about 1 litre/2 pints a day, but you don't need to regulate how much fluid you drink – your body will let you know, through thirst.

*You should take care **what** you drink though. Mineral water is preferable to tap water, which may be contaminated by lead or other pollutants. If you do drink tap water, let it run for at least 10 seconds before filling your glass, especially first thing in the day, or when you get home.*

Most people will take wine or water with a meal. There are schools of thought that abjure alcohol, and others which frown upon water at meal times as they believe it to dilute the digestion. The latter I take for an outré argument, and give little credence. As for wine, it is known to stimulate and benefit the digestion.

Herb teas and tisanes can be refreshing, and lassi (see page 209) makes a noble drink with all curries, especially in summer. Chilled soya milk mixed with yoghurt is also delicious.

Reduce intake of	Drink	Eat
● Refined foods	● Skimmed milk	● As varied a diet as possible
● Dependence on dairy foods for protein	● Mineral water, fruit or vegetable juice	● As many fresh, whole or raw foods as possible
● Fizzy soft drinks (they usually contain additives and sugar)	● Herb teas	● Small, frequent meals
● Milk and milky drinks (they are high in fat)	● Decaffeinated coffee	● Varied protein sources
● Coffee and tea		● Complementary proteins in one meal
		● A wide range of foods

The ingredients of the vegetarian meal above will all combine to provide the necessary supplies of protein, carbohydrate, fats, vitamins and minerals. They are all good sources of the nutrients listed.

Clockwise from top left:
High protein wholewheat roll containing Mushrooms in red wine and mustard: *iron, zinc, copper, magnesium, fibre, niacin, vitamins B_1, B_2, and B_6.*
Gratin Dauphinois: *carbohydrate, vitamins A, B_{12}, C, D and E.*

Leek and parsley pâté croquettes: *fibre, iron, calcium, carotene, vitamins B_6, B_{12} and C.*
Ratatouille: *iron, fibre, unsaturated fats, vitamins B_6, C and E.*
Green salad: *carotene, vitamin C, fibre, folic acid.*
Melon with mango purée: *carotene, vitamins and fibre.*

Protein

New vegetarians need have no worries today either about the amount of protein in their diet, or its quality. Views on protein have changed. In the past it was believed that the protein intake necessary for health was much larger than we now think. People were told to eat too much protein and, in affluent societies, most still do. It is said that Americans pass the most expensive urine in the world – the result of excess protein in their diet.

Until recently, too, protein from animals was thought superior to that from plants – they were even, misleadingly, termed first and second class proteins. Such entrenched opinions were largely the result of ignorance – meat, eggs, milk and fish were familiar protein sources, whereas the varied vegetable protein foods were less common in Western diets – legumes (especially soya beans), nuts, whole grains, root vegetables and seeds – particularly the protein-rich sprouted seeds like alfalfa. Nowadays, stores offer a great range of these foods, from all round the world.

Protein is a part of every cell in our bodies. It is always in a state of flux, being broken down and remade in the ceaseless work of repairing and building tissues, regulating body chemistry, and defending against infection. In digestion, the protein foods we eat are broken down into the twenty-odd amino acids of which they are made. Eight of these amino acids (nine in children) are not produced by living tissue, but must be obtained in the diet. 'Complete' protein foods have a correct balance of these essential dietary amino acids, egg yolks being the standard example. Soya milk, tofu, miso and TVP (textured vegetable protein) are also complete – as are all dairy products.

We can also obtain complete protein by the combination of two or more 'complementary' protein sources in one meal – rice with wheat, beans or sesame seeds, for example, or beans with corn, barley or oats. Each supplies the amino acids the other may lack. The classic example always given us is beans on toast – homemade baked beans, of course, on wholewheat toast. If you ponder a moment on this mix of complementary proteins, you will see how naturally we use it in many of our favourite meals. A vegetable curry, for example, is served with rice and a lentil dahl. We soak up hummus with pitta bread. We eat peanut butter sandwiches. Many more enticing examples are given in the recipe sections of this book.

Facts
- *There is no danger of protein deficiency in a balanced vegetarian diet.*
- *Most people still eat twice as much protein as they actually need.*
- *There is no organ in the body for storing excess protein. Any surplus is expelled in the urine.*
- *Protein requirements decrease with age.*
- *Excess protein can make you fat.*
- *Old people, and any person with weak kidneys, cannot handle excess protein in the diet. Babies, children and adolescents need more protein, weight for weight, than adults, because they are growing.*

INCOMPLETE PROTEINS	Eaten alone	Eaten in combination with:				Suggested dishes
		Grains	**Legumes**	**Nuts & seeds**	**Dairy**	
Grains Brown rice, Wheat, cracked wheat and wheat flour, Barley, Oats and oatmeal, Rye, Bread, Corn, Millet, Buckwheat.	⊂ – – – – ◁ (Grains) ⊂ – – – – – – – ◁ (Dairy)					**Grains and dairy** Muesli with milk or yoghurt Pasta with cheese sauce Bread and cheese Rice pudding
Legumes Lentils, Mung beans, Aduki beans, Black eyed beans/peas, Haricot/navy beans, Kidney beans, Broad/fava beans, Flageolet/lima beans, Chick peas, Dried peas.	⊂ – ◁ (Grains) ⊂ – – – – ◁ (Nuts & seeds)					**Legumes and grains** Baked beans on toast Bean or pea risotto Bean and vegetable casserole with barley Vegetarian cassoulet
Nuts and seeds Sunflower seeds, Sesame seeds, Pumpkin seeds, Tahini, Cashew nuts, Peanuts, Almonds, Hazelnuts, Brazil nuts, Chestnuts, Coconuts, Pine nuts, Pistachios.	⊂ – – – ◁ (Legumes)					**Nuts or seeds and legumes** Chickpea patties with tahini Lentil and nut roast Bean salad with toasted sunflower seeds Granola

COMPLETE PROTEINS	
Eggs	◯
Dairy products Milk and dried milk, Yoghurt, Cheese, Quark.	◯
Soya products Soya beans, Tofu, Miso, Shoyu and tamari, Soya milk, Soya flour.	◯

By combining your foods wisely you can increase the quality of the protein you eat in any meal by as much as 50%. Beans (a legume) and wholewheat toast (a grain), for example, have complementary strengths and weaknesses in amino acids. Eaten together, they give you a proper protein balance. The most useful of these complementary protein combinations are illustrated above. The foods in the left-hand column above yield incomplete protein when eaten alone. To complete the protein you can eat them in combination with other protein foods as shown by the linked symbols. Dairy and soya products and eggs are already complete proteins as shown left; combine them with food of any of the other groups to increase a meal's nutritional value.

Carbohydrates

Carbohydrates have a poor public image. We tend to think of them as pure stodge – filling, fattening and not much else. And when you consider what's been done to them in the name of convenience, appearance and palatability, it's little wonder that this has come about. But recently, just as popular thinking about protein has changed, so too, has the regard for carbohydrates.

Carbohydrates have two main forms – starches and sugars – and a third kind, fibre, the indigestible parts of food, such as cellulose, whose importance in health terms is now recognized (see page 16). Over the last thirty years, refined carbohydrates have become alarmingly commonplace. Stripped of their fibre, vitamins and minerals, they supply very little nutrition.

In their natural, unrefined state carbohydrates are a very important source of energy and nutrition. The humble potato, for instance, contains protein, iron, phosphorus, thiamin, niacin, vitamins C and B_6, as well as many minerals. And that's not all. Carbohydrates are *not* fattening in themselves. Potatoes, for example, weight for weight, have fewer calories than steak. They are only fattening when eaten in excess of the body's energy needs with fat, as a baked potato often is with butter or sour cream. Eat your carbohydrates with low-fat spreads and in as natural a form as possible and they are an excellent source of nutrients and dietary fibre.

Facts
● *Carbohydrates are **not** in themselves fattening.*
● *High-carbohydrate-foods are very nutritious. They are a valuable source of energy and, if eaten in their unrefined state, contain fibre and many other nutrients.*
● *Sugars, in any form, are totally lacking in nutrients.*

To get the most from carbohydrates:
1 Eat them in an unrefined form (whole grains, pastas, legumes and potatoes are all good sources).
2 Follow the instructions on pages 50–53, and 17 for preparing and cooking carbohydrate foods, and for cutting down on sugar.

*Here is a selection of foods high
in carbohydrates and protein. Unusual
ones may be found in the Glossary
(see pages 59–93).*

Fats, good and bad

Fats are divided chemically into three kinds: the saturates and polyunsaturates, now so familiar, and the less publicized monounsaturates. Saturated fats are the baddies, furring the arteries by raising cholesterol levels until a clot or blockage leads to a heart attack. Polyunsaturates don't fur blood vessels, and may even, it is thought, act as an antidote to the process (though this is not yet proven). Polyunsaturates also supply us with the essential fatty acids (EFAS: linoleic, linolenic and archidonic acids) which are necessary to healthy blood flow and blood vessels. Monounsaturates are neutral in health terms.

Distinguishing the good fats from the bad is not always easy. Broadly speaking, saturated fats tend to be solid, unsaturated fats liquid. In terms of food source, the saturates are found mainly in animal fats, such as butter, cheese, meat, fowl and eggs, the polyunsaturates in fish, nuts and vegetable oils, and the monounsaturates in nuts, and especially olive oil. However, coconut oil is vegetable, but solid and saturated, and palm oil, though vegetable and liquid, is also saturated.

Most fats, and foods of all kinds, actually contain a varying proportion of all three types; it is the proportion that matters. To take palm oil again, it is 48% saturated, 44% monounsatured and 8% polyunsaturated. To complicate matters further, when polyunsaturated oils are hydrogenated (heated under pressure with hydrogen) to make them solid – which happens in the manufacture of most margarines – they become, in effect, saturated.

We do need fats. They are a concentrated source of energy, supply us with essential fatty acids and fat-soluble vitamins make food palatable, and help satisfy the appetite by slowing digestion. Be sure to buy from the marvellous range of polyunsaturated oils now available.

Facts
- *The body needs fats to some extent, but we should try to reduce our consumption of saturated fats by 25%.*
- *If you cut down on saturated fatty acids, the blood cholesterol level will automatically be reduced.*
- *Fat is a concentrated source of energy.*
- *Fat can change in nature when it is heated.*

To get the most from fats:
1 Eat polyunsaturated fats whenever possible – they are a source of essential fatty acids. Use polyunsaturated oils such as safflower and sunflower oil, and follow the recommendations on the opposite page.
2 Monounsaturated fats (found in nuts, seeds and olive oil) make a good substitute for saturates.
3 Use cold-pressed oils where possible, as they retain their flavours and vitamins.

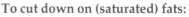

To cut down on (saturated) fats:
- *Use low-fat dairy products.*
- *Serve cereals with fruit juice, or skimmed milk.*
- *Drink tea with lemon, not milk.*
- *When you do fry, use a non-stick pan (which requires less oil), and use polyunsaturated oils – but don't let them get too hot or they may become saturated. (Corn oil is the most stable at high temperatures.)*
- *Limit your egg consumption to two or three a week.*

Low fat, low cholesterol

For many years people in affluent societies have consumed far too much fat – saturated fat in particular. Excess saturated fat in the diet is implicated in cancer, diabetes, and most of all, heart disease. We are now advised to cut down our intake by one quarter.

Vegetarians start with a plus in this matter, avoiding the high proportion of saturated fats in meat. But, except for vegans, there are still the dairy foods, high in saturates – so watch your intake of these, as well as of eggs which have concentrated levels of saturated fats in their yolks. Change over to skimmed milk, cook in oils high in polyunsaturated fats, and for butter substitute a margarine high in polyunsaturates – though I would still tend to keep butter for its flavour in cooking. I would personally rather cut down on cream and high-fat cheeses. Many processed foods also have an unexpectedly high proportion of saturated fats. Cakes, biscuits, pies, some canned and frozen meals have a lot of added fats in them – read the labels carefully.

The cholesterol factor

Cholesterol is a form of fat naturally present in animal tissues and made mainly by the liver. We hear much about its harmful effects, but in fact it does have vital functions – in the manufacture of vitamin D, hormones, cell walls and bile acids for digestion.

Recent evidence suggests that there may be 'good' and 'bad' cholesterol forms in the body. The key lies in the way it is transported. Cholesterol travels through the blood in the form of a pocket of fatty protein, known as lipoprotein, of which there are three kinds: high density (HDL), low density (LDL) and very low density (VLDL). It is LDL which is considered harmful, in that it clogs up the arteries contributing to heart disease. HDLs, on the other hand, actually seem to protect against clogging, by removing cholesterol and returning it to the liver, where excess can be excreted as bile.

When the diet is high in saturated fats, the liver produces large amounts of VLDLs and LDLs. Cholesterol-laden saturated fats are largely found in animal products. Vegetarians therefore have an automatic advantage – their only concern need be egg yolks, which are high in cholesterol.

Useful low-fat substitutes

Dairy Low-fat milk, cheese and yoghurt, Quark (see page 45), cottage cheeses, and Smetana/low-fat sour cream.
Non-dairy Soya milk, tofu
Mainly non-dairy Margarine high in polyunsaturates (Make sure it says 'high in polyunsaturates'. If it just says 'low in cholesterol', it could still be made from oils which are high in saturated fats.)

● *Instead of cream, try low-fat yoghurt, Greek yoghurt or Smetana/low-fat sour cream as a topping, Quark, curd cheese or puréed cottage cheese in cooking.*
● *Instead of butter, use polyunsaturated margarine, and on vegetables try cottage cheese, Smetana/low-fat sour cream or yoghurt.*
● *Instead of milk, try soya milk or, in thickening sauces, plain water with cornflour/cornstarch.*
● *Instead of mayonnaise or thick salad creams, make dressings based on low-fat yoghurt, cottage cheese, Quark, or a combination of these.*

Reduce intake of
● Full-fat milk
● Cream, butter and high-fat cheeses
● Processed foods with fat near the top of the listed ingredients
● Pastries, pies, cakes, potato snacks, chocolate, peanuts and blended oils.
● Frying food

Vitamins

It's currently very fashionable to worry about vitamin intake. But in fact we need vitamins in such small amounts that we are very unlikely to suffer from deficiency as long as we eat a varied diet.

There are about thirteen recognized vitamins in all, and they fall into two main groups: water-soluble (B group vitamins, vitamin C and folic acid) and fat-soluble (vitamins A, D, E and K). Water-soluble vitamins dissolve in the blood and tissue fluid and cannot be stored in the body for long. They are also easily lost in cooking, so a regular daily intake is essential. Fat-soluble vitamins, on the other hand, are stored by the body in the liver and fatty tissues and therefore don't really need to be consumed in daily amounts. They are also easier to retain in foods as they are more stable in cooking and processing. Vitamin requirements will depend on a number of factors such as age, sex, occupation, diet and lifestyle. Requirements for special needs are given on Chapter 6. A breakdown of the individual vitamins and their functions is on page 32.

It's worth remembering that alcohol, cigarettes, tea, coffee, aspirin, and the contraceptive pill all increase the vitamin requirement of the body. If you take any of these things, you might be well advised to take a small multi-vitamin supplement too. An additional, but slight concern, that applies solely to vegans, is the problem of B_{12} deficiency (see page 33).

But on the whole, a far greater danger than inadequate foods is vitamin loss through incorrect cooking, or through eating over-refined or processed foods. Follow the tips given on page 53.

Facts
- *If you eat a balanced diet you are in no danger of vitamin shortage, though vegans need to be careful about adequate B_{12} consumption.*
- *Vitamins can be destroyed during storing, cooking and processing, but freezing has virtually no effect. Fat-soluble vitamins are on the whole more stable than water-soluble vitamins.*

To get the most from vitamins:
1 Eat food as soon after it is picked (or bought) as possible.
2 Keep fruit and vegetables somewhere cool, dark and dry. (Fat-soluble vitamins are sensitive to light.)
3 Eat wholefoods – refined foods have fewer vitamins.
4 Check that skimmed milk is fortified with vitamins A and D, as these are removed with the fat.
5 Make sure you use a healthy cooking method (see page 53).
6 Avoid prolonged soaking of vegetables, and don't wash rice before cooking – you may wash all the vitamins out of it.

Minerals

They may not conjure up much to most people, but minerals are vital for our well being. They form part of our enzyme and hormone systems and, as soluble salts, can affect the composition and balance of body fluids. They also enable muscles and nerves to work efficiently.

Minerals make up about four per cent of our bodyweight. There are about 100 in all, of which twenty or so are believed to be essential. Of these six are needed in large quantities and are called *macrominerals*: sodium, chloride, potassium, calcium, phosporus and magnesium. The other fourteen are only needed in tiny amounts and are called *microminerals* or *trace elements*: iron, manganese, zinc, copper and iodine, but there are several more.

Like some vitamins, some minerals are water-soluble and can easily be cooked out of foods. An individual breakdown of minerals and their functions is overleaf.

Facts
- *Minerals must be correctly balanced in the body to work efficiently.*
- *Minerals can be destroyed by many factors such as smoking and caffeine.*

To get the most from minerals:
1 Cereal fibre, particularly wheat fibre, reduces the availability of minerals in the body. Eat fibre from other sources to counteract this.
2 Vitamin C increases iron absorption.

These foods are good sources of vitamins and minerals. For more specific details, see the Glossary (pages 59–93).

Vitamins

Vitamin A
Fat-soluble. Important for the growth and repair of tissues and eye health. It also protects from infection.
Good sources: carrots, broccoli, spinach and milk products.

B-group vitamins
Important in the metabolism of carbohydrates, fats and proteins in the body. The individual B vitamins, their functions and sources, are given below.

Vitamin B1 (thiamin)
Helps release energy from carbohydrates. It also improves mental and nerve function and promotes growth.
Good sources: whole grains and cereals (including pasta and bread), wheat germ, oatmeal, nuts, most vegetables.

Vitamin B2 (riboflavin)
Water-soluble. Contributes to healthy eyes, skin, nails and hair and aids growth and reproduction.
Good sources: green vegetables, eggs, whole grains and cereals, mushrooms, yeast.

Vitamin B3 (niacin)
Water-soluble. It helps to regulate blood sugar and cholesterol levels. It works in combination with vitamins B_1 and B_2 in assisting energy production in cells.
Good sources: nuts, whole grains and cereals, eggs, avocados, yeast, dried beans and peas. It is also produced by the body.

Vitamin B6 (pyridoxine)
Water-soluble. Essential for production of red blood cells, antibodies and for protein manufacture. It also helps the body use fats and may relieve pre-menstrual tension in some women.
Good sources: whole grains and cereals, avocados, green beans, bananas, nuts, potatoes, leafy vegetables, fresh and dried fruit, wheat germ.

Vitamin B12
Water-soluble. Important for iron metabolism and to maintain cell life and a healthy nervous system.
Good sources: eggs and dairy products, yeast extract and fermented foods, such as miso. Vegans – who take in no animal products – may suffer from a deficiency.

Folic acid
Water-soluble. It is important in the prevention of anaemia and for a healthy cell life. Particularly important for pregnant women.
Good sources: leafy vegetables, carrots, pumpkins, avocados, apricots, whole grains and egg yolks.

Vitamin E
Fat-soluble. A component of all cell membranes, it protects unsaturated fats in the body from damage. It also protects the circulatory system cells and is believed to delay aging.
Good sources: vegetable oils, dark green vegetables, wheat germ, whole grains, nuts and eggs.

Vitamin C (ascorbic acid)
Water-soluble. It is vital for many body functions including wound healing, and resistance to disease. It also helps increase absorption of iron. Extra supplies may be needed when the body is under stress. *Good sources:* leafy vegetables, potatoes, tomatoes, fruit (particularly citrus and berry fruits).

Vitamin D
Fat-soluble. It is essential for maintaining normal levels of calcium and phosphorus in the blood, thus enhancing the healthy formation of bones and teeth. It is especially important for pregnant women and young children. *Good sources:* dairy products. It is also produced by sunlight.

Vitamin K
Fat-soluble. Vital for blood clotting. *Good sources:* egg yolks, yoghurt and leafy vegetables.

Note to vegans
When adopting a vegan diet the main worry is the possibility of a B_{12} deficiency, since this vitamin is found mostly in animal products. This need not concern you if you have been a meat-eater for most of your life and then change to a vegan diet, for you will already have good stores of B_{12} in your body which will take many years to deplete. In any case, it seems that many vegans can survive adequately on the marginal intakes that their natural diet provides. Sources of B_{12} occur in our intestines and fermented foods, such as yeast extracts, miso and shoyu, apart from dairy products. In addition, many manufacturers of other foods, such as cereals, have added it to their products.

There are certain situations, however, where a vegan's B_{12} requirements might increase, for example if you are pregnant, or if you suffer from gastro-intestinal disorders, in which case, your doctor may recommend a supplement. Special supplements may also have to be given to infant vegans (see page 232).

Minerals

Calcium, phosphorus and magnesium
Calcium is important for strong bones and teeth, and the proper functioning of enzymes. Good sources are spinach, milk and cheese. Phosphorus is essential for heart and kidney function and normal bone structure. Good sources are whole grains, seeds, nuts, eggs and soya. Magnesium is needed for cells, muscle and nerve function. Good sources are vegetables and grains.

Potassium and sodium
Potassium is essential for the normal functioning of hert muscles, kidneys, blood circulation and the nervous system, and also helps maintain fluid levels. Good sources are fresh and dried fruit, vegetables, milk and legumes; sodium helps maintain nerve and muscle function and normal fluid levels. It occurs naturally in most vegetables, and is often added in the form of salt (see page 64).

Iron and zinc
Iron is needed to form haemoglobin which carries oxygen in the blood. Good sources are dried fruit, legumes, sesame seeds, turnips and cabbages. (Absorption of iron is increased by vitamin C.) Zinc is important for growth and for the synthesis of proteins. Also for wound healing and for maintaining hair, skin and nails. Good sources are eggs, milk, cheese, whole grains and legumes.

CHAPTER 2

The Vegetarian Cook

The transition to a vegetarian diet is often a gradual one. Very likely, many of us will never give up meat entirely, but eat it only occasionally. This is the way the trend in food appears to be going. People are not coming to an ethical and dramatic decision, but rather being swayed by notions of a healthier diet which does not exploit the land or animals.

As meat and meat products are abandoned, they can leave gaps in your diet and store cupboard that must be filled. Once the decision has been taken to avoid meat, various sensible procedures can take place. For example, it is wise to tell family and friends about your change of diet to avoid the embarrassment of being served meat and having to eat it out of politeness. Becoming vegetarian is now so widespread that your announcement will probably cause little surprise. Most people who cook and entertain frequently generally take the precaution of checking in advance whether their guests have any dietary preferences.

Another sensible step for the new vegetarian is to take a fresh look at your neighbourhood shops to see if they stock a good range of wholefoods. If not, ask them to start. While specialist 'health food' shops cater for most requirements, it is encouraging to note that big supermarkets are increasingly aware of the trend and now stock a range of healthier foods - high in fibre, low in saturated fats, salt and sugar.

It is a good idea to take a fresh look at restaurants too. Even very recently it was not uncommon for distinguished restaurants to offer only an omelette or salad when asked for a vegetarian meal. Once, at a four-star hotel, I was given a plate of boiled vegetables, which was one of the most unappealing dishes ever set before me. This, of course, is a pathetic state of affairs. Vegetarians should insist on their right to a gourmet meal, as much as any meat-eater.

However, the most important task for a new vegetarian is to review the store cupboard. Within weeks this can change your cooking and add hundreds of new dishes to your repertoire. On the following pages I list what I consider to be essentials, with the emphasis on natural herbs, flavours and spices. For too long vegetarian food has had the reputation of being bland and stodgy. While it is certainly capable of being both, it does not have to be; imaginative use of ingredients and seasoning can create meals which are enticing in their own right.

 *Pâtés look doubly enticing if shaped into quenelles and circles. Try rolling the outside in chopped nuts or herbs. (See page 57 for the technique.)*

The Store Cupboard

Oils

Good oils are expensive, but they contribute so much flavour and nutrition that it is money well spent. Besides, you are saving money on buying meat.

Extra virgin olive oil is the first essential. It is made from the first pressing of olives, so it is thick, green and powerful in flavour. Use it for vinaigrettes, mayonnaises, and cooking vegetables.

Walnut oil and **hazelnut oil** , cold pressed from ripe nuts, are delicately flavoured and magnificent with salads, sauces and mayonnaises. They are expensive, so most of us use them sparingly, but if you can afford it, be as liberal as you would with olive oil.

Toasted sesame oil is another useful addition to the store cupboard, particularly as it is high in protein. The oil is extracted from toasted sesame seeds, giving it a pungent and strong flavour, so mix it with other oils; a mere half teaspoon will be enough to flavour a salad. This oil is often used in stir-fries, but even then only 3-4 drops are used with a blander oil made from corn or sunflowers.

Corn oil has hardly any flavour, but it is light and perfect for stir-fries and deep-frying.

Fats

Cutting down on saturated fats is probably desirable for all of us, and is easy to do when you think of all the polyunsaturated fats available. In health terms, it is wise to avoid hard fats as this is the form in which saturated fats are generally available. However, there is no need to avoid them entirely.

Butter is an essential ingredient in some dishes because it gives a richness of flavour that no other fat can match. It may also be mixed with oil for frying to prevent burning. Use unsalted French butter when required.

Margarine is a butter substitute made from animal or vegetable fat, or a mixture of both. It is available in solid form, which contains a higher proportion of saturated fat, and in soft form, which contains a higher percentage of water. It may be used for spreading, baking and frying, but is not a patch on butter for flavour.

Polyunsaturated margarine is made from vegetable oils, so it is lighter in texture and flavour than solid margarine. It spreads very easily, but is not so successful in baking.

Pastry shortening I use a hydrogenated vegetable shortening, which is high in saturated fats, but gives the essential 'shortness' that pastry requires. I think this is justifiable as the flavour is better than margarine, and each person has only a small portion, so the fat intake is not horrendous.

Suet is the fat surrounding the kidneys of sheep and beef. A vegetable variety is now available in Britain, but all types of suet are high in saturated fats. It is usually sold shredded for easy rubbing in and the dough is most often used in steamed puddings. If you have difficulty in finding vegetable suet, you may substitute hard vegetable fat which you should grate before using.

Ghee is clarified butter used in Indian cooking. It does not burn so easily as ordinary butter.

Vinegars

Do not think of flavoured vinegars solely in relation to salads. A tablespoon added at the last minute to a stir-fry allows the vegetables to steam briefly and absorb some of the vinegar's flavour.

Good red and white wine vinegars are a fine start to your collection.

Cider vinegars, flavoured with herbs such as tarragon, mint, thyme and basil, should be your next additions. Cider vinegar flavoured with mint and beaten into sour cream is perfect for topping new or baked potatoes.

Raspberry vinegar, **sherry vinegar** and **Chinese black bean vinegar** have unusual and delicious flavours that are well worth experimenting with.

Balsamic vinegar is made in northern Italy and is kept for ten years or more in wooden kegs made fom oak, chestnut, mulberry or juniper. It has a strong, dense flavour and is reddish-brown in colour. Use it in salads and sauces.

Homemade herb vinegar
Rinse and dry a handful of mixed fresh herbs, or use half that amount of dried herbs. Place in a 1-litre/1¾-pint/1-quart jar or bottle. Add 10 whole peppercorns, 2 peeled shallots and 1 teaspoon celery seed. Fill up with cider vinegar, then seal and store for 2 weeks. Strain through muslin/cheesecloth and bottle.

Legumes

Also known as 'pulses', this group includes all types of beans, peas and lentils. They are high in protein and are a useful source of fibre. However, beans have always had a bad press, as they have long been considered a cause of 'nether wind'. It is sad that beans have taken much of the blame for flatulence. In fact, fifteen per cent of *all* carbohydrates have the same effect because part of them cannot be absorbed by the small intestine. The result is that the bacteria in the stomach and colon convert the food into gas to make it digestible. As we are all individual, our intestines produce different amounts of bacteria, so some people are more flatulent than others; beans have little to do with it. Legumes add texture, taste and protein to the diet, so don't avoid them because of their reputation.

Try to keep several types of legumes in your store cupboard to give colour and variety to your meals. However, it is a mistake to keep too much in either range or quantity. Legumes become tough when old and need lengthy cooking to tenderize them. To ensure freshness, buy from shops which have a steady turnover, do not buy more than 450 g/1 lb at a time, and store them in airtight jars.

My favourites are *broad/fava* beans, which people are either excessively fond of, or dislike intensely. However, do try *aduki, butter/lima, haricot/navy, mung* and *soya beans*. The haricot family is very large and includes many different varieties (see page 80). As far as I am concerned, the greatest disappointment in this selection is the soya bean. For many years I have tried to create flavoursome soya dishes by casseroling them with garlic, ginger, herbs and practically everything growing in the kitchen garden, but the soya bean tastes resolutely only of itself - bland and insipid. Nonetheless, they are rich in nutrition and should not be dismissed.

Peas

Believed to have been cultivated as far back as Neolithic times, peas have veered in and out of fashion. In the Middle Ages dried peas were commonly used in cooking, particularly meat and fish dishes. In seventeenth-century France Louis XIV became addicted to fresh peas, consuming large platefuls of them and causing his mistress to confide to her diary, 'This passion for peas is a madness!' The fashion spread to England and peas became a rare delicacy.

Peas
As peas have such a short season, *dried peas* are a useful part of the store cupboard.
Chick peas do not resemble garden peas at all, but they have a good nutty flavour and are well worth keeping in stock. There is a legend that the plant was cursed by the Virgin Mary because it refused to hide the Holy Family. As the plant grows to only 45 cm/18 inches in height, the Holy Family would have had to be dwarfs to be hidden at all.

Lentils

Although high in nutritional content, lentils lack some of the essential amino acids, so they are not a complete protein (see page 25). They have been widely eaten in the Far East, India, the Middle East and North Africa for thousands of years, but since World War II they have become one of the most popular legumes in Europe and the US. I enjoy the versatility of lentils; they make good soups, salads, pâtés or casseroles, and do not need much preparation. I find a ten-minute soak is ideal as it allows them to absorb some water and thus cuts down on cooking time.

Grains

We are most used to eating grain in the form of bread, or drinking alcohol brewed from it. However, there are many types of grain which can be prepared in a number of ways to add colour, texture and taste to any meal. Most are available in several forms, ranging from the whole, unrefined grain to freeze-dried flakes (see page 85). Barley, buckwheat, bulgar, corn, millet, oats, rye and wheat are the grains I most often use. If you keep a small supply of each of these, or any of their by-products, you will always be able to conjure up tasty and nutritious meals.

Nuts

Being high in protein and essential fats, including linoleic acid, which is helpful in controlling cholesterol, nuts are good news for vegetarians. However, their unimaginative use in the past has made them the *bête noir* of all gourmets, as they so often turned up in stodgy loaves, muddy soups and slushy sauces. The golden rule must be to use this valuable and delicious food with discretion. I suggest you keep a variety of nuts in your store cupboard. They add taste and texture to all sorts of dishes.

For new vegetarians in particular, who may still miss the substantial texture of meat, nuts can be a great help in 'bridging the gap'. Do not use a coffee grinder or food processor to break them up, or they will become at best gritty, and at worst powdery. It is worth investing in a hand-operated mincer or food mill that clamps to the table. This creates a coarser texture and gives the jaws more to work on.

Flours

It is possible to make flour from almost any pulse or grain.
I recommend that you keep a good variety in smallish
quantities in your store cupboard. This way you can
experiment with them singly or in combination for texture
and flavour. Flour begins to lose its nutritional value after six
months, so do not buy or store it in bulk. Apart from wheat
flours, you will generally find other flours do not contain
enough gluten to leaven bread on their own. Gluten is a
protein present in many flours. When mixed with water and
kneaded, it is gluten that makes the dough stretch. If yeast
or baking powder is added, the mixture produces bubbles of
air which the gluten traps. It is this process that makes the
dough rise. People who suffer from an allergy to gluten can
eat bread and cakes made from rye flour.

A comprehensive list of flours is included in the Glossary
(see page 84). Note that it is not always possible to give exact
UK or US equivalents for certain flours. For example,
American all-purpose flour is the nearest equivalent to
British plain flour, but unlike plain flour, may be
successfully used for making bread. Granary flour, which is
becoming increasingly popular in the UK, is not available at
all in the US. As it has such a good flavour, it is worth
making your own if you cannot find it (see right).

Granary flour
Heat 4 tablespoons broken wheat
kernels in 1 tablespoon malt extract
in a small saucepan. This will
caramelize the grains. Add them to
450 g/1 lb/4 cups bread flour
(wholewheat, strong or all-purpose
flour) plus 1 tablespoon bran.

Thickeners

The following items are essential ingredients to many
sauces, stews and gels. Most will keep for several months if
stored in airtight containers in a cool, dry place.

Agar agar, available in sticks or
powder form, is the vegetarian
substitute for gelatine. It is very
important to ensure that it is
completely dissolved before
cooking, so stir it into boiling water
and simmer for 5 minutes. It sets in
about 1 hour at room temperature
and may be reliquified in a
microwave or double boiler.
8 g/⅓ oz agar agar will jelly 250 ml/
8 fl oz/1 cup of liquid.

Arrowroot is a fine white flour used
for thickening sauces.
Flour Most types of flour can be
used for thickening (see page 84).
Kuzo is available as a white powder,
and is much used in Oriental
cooking. It is far superior to
arrowroot and cornflour/cornstarch
as it contains protein.

Raising agents

Bread and cake-making are two very satisfying tasks. Both depend for their success on raising agents which alter the chemical composition of the mixture.

Baking powder is useful in making cakes and soda bread, although I do not much care for the slight flavour or texture it bestows. You can make your own by mixing 3 parts of bicarbonate of soda to 2 parts of cream of tartar.
Fresh yeast is moist and bought in small slabs. Keep it covered in plastic wrap in a refrigerator for up to 2 weeks.

Dried yeast comes in sachets, usually enough for a 450 g/1 lb loaf, and sometimes has a stronger flavour than fresh yeast. It needs to be mixed with a little water before using. (Although the instructions on the packet say it should be mixed with a little sugar, I think this is unnecessary.) Bread made with this yeast needs two risings before baking to ensure the yeast is evenly distributed and working properly. Only half as much dried as fresh yeast is needed in a recipe.

Micronized/active dry yeast is dried and resembles tiny ball bearings. It requires no preparation and is simply mixed with the dry ingredients before liquid is added. It requires only one rising.
Note: In the US, **active dry yeast** may also be prepared in the same way as *dried yeast* (see left). To save time and fuss, I recommend you try using it straight from the packet and compare the results.

Flavourings

This section covers the powders, liquids and pastes that you may well use every day.

Black peppercorns contribute aroma and flavour when freshly ground; pre-ground they add only heat.
Dijon mustard is a French mustard which is very useful in cooking as its flavour is fairly 'pure'; unlike many other French mustards, it contains no tarragon, sugar or vinegar.
English mustard powder To use as a condiment, mix it to a smooth paste with a little cold water. Do not use vinegar, boiling water or salt as these will destroy the enzymes and make it bitter rather than hot. I like to add a little of this powder to mayonnaise (see page 129).
Garlic I could write a book about garlic. It is one of the most vital flavourings, and as an added bonus has many medicinal properties.
Lemon juice I could never be without the lemon; I rely on its juice and zest to enhance many dishes. The peel of most citrus fruit is treated with a fungicide to add

sheen. This can apparently be dissolved with gin or by cooking. I don't believe the amount we might absorb would be injurious to health.
Meaux mustard This is a grainy French mustard made from whole crushed mustard seeds. If you find it difficult to get hold of, any other wholegrain mustard may be used.
Sea salt is preferable to ordinary table salt as it has no added preservatives. Alternatives to salt are given on page 18).
Soy sauce I prefer the natural fermented sauce called 'shoyu'. The Japanese version is called 'tamari'. Beware cheap soy sauce; it is made from chemicals.
Sugar There are many types of sugar, the most common being white granulated. The only one to have any nutritional value is raw cane sugar - but even this has only a trace of natural minerals, so it can hardly be considered a useful part of

the diet. Where castor/superfine sugar is required in the recipes, it is possible to make your own by whizzing granulated sugar in a blender until it is in very small crystals, not a powder. However, all sugars are cariogenic, and therefore best avoided.
Tabasco is a very hot sauce made from chillies, vinegar and salt. It is a useful standby if you have run out of dried red chillies or chilli powder, but only *a few drops* are required to flavour a dish.
Wasabi (Japanese horseradish) is hotter than European horseradish and is useful for dishes that need an extra sharp pungency.
Worcestershire sauce contains anchovies, so strict vegetarians will eschew it. It can be useful as an extra flavouring in some sauces, soups and stews, though I personally prefer it with tomato juice and vodka.

Herbs and spices

You will probably already have a selection of herbs and spices in your store cupboard, so do not be daunted by the length of my list. This variety is necessary if you intend to make your own curry powder. Buy herbs and spices from shops with a fast turnover to ensure freshness. Buy in small amounts, say 50 g/2 oz sachets, and keep them in airtight jars hidden from the light. When adding them to dishes, keep the jar away from the steam to prevent the contents getting damp.

Essentials
Allspice, Anise, Star anise, Asafoetida, Basil, Caraway seeds, Cardomom, Cassia, Cayenne pepper, Celery salt, Chervil, Chilli, Cinnamon, Cloves, Coriander seeds, Cumin, Dill, Fenugreek, Garlic salt, Ginger, Juniper berries, Mace, Marjoram, Mixed/apple pie spice, Mustard seeds, Nutmeg, Oregano, Paprika, Parsley, Peppercorns, Rosemary, Sage, Savory, Tamarind, Tarragon, Thyme, Turmeric.

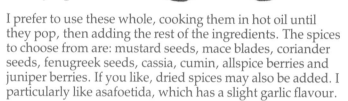

Curry spices

I prefer to use these whole, cooking them in hot oil until they pop, then adding the rest of the ingredients. The spices to choose from are: mustard seeds, mace blades, coriander seeds, fenugreek seeds, cassia, cumin, allspice berries and juniper berries. If you like, dried spices may also be added. I particularly like asafoetida, which has a slight garlic flavour.

Curry powder Purchased curry powder is not a good idea, as it does not keep well. Make your own in small amounts as you require it. Although it is time-consuming, the final flavour of your curry will be much better. If you prefer to make curry paste, mix your ground spices with corn, sunflower or safflower oil. If bottled, this paste keeps well for many months. Use any five of the following spices: the permutations are endless. Black peppercorns, chilli, cloves, cinnamon, cardomom, mace, poppy seeds, coriander, cumin, curry leaves, fenugreek, ginger, mustard seed, turmeric.

Apart from chilli, cardomom, curry leaves and ginger, it is essential to roast each spice separately as some cook more quickly than others. Do this in a heavy, dry pan on top of the stove, being careful not to overcook; this causes bitterness. The spice is done in one or two minutes when it begins to change colour and exude its aroma. After the spices have each been roasted they can be mixed together and ground into a powder.
Garam masala Like curry powder, this is best when homemade in small quantities. It is a mixture of several ground spices, which may be used in addition to curry powder. The basic formula is an equal measure of

black pepper, cloves and cinnamon, and a double measure of coriander and cumin seeds. They are roasted and ground in the same way as curry powder.
Chillies Take care (or wear gloves) when preparing fresh chillies. If you handle the seeds and then happen to touch your eyes, it can be painful. I find dried red chillies are most practical; they store well, give the required heat and there is no problem in preparation. However, there are many kinds available (see page 60).

Seeds

It is useful to keep a variety of seeds to add texture and crunch to certain dishes. They also help to create an attractive appearance when sprinkled on top of loaves and rolls. In my opinion *sesame seeds* are the most delicious of all, but I also keep *linseeds*, *poppy seeds*, *pumpkin seeds* and *sunflower seeds* in the cupboard.

Spreads

Honey is the most ancient form of sweetener. Use in preference to sugar, but do not deceive yourself about its cariogenic properties. Honey with yoghurt has become a simple classic. Even better is the Scottish classic of honey with whisky, cream and oatmeal called 'atholl brose'.

Molasses is a very sweet and strongly-flavoured by-product of sugar. It is often used in cakes and desserts.

Peanut butter This is a paste made from peanuts (minus their skins). It may be added to some stews or casseroles (see page 151), but should be used sparingly as it has a powerful flavour.

Pure fructose syrups and spreads These are a fairly recent development but are available in many health food stores. They are made by reducing fruit to the essential fructose and are very useful for puddings and desserts and as a general sugar substitute. They come in various natural fruit flavours. If you have difficulty in finding fructose products, you may substitute honey or sugar instead.

Tahini (sesame spread) is an oily paste made from sesame seeds. It is sometimes added to hummus (see page 188) and may also be mixed with miso (see page 138). It is highly nutritious and delicious.

Yeast extracts There are many types of yeast extract available under different brand names, Marmite, Yeastvite, Savorex, Vecon, to name just a few. All are high in salt. Vegetarian cooking in the past has been destroyed by the use of these brown pastes, as they have such a harsh and pervasive flavour. If you happen to like the taste, use yeast extracts as a spread on toast or sandwiches, but avoid cooking with them.

Canned foods

Canned stores are useful standbys. Artichoke hearts, beans, carob powder, laver seaweed (sometimes frozen), oyster mushrooms, sweet peppers, tomato purée/paste and tomatoes can make useful contributions, but should not be relied on.

Pasta

This must surely be one of the most versatile foodstuffs ever devised. It is usually made from a simple mixture of flour, eggs and water, but the flour may be white, wholewheat or buckwheat. Pasta is made in an enormous variety of shapes and sizes, ranging from large lasagne sheets, to tiny stars. It may be boiled, baked or added to soups. A few packets of dried pasta are essential to any well-stocked store cupboard.

Pickles

To my mind nothing conjures up images of plenty, good food, love and security more than shelves bent a little under the weight of large jars of homemade pickles. Some of the following are commercial preparations, but still worth having: capers, garlic, gherkins, green peppercorns, olives, plums, quinces, seitan (see recipe on page 55), shallots, umeboshi plums and walnuts (perfect with cheese).

Dried vegetables

The only method of preserving vegetables which retains all their nutrients is drying, so there would always be a couple of packets of dried vegetables in my larder. The following selection will add variety and protein to the vegetarian diet.

Funghi A wide variety of Chinese, Japanese, Italian and French mushrooms are available. They are better value for money than they appear as they absorb a huge amount of water when soaked (see page 92).

Sea vegetables This is the general name for seaweed. Depending on the variety, it can be grilled/broiled until crisp, cut and added to soups, stews and salads, stir-fried, or cooked to soften and wrapped round moulds. Like dried funghi, seaweed expands considerably when soaked, so only a little is needed. The types and methods of preparation are described in the Glossary on page 59.

Dried fruit

A selection of dried fruits is a must. Apart from tasting delicious, they are high in nutritional content, particularly apricots. Apples, apricots, bananas, currants, dates, figs, pears and raisins are most widely used in both sweet and savoury dishes. Try mixing them with nuts and celery to stuff root vegetables.

Dairy produce and non-dairy substitutes

The new vegetarian's preoccupation with replacing the protein gap left by meat is a misguided one. There are many other sources of protein and the body does not require huge amounts of it anyway. Many vegetarians are happy to consume milk, cheese and eggs for their protein intake, but these products are not the answer if you are allergic to them, or if you follow a vegan diet. For people in this dilemma, it is possible to buy milk extracted from soya beans, vegetarian cheese made from plant rennet, and a vegan egg substitute. The latter is particularly useful for binding dishes, such as pâtés and moulds, which traditionally rely on eggs to help keep their shape.

Eggs
Free-range eggs are considerably better in flavour than battery produced eggs, and you have the additional bonus of knowing that they are reared in humane and natural conditions. When broken open a fresh egg should sit on a cushion of white. The colour of the yolk is no indication of freshness.

It is possible to buy a vegan substitute for eggs, which is useful in baking. The nearest substitute in appearance and protein content is probably tofu (see page 46). As I have said before, there are many other sources of protein, so do not worry if eggs are not part of your diet.

Personally, I cannot imagine life without eating good cheese with homemade breads and pickles. Equally, I cannot imagine cooking without cheese. Below I list the dairy items I find most useful in my kitchen, but do not be afraid to make changes and substitutions to suit your particular needs. Fat content alone is a major consideration for many people, and most of my recipes in this book reflect the trend towards less fat in the diet. In the few recipes where I have used cream, it is often possible to use an alternative (unless I have expressly stated otherwise). Try substituting yoghurt and Smetana/low-fat sour cream, both of which are approximately the same consistency as cream, but which have a sharper flavour. If a thicker alternative is required, try a skimmed soft cheese and thin it with a little milk if necessary. A non-dairy soft cheese, made from soya beans or nuts, is also available from health food stores.

I find soft, low-fat cheeses indispensable as they can be used instead of eggs to bind purées and other dishes. If you find them lacking in taste, try augmenting them with a tiny amount of Parmesan, Pecorino or mature Gouda.

Milk

Cow's milk is available in many forms and has many by-products. For health reasons it is preferable to use *skimmed milk*, which has all the goodness but only 1% of the fat of whole milk. The flavour and consistency are quite thin, but it is possible to get used to both, given time. *Dried low-fat cow's milk* is useful in baking, and may be used for enriching soups and skimmed milk.

Goat's milk has a sharper taste than cow's milk and is a good substitute for those allergic to it. It may be used in exactly the same ways as cow's milk, and makes some very good cheeses.

Soya milk is extracted from soya beans and is available in liquid and dried forms. It has a nutty taste, which I find very pleasant, and it can give additional flavour to soups. It is not so successful in tea and coffee. It makes a refreshing summer drink when mixed with mint and a dash of salt. It also makes excellent lassi mixed half and half with yoghurt (see page 206).

Yoghurt is made from milk which has been thickened by the action of certain bacteria. I particularly like Greek yoghurt which has been strained to make it thick and smooth. If you find it difficult to get hold of, you can strain ordinary plain yoghurt through muslin/cheesecloth. Eat it plain, or with fruit and honey, or use it in cooking in place of cream. When mixed with cucumber and mint it makes a refreshing side dish with curries (see page 190).

Butter (see page 36)

Cheese

It is now possible to find a huge range of cheeses in the shops, and they can add a great deal of interest to the vegetarian diet. However, they are made with animal rennet, so pure vegetarians should stick to those made from plant rennet (see below). The ones I make a point of keeping to hand are used mainly in making sauces.

Hard cheeses, such as *Cheddar*, *Gruyère* and *Parmesan* are particularly useful. Try to buy cheese freshly cut, rather than pre-packed from a supermarket. It will cost more, but taste considerably better.

Vegetarian cheese is made with plant rennet. The most common is called *Galium verum*, popularly called 'lady's bedstraw' in the UK. The cheese is available in hard and soft forms and may be used in exactly the same ways as Cheddar and Ricotta. As public demand increases, many more vegetarian cheeses are becoming available, so keep your eyes open for them.

Soft cheeses, particularly French ones, are legion. Some, like *Brie* and *Camembert* may need 'ripening' before you eat them. If the rind on the outside does not 'give', leave them out at room temperature for a few days. Never cut a whole Brie or Camembert before it is ripe for, once cut, it cannot mature. (Slices of Brie will soften and become yellow, but the flavour does not improve without the rind.)

Soft cheeses Try to keep *curd/small curd cottage cheese, Quark, Smetana/low-fat sour cream, Ricotta* and *cottage cheese* to hand. They are all low in fat and the first four have useful binding qualities in cooking. As there is no US equivalent to Quark, or low-fat curd cheese, like fromage frais, it is acceptable to substitute puréed cottage cheese wherever these ingredients occur.

Meat substitutes

For the new vegetarian in particular, meat substitutes can be a useful addition to the store cupboard. Although there is no lack of fibre and texture in a good vegetarian diet, some people miss meat a great deal. There are several types of meat substitutes available, but with a little imagination vegetables can be successfully used to create the colour and texture of the missing meat.

TVP (Textured vegetable protein) is the name given to soya mince and chunks. It is used in the same way as minced/ground beef. To prepare, simply follow the instructions on the packet.

Tofu is a white bean curd made from soya beans which has the protein equivalent of eggs. The smoked variety has a subtle flavour, but the plain white variety is completely tasteless. If using packaged tofu, drain it and dry it on absorbent paper - it will then be easier to cook. When stir-fried and tossed in flavoured oils and spices, it becomes a tasty and versatile ingredient. For sweet dishes, beat in some concentrated fruit juice, or use in soufflés and cold puddings.

Tempeh is fermented tofu. It is available as a densely packed cake and is used in stir-fries and soups in much-the same way as tofu.

Soya grits and flakes are processed in much the same way that oats are rolled. In these forms they can be added to herb, vegetable and grain mixtures for rissoles or croquettes.

Established vegetarians will, no doubt, have many ideas for non-TVP variations and substitutions in traditional meat dishes, but for those who lack the experience, the following ideas work well in moussaka, pasta dishes, risotto and stuffings. They could be particularly useful if you are feeding non-vegetarians.

Substitutions for 450 g/1 lb minced/ground beef in recipes

● *225 g/8 oz grated carrot, pumpkin, turnip, swede/rutabaga or other root vegetable, and 225 g/8 oz minced/ground nuts, especially hazelnuts, filberts, cashews, walnuts, flaked/slivered almonds and pecans.*

● *225 g/8 oz minced/ground root vegetable, and 225 g/8 oz of legumes, such as chick peas or lentils.*

● *225 g/8 oz minced/ground nuts, plus 100 g/4 oz buckwheat or millet, and 100 g/4 oz minced/ground root vegetable.*

If you want to match the texture of minced/ground beef, use a coarse mincer, not a grinder.

Substitutions for white chicken pieces in recipes

● *Try using coarsely minced/ground white root vegetables, such as parsnips and turnips, pine nuts, flaked/slivered almonds, artichoke hearts and water chestnuts.*

Substitutions for white fish or seafood in recipes

● *Try using white vegetables, such as leeks, celeriac, baby turnips, sea vegetables (particularly laver), capers, funghi, tofu (plain and smoked) with some white wine.*

Cooking equipment

It is possible to cook adequately and healthily with only one saucepan and a wooden spoon on a single gas ring. However, it is preferable to have a little more to hand, simply to make life easier and allow you to cook more than one thing at a time.

Electrical equipment

The range is now so vast that we are spoilt for choice. Below I list the items that I find particularly useful, but no doubt you will have your own favourite and indispensable items.

Blender or *liquidizer* This has to come top of my list as it has revolutionized the making of purées, cutting the process from about 30 minutes to 30 seconds.

Food mixer A close second in my choice of equipment. I find the dough hooks particularly good for bread-making, saving me the arm-aching chore of kneading. It also whips cream and egg whites in a trice.

Food processsor This item incorporates a blending device and has many other functions, which makes it a useful kitchen companion. The only drawback is that, even for a simple task like making breadcrumbs, the subsequent dismantling, washing and reassembling of the machine takes considerably longer than the task itself.

Coffee grinder Apart from being essential for making good, fresh coffee, it is also useful for grinding nuts, and herbs and spices for curries.

Manually-operated equipment

The professional cook gathers a huge amount of equipment in a lifetime, most of which is unnecessary. The items I list below are essentials and I recommend that you buy the best you can afford. They will reward you with a lifetime's reliability.

Cheese grater Choose one which is triangular in shape so it sits squarely on the working surface.

Garlic press It is useful to have a press that takes several cloves at once. Some now have removable parts which makes them easy to wash.

Grinder/mincer This is particularly useful for making coarse mixtures of nuts and root vegetables. Choose one that clamps to the table and has a choice of blades for various textures.

Knives Money spent on good carbon steel knives is an investment as they will last a lifetime. Keep them hanging up or slotted into a wooden block. They rapidly lose their sharpness if jumbled together in a drawer.

Implements Keep things simple. Have a selection of wooden spoons and spatulas, with some additional metal items, like a slotted spoon, a palette knife, a ladle, a sieve and a balloon whisk.

Measuring jug/cup Choose one made of glass with clear markings so you can read it accurately.

Kitchen scales Experienced cooks rarely use scales as they can usually judge quantities by eye. However, a pair of scales clearly marked in ounces and grams is a useful item for many people.

Pans and dishes

Saucepans should be heavy-based with a non-stick surface and tightly-fitting lids. Three different sizes are sufficient. Do not use aluminium. It reacts badly with metal implements and food which has a wine or acid content.

Steamer If you want to preserve the nutritional value of your food, a steamer is essential. There are many types available.

Frying pan I find a copper-bottomed frying pan particularly useful as copper spreads heat well and helps prevent food burning.

Pressure cooker This can be a very useful item as it cuts down on cooking time and saves fuel in the process. It is especially good for cooking beans (see page 51).

Wok Excellent for stir-fries, needing very little fat.

Baking pans For this book the requirements are very simple: a baking sheet, a bun tray/muffin pan, a 23-cm/9-inch tart pan, a 17-cm/7- inch spring-release cake pan and a 450 g/1 lb loaf pan.

Casseroles Earthenware casseroles are, for me, quite the best, but some people swear by enamelled cast-iron casseroles, such as the ones made by Le Creuset. Like so many things in life, the choice is highly subjective.

Gratin dishes/tians are shallow baking dishes, usually with two fluted handles. They can be made from cast iron, copper or earthenware, and are available in all sizes.

Soufflé dishes All the soufflés in this book require a 2.75-litre/5-pint/3- quart dish, 24 cm/9 inches in diameter. It is also useful to have one of half this capacity.

Ramekins are small earthenware pots. Have one per person.

Mixing bowls Available in earthenware or plastic. Have a variety of sizes.

Pudding basin/steaming mould In this book I use a 1.7-litre/3-pint/7½-cup basin for all the steamed puddings. This will give 6-8 servings, so you may find it useful to have smaller ones available too.

Wooden salad bowl Usually made of hardwood, such as teak, these bowls retain the flavours from the dressings. They should never be washed, but simply wiped with absorbent kitchen paper.

Pastry

If you find wholewheat pastry crumbly and difficult to roll out neatly, try the following technique.

How to roll out wholewheat pastry
Place a piece of plastic wrap on the rolling surface roughly the size you want the pastry to be. Roll the pastry out on top of it, then pick up the plastic wrap base and carefully turn the pastry into the baking pan or pie dish. Make sure it is accurately positioned before peeling off the plastic wrap.

How to bake blind
The purpose of this exercise is to make a cooked pastry case which can then be filled. In order to stop the base of the pastry case rising it is lined with foil or greaseproof/waxed paper and covered with a weight. The weight is normally dried beans, but you can now buy ceramic beans which serve the purpose very well. They hold and generate heat very efficiently, thus cooking the pastry a little quicker than dried beans. Bake the case in a pre-heated oven at 200°C/350°F/Gas mark 4 for about 10 minutes. Remove the weight and foil, then return the case to the oven for 2-3 minutes to dry out.
Note: If you are making a cool tart, it is a good idea to seal the pastry case with egg white before the final drying out to prevent the pastry becoming soggy when it is filled.

Breadcrumbs and croûtons

Although the name is misleading, fresh breadcrumbs are *not* made from fresh bread. In order to grate easily, the bread should be slightly stale, say two days old. It is also best to make croûtons from slightly stale bread. Do not use very stale bread or you will end up with croûtons that are too hard and crisp.

How to make toasted breadcrumbs
Place your breadcrumbs on a baking sheet in the oven pre-heated to 180°C/350°F/Gas mark 4, and bake for 10-15 minutes, or until golden brown.

How to make croûtons
To make croûtons cut a slice of bread about 1 cm/½ inch thick and remove the crusts. Cut the bread into dice about 1 cm/½ inch square. Heat 2 tablespoons of olive oil in a pan and fry the cubes briskly, turning them over in the oil so each side becomes golden. (You might find it useful to use the sautéeing technique of shaking the pan quite violently.)

How to make garlic croûtons
For garlic croûtons, add 1 or 2 crushed garlic cloves to the olive oil. The garlic fries with the bread and crusts the croûtons rather pleasantly. I happen to like the taste of fried garlic, but some people do not, so discard the garlic after cooking if you are uncertain.
Note: Classic French croûtons are diced very small - about the size of a little finger nail.

How to make pasta

This recipe may be made by hand or in a food processor. It makes enough for 6-8 generous servings.

75 g/3 oz/³⁄₄ cup wholewheat flour
100 g/4 oz/1 cup white unbleached flour
¼ teaspoon sea salt
2 large eggs

Sieve the flours and salt into a mound on a clean, dry board and make a well in the centre. Crack in the eggs and mix with a fork, using your free hand to prevent the flour going everywhere. When the eggs have absorbed as much flour as possible, sprinkle with a little water if necessary and knead the dough for 5 minutes. It will be sticky and elastic. Wrap the dough in a damp cloth and refrigerate for 30 minutes. Divide the dough into two pieces and roll out as thinly as possible on a floured surface.

How to make ravioli

1 Cut the pasta into strips 10 cm/4 inches wide. Place teaspoonfuls of filling at 5-cm/2-inch intervals.

2 Brush a little egg yolk mixed with milk between each bit of filling and along one edge of each strip.

3 Fold the dough over the filling, pressing firmly between the filling and along the edge.

4 Cut the ravioli apart with a knife or a pastry wheel.

How to cook pasta

You should always cook pasta in plenty of boiling water, adding a little salt or lemon juice to taste. Aim to serve it al dente - cooked through but still slightly firm to the bite. If using dried pasta, follow the instructions on the packet for cooking times. Wholewheat pasta, which is brown, takes a little longer to cook than the common yellow egg pasta. Buckwheat pasta will cook within 2 minutes - the quickest of all the dried pastas.

Fresh pasta takes less time to cook than dried, perhaps only a minute or two for noodles, and 7-8 minutes for something like tortelloni.

Is it done?
Some people believe that it is possible to test spaghetti and noodles for readiness by hurling a strand at the wall - the idea being that if it sticks, it's done. This is far from accurate. It would have to be sticky, and therefore overcooked, in order for it to cling.

Preparing rice and grains

The three types of rice - long, medium and short grain - do not need to be washed before cooking, as some people claim. Do be sure though to cook them al dente.

On the whole, grains do not need soaking, although cooking times will be shortened somewhat if they are soaked. Bulgar and cous cous are exceptions in always needing some form of treatment. Treat grains as you would rice, cooking so that they are al dente rather than soft. See the chart below for full details.

How to cook perfect rice
I don't bother to wash the rice before cooking it. Cover the grains with about 2 cm/1 inch cold water, and add a pinch of sea salt. Bring to the boil, then cover and simmer for 5-6 minutes. Bite into a grain and if not quite done, simmer for 2 more minutes. Drain the rice in a colander and rinse with hot water. Transfer the rice - still in the colander - to a warm oven (160°C/325°F/Gas mark 3) for 8-10 minutes to dry out. Stir the rice and turn out into a serving dish.

GRAIN	Soaking time	Cooking time		
		Oven	Hob	Pressure cooker
Pot barley	60	80	60	20
Pearl barley	15	40	30	15
Buckwheat groats	—	15	10	3
Bulgar	30	—	3	—
Corn meal	—	15	10	3
Cous cous	wash, drain and leave	—	steam 20	—
Millet	—	25	20	10
Oat groats	20 or overnight	90	60	25
Jumbo oats	overnight if eaten raw	20	20	10
Rolled oats	—	—	5	2
Oat grains	15	15	10	5
Rye flakes	—	—	5	2
Cracked wheat	15	15	12	5

RICE	Cooking method	Timing once boiling
Arborio/ Italian	Simmer, covered	8-10
Basmati	Simmer, covered	8-10
Brown	Simmer, covered	45
Patna/ long grain	Simmer, covered	8-10
Wild	Simmer, covered	5
	Remove from heat but leave in water	60
	Return to boil and simmer, covered	5

Note: As all these grains are processed by different manufacturers and then packaged by different retailers, they might have cooking instructions which differ from those given above. Compare the packet with the chart, and if there is a difference, follow the packet. Cooking grains is often a matter of trial and error, but if you are in any doubt, follow the chart. All timings are given in minutes.

Preparing legumes

It is impossible to be precise about the amount of liquid and the length of time that different beans need to cook in. The chart below is a guide, but do not take it as precise to the last minute. Both the time and water factors depend on the age of the bean - the older the bean, the longer it takes to cook - but there is no way of telling how old a dried bean is. As a safeguard, buy from shops with a steady turnover, and do not buy wrinkled beans that have no sheen.

Pressure cookers tend to inspire strong emotions in people; you either love them or loathe them. I admit that I have stopped using a pressure cooker, but only because I have burnt two by forgetting they were on the stove when pruning out in the garden. Pressure cookers cut down considerably on cooking time, which can mean a great saving on fuel; and contrary to popular belief, they do *not* destroy vitamins in food.

Toxins
Most of the kidney bean family have a toxin in the skin which must be destroyed by fast-boiling for 10 minutes and then throwing the water away. Never cook beans in a slow cooker and never attempt to eat them raw. It sounds silly, I know, but the toxins in red kidney beans were discovered by someone eating beans that had been soaked but not cooked. However, do not let this alarm you unduly. There are tiny amounts of toxins in most foods and generally they do us no harm.

LEGUME	Soaking time		Fast boil	Cooking time		
	Boiling water	Cold water		Oven	Hob	Pressure cooker
Aduki	60	overnight	5	75	60	10
Black-eyed	60	overnight	5	75	60	15
Borlotti	60	overnight	5	75	60	15
Broad/fava	60	overnight	10	75	60	15
Butter/lima	60	overnight	5	75	60	15
Cannellini	60	overnight	5	90	75	15
Chick peas	180	overnight	10	130	120	20
Dried peas	60	overnight	5	40	30	10
Flageolet	—	60	3	50	45	10
Ful medames (brown beans)	60	overnight	5	120	90	20
Haricot/navy	60	overnight	5	90	60	15
Kidney (all varieties)	60	overnight	10 (then discard water)	100	75	15
Lentils	—	10	2	40	30	8
Mung	30	overnight	3	50	45	10
Pinto	60	overnight	10	100	75	15
Soya	60	overnight	—	120	90	20

Preparing vegetables

Clean vegetables briefly and try to avoid peeling them, as much of the goodness is in the peel. If you must peel vegetables, do so just before eating and use the peelings to make stock for soups and stews. (That is the advice of the economical cook, but I must admit I rarely follow it myself.) Cook vegetables as briefly as possible, preferably steaming rather than boiling to retain goodness. If you do boil vegetables, use the water to make soups or sauces.

It is best to cook without sugar and salt, adding them at the table if you really miss them. Remember, if you keep the heat very low and the pan covered, vegetables will cook in a tiny amount of oil or water without burning.

Cutting The Chinese method of diagonal cutting is the best. This ensures the maximum amount of surface area is exposed to the heat, thus allowing it to cook quickly with minimal loss of nutrients. A good rule is to 'cut to the character' of the vegetable: cut long root vegetables diagonally down the stem, and cut round vegetables across.

Slicing To slice is to cut thinly. Occasionally, for such things as Chinese soups, you may need to 'julienne' vegetables. This means to slice into thin strips resembling fine matchsticks.

Dicing This means to cut into square, box-like shapes about the size of a die.

Chopping This means to cut into small pieces with no regard for shape or size. When fine chopping is specified, it is usually in relation to herbs and means that they should resemble breadcrumbs in size.

How to salt vegetables to remove moisture (and bitterness)
Certain vegetables, such as aubergines/eggplants, cucumber and courgettes/zucchini cook more easily, absorb less fat and become more digestible if some of their water content is removed. To do this, slice but do not peel the vegetables to the desired size. Sprinkle each slice with a little sea salt and place in a colander or on a platter for about 60 minutes. Rinse the salt off under running cold water, then pat dry with absorbent paper. Note: After rinsing, grated courgettes/zucchini can be squeezed dry in a colander. When you have removed as much liquid as possible, pat them dry with a clean cloth.

How to skin tomatoes, garlic, onions, shallots and chestnuts
The best method of doing this is by blanching. Put the items to be skinned in a bowl and pour boiling water over them. Leave for a few minutes or until the water is cool. Nick the skin with a sharp knife and it will peel away like a glove. Note: Dried chestnuts can be tricky even after this process, as the nuts have a dark, wrinkled inner skin which is sometimes rather obstinate. If you find this to be the case, repeat the blanching process.

How to peel peppers
This is a useful technique for such things as salads and piperade (see page 144). Impale the pepper on a fork and hold over a flame until it is blackened and blistered all over. Peel off the skin, then seed, chop and use.

Alternatively, roast the peppers in the hottest possible oven for about 30 minutes, or until very brown. Transfer to a plastic bag, close it tightly, and leave for 10 minutes. The peppers will be very easy to peel.

Cooking vegetables

There are many methods of cooking vegetables, some of which are outlined below, but do remember that food does not necessarily have to be cooked to be edible. Many vegetables simply need peeling, slicing or grating, and may be served as a salad or as crudités with a sauce or vinaigrette.

Boiling There is a theory that root vegetables should be placed in cold water and brought to the boil, while all others should be placed in boiling water. I can see no reason for this practice, and believe that putting root vegetables in cold water prolongs the cooking time and encourages them to leach out more of their goodness. I put *all* vegetables in boiling water and recommend that you do the same. Use as little water as possible, but watch that it does not evaporate. Serve vegetables 'al dente' - cooked through, but retaining a little 'bite'.

Steaming It generally takes twice as long to steam vegetables al dente as it does to boil them, but they retain much more of their nutritional content. There are many types of steamers available, but a makeshift one can be made by sitting a colander over a pan of boiling water and covering it with a lid or a plate.

Papillotes are another method of steaming, but can also be used for baking. The food is wrapped in a bag of paper or foil before cooking to keep in all the flavours.

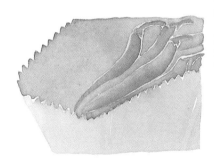

Simmering This means to keep the liquid just on the boil, moving slightly and emanating a little steam.

Blanching There are two methods of blanching. Food may be plunged into a pan of boiling water which is then taken from the heat, or boiling water may be poured over the food in a bowl. In both cases, leave the food in the water for 1-5 minutes, then drain carefully. Blanching is a technique often used for removing difficult skins.

Frying involves cooking food in fat, usually butter or oil. Try to use a polyunsaturated oil like corn or safflower, and use only a little. This technique is called shallow- or pan-frying. If you use a wok, even less oil is required. The food must be constantly moved round the pan, and vegetables require no more than 3 minutes. This is called stir-frying. Deep-frying is a technique used for such things as rissoles, and means that the food is submerged in hot oil and cooked until crisp.

Sautéeing is similar to shallow-frying, but the food is constantly moved round the pan and cooked until brown and crisp.

Sweating means to cook gently in a covered pan with a little butter or oil without browning or frying.

How to make a bain marie
A bain marie is a water bath, used to help things bake gently without drying. Although you can buy special utensils, I find a roasting pan quite adequate for the purpose. Place the dish(es) to be baked in a roasting pan and pour in enough boiling water to come two-thirds of the way up the dish(es). Place in the oven and bake as directed.

How to prepare eggs

Eggs are extremely versatile, but often the simplest methods of preparation can be the best. Here are the basic ways of cooking eggs which deserve to be mastered.

Soft-boiled eggs

Eggs should be placed in boiling water; a soft-boiled egg (firm white and runny yolk) needs 3½ - 4 minutes. However, the timing depends on the size of the egg and how fresh it is. Fresh eggs need to boil a little longer and a large fresh egg takes all of 5 minutes to be soft-boiled. In France soft-boiled eggs are called *oeufs mollets*. They are most often peeled, placed in ramekins and covered with a sauce. To peel a soft-boiled egg place it in the palm of your hand and tap it lightly all over with the back of a spoon. Peel carefully under gently running cold water. The shell should come off with the inner membrane.

Hard-boiled eggs

The perfect way of making firm but non-rubbery eggs is to put them in a pan of boiling water, cover with a lid and turn off the heat. In 10 minutes the eggs will be perfectly hard-boiled.
Quail's eggs should be placed in cold water, brought to the boil and cooked for 2 minutes. Drain and then plunge into iced water to cool.

Shirred eggs

Grease a shallow fire-proof dish with butter or oil, and break in your eggs. Let the white set over a flame, then place the dish under a hot grill or broiler and allow to cook for another minute or two until just set.

Coddled eggs

These are steamed eggs, usually made in individual china bowls with screw lids. Lightly butter the inside of the coddler, break in the egg, screw the top on, and place in a saucepan one-third full of boiling water. It is also possible to make coddled eggs in a soup plate, which is covered with a lid and placed over a saucepan of boiling water. It takes about 8 minutes to soft-steam them.

Baked eggs

These are usually made in individual ramekins, covered with a little cream and baked in the oven. Put them on the top rack of the oven, pre-heated to 200°C/400°F/Gas mark 6 for 3-4 minutes. To ensure firm whites and runny yolks I prefer to steam the eggs in ramekins in a large frying pan filled with simmering water, so I can see their progress. This will take about 3-4 minutes.

Poached eggs

How rare it is to get a perfectly poached egg. I have tried in the most distinguished restaurants in the world, where whirlpools are made in lightly salted or vinegared water, the egg is slipped in and cooked for 4 minutes. It is then taken out with a slotted spoon and its dismal skeins of white snipped. Its final appearance may be aesthetically pleasing, but still the egg tastes watery and sometimes, on being punctured, will let out a gulp of cloudy water, ruining the delicate sauce it is covered in. I shall be a heretic about poached eggs. I believe in using a poaching pan. I enjoy the concave little eggs cratered with pockets of air and lightly smeared with butter. Lightly grease each poaching cup with a little butter, add the eggs and cook for 4 minutes.

Scrambled eggs

There are many people who refuse to cook scrambled eggs because it mucks up the saucepan. It is absurd to use a saucepan in the first place. Scrambled eggs are best done in a frying pan. Break the eggs into a bowl, add seasoning, herbs or any other ingredient you wish, and beat them briskly so that the yolk and white are just blended. Melt 2 tablespoons of butter in a frying pan and swirl it around to cover the base evenly. Pour in the eggs and continue to beat as they cook. The scrambled eggs will leave the pan quite clean if you use this method. Note: Chilled scrambled eggs make a surprisingly refreshing summer lunch with a plain green salad.

Homemade seitan

This recipe makes 225 g/8 oz of gluten. Eat it as a cocktail snack, or use like tofu - stir-fried with vegetables. It is a fascinating experience to make seitan dough and see it change its appearance as the starch is washed away.

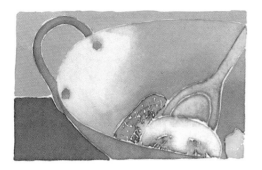

450 g/1 lb strong white/all-purpose flour
2 teaspoons salt
scant 300 ml/10 fl oz/1¼ cups water

Mix all the ingredients together to make a dough and knead well for 5 minutes. Fill a large bowl with cold water and mix in 2 more teaspoons salt. Immerse the dough in this water for 30 minutes. Transfer the dough to a colander and rinse under cold running water, squeezing the starch away with your fingers. Gradually the dough becomes hardier and elastic. This is the gluten, which must remain under the running water until it gives off no more starch. Allow the gluten to stand for another 30 minutes, and then steam it over a flavoured stock for 30 minutes. Leave to cool, then slice thinly and bottle in the stock, much reduced and flavoured with shoyu.

Homemade Ricotta

This is very easy to make at home. The following recipe will make 150 g/5 oz/ 1 generous cup of cheese.

1 litre/1¾ pints/1 quart milk
1 teaspoon sea salt
juice from ½ a lemon

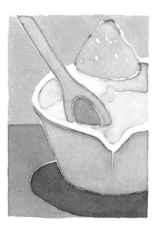

1 Heat the milk to boiling boiling point, then add the salt and lemon juice. Simmer for 15 minutes, stirring now and again.

2 Line a colander or sieve sieve with a double layer of muslin/cheesecloth and place over a large bowl or saucepan. Pour in the milk.

3 Leave for 1 hour so the whey drains off, leaving the curds behind.

Herbs

For cooking purposes, herbs should be finely chopped. I like to use a large cleaver on a thick wooden board, but other people swear by a 'mezzaluna', a two-handled semi-circular blade. However, an ordinary sharp knife will do the job perfectly well if held in both hands. Hold the handle firmly in place while moving the blade up and down in short, chopping gestures. If fresh herbs are to give out their most fragrant flavours, the finer they are chopped, the better.

If you have a glut of fresh herbs, it is worth drying them for future use. Tie them in bunches and hang them upside down somewhere cool and fairly dark for 3-4 weeks. Then crumble the seed pods or leaves over paper before packing them into airtight containers. Recently dried herbs are more pungent than fresh, so only use them in small pinches. If more than six months old they are less pungent than fresh.

Some herbs, such as parsley, mint or basil can be frozen. Chop them up, place them in an ice cube tray, cover them with water and freeze. Alternatively, tie them in bunches and freeze them as they are. They look a bit dismal when thawed, so are not suitable for garnish, but they are perfect for cooking and much nicer than dried herbs.

My favourite way of preserving basil is to chop a fresh handful of it, add the juice of 1 lemon, 2 or 3 crushed garlic cloves and blend to a chunky purée. Add just enough olive oil to cover, then bottle it and store in the refrigerator or freezer. This mixture can be used to make pesto (see page 120) or a salad dressing, if a little vinegar is added.

How to sprout seeds and grains

It takes between four and five days for them to sprout, and those most commonly used are alfalfa, aduki, barley, fenugreek, lentil, mung, pea, soya and wheat. It is possible to buy special sprouting utensils which work very well but a method that many people swear by is to place the seeds in a jam jar and stretch a piece of muslin/cheesecloth over the top, secured with an elastic band.

How to roast nuts and seeds

The best way of roasting nuts and seeds is to dry roast them in a saucepan. Use just enough seeds or nuts to cover the bottom of the pan, place over a high flame and, once hot, shake violently to keep the contents moving. They are done when they smell aromatic and change colour. This method is safer than roasting them on a baking sheet in the oven where they take longer and can sometimes be entirely forgotten until the smell of burning alerts you.

How to make bouquet garni
You can buy sachets of bouquet garni, but it is far cheaper to make your own. Simply tie a small bouquet of herbs together with string. A collection of three to five herbs will do - generally bay, rosemary, thyme and parsley - but ring the changes. A Victorian recipe I know suggests using cinnamon, garlic, mace and red pepper among ten or twelve others - hardly a bouquet, more a cornucopia.

- Beans and grains will sprout in a dark or light place, but they like a pleasant room temperature (13°-22°C/55°-70°F).

- They must be washed with fresh water twice a day, then drained thoroughly or else they will rot.

- After the sprouts have been harvested, they can be kept in the refrigerator for up to a week.

Serving and presentation

If food is perfectly cooked, it needs little done to it to look attractive. However, simple garnishes of fresh herbs, chopped nuts or triangles of toast, can add an appealing finishing touch to such dishes as soups, pâtés and terrines.

Occasionally, if you feel like making the effort, you can achieve stunning effects by cutting vegetables into pretty shapes. For example, cut a spring onion/scallion into 5-cm/2-inch lengths and make fine lengthways cuts at one or both ends. Make sure you leave one end or the middle of the onion/scallion uncut so it doesn't fall apart. Put the onions/scallions into ice-cold water and they will fan out into pretty tendrils in about 30 minutes.

Contrived garnishing, as in tomato roses, makes food look vulgar. Spend your time instead on quicker and simpler presentation ideas. Make knotted bunches of chives (see page 23), or thread broccoli and carrots through rings of courgettes/zucchini. These are easily achieved and can do much to enhance a meal. Here are a few simple rules to follow about presentation.

- When preparing a meal, try to think about colour balance, so you can avoid colour clashes, like beetroot/beet and tomatoes on the same plate.

- Never crowd a plate or platter. Nothing deadens the appetite more than an overcrowded plate of untidily-heaped food.

- Choose your china and glass with care. Hectically-patterned plates under a variegated stew can be very off-putting. However, I do think it is a good idea to make a collection of odd Victorian plates and dishes. Even if chipped or cracked, they can still make food look very enticing.

Quenelles

Quenelles are small, moulded shapes made by rolling pâtés, mousses or even mashed potatoes between two wet spoons (see page 35). Gnocchi are made using this technique, but they are then curved into crescents with the back of one spoon, and indented with the prongs of a fork. Quenelles can be used in sweet dishes if the mousse or filling is firm enough to mould. If arranged on top of a tart, for example, they could be made in graduated sizes for a stunning effect.

As an alternative, try making pâtés into fat sausage-shapes and rolling them in a mixture of finely-chopped nuts, or herbs. Wrap them in foil and keep refrigerated until needed. Cut into slices with a knife dipped in hot water and serve (see page 35).

1 This technique requires a jug of warm water and 2 spoons. Wet one spoon and scoop out a generous amount of pâté.

2 Roll the pâté into another wet spoon, pressing lightly to shape it. Keep wetting the spoons and rolling the pâté until you have created a satisfactory shape.

Shaping butter
Use a melon scoop to make butter balls, ensuring that the butter is neither too hard nor too soft. Then roll them in spices, herbs or citrus zest (see page 141).

I prefer to make rolls of butter, in much the same way as pâté rolls. They are easier to store and slices can be cut off as needed.

Removing zest

The zest of a citrus fruit is the very outer coloured part of the skin. There are various methods of removing it, but I think it is best to use a zester—a tiny metal implement which has a blade divided into several holes. When the zester is drawn across the skin, small strings of zest curl through the holes.

Frosted flowers or leaves

As a decorative touch for a special occasion, you might like to add some frosted leaves or flowers to a cake or dessert. This is a simple technique and can make any occasion seem celebratory.

Use a leaf or petal which is tiny and nicely shaped, or any small flower: rosebuds, pinks, pansies and violets, or fruit and herb flowers. Trim off any straggly green bits. Hold the leaf or flower in a pair of tweezers and paint with lightly whipped egg white, then dip into castor/superfine sugar. Place on a tray in a warm spot to dry. Pack lightly between sheets of waxed or greaseproof paper in an airtight container and use as required.

Marbling eggs

For me the pretty appearance of these eggs is flawed by the fact that I find them rather hard and indigestible. However, some people love them, and they are the traditional accompaniment to Ful medames (see pages 11 and 152).

Hard-boil your eggs as described on page 54. Gently crack them all over with the back of a spoon so that they are covered with hairline cracks. Make a marinade of strong tea mixed with rose water and vanilla or cinnamon, and bring to the boil. Simmer the eggs in this mixture for 15-30 minutes, depending on how dark you want the colour to be. Allow the eggs to cool and then shell them.

Note: The marinade can also be made from beetroot/beet or spinach water to give red or green marbling, or from soy sauce which will flavour the eggs as well as darkening the pattern.

Melba toast

As an accompaniment to soup or pâté, wafer-thin slices of toast are ideal, and quick to make. Use sliced bread which is a day or so old. Toast both sides, then while still warm, cut off the crusts and slice the toast horizontally through the middle so you have two thin slices. Cut these in triangles and toast the untoasted sides. The toast will curl up, but watch carefully that it doesn't burn. Once cool it can be stored in an airtight container.

Note: Melba toast must be made under a grill or broiler. It cannot be made successfully in a toaster as there is no room for it to curl up.

CHAPTER 3

Glossary

Knowing your ingredients is the basis of good cookery. There was a time when vegetarian food was limiting - some would even have said boring - in what it had to offer. But over the last decade the picture has changed dramatically. As international markets have opened up, new and exciting foods have become available fom Asia, Africa and the Tropics. So dramatic has been the change, in fact, that the resulting array of foods before us can often seem overwhelming, not to say confusing. And confusion increases as names are changed, or added to, and as experiments with fruit and vegetables lead to hybridization.

The glossary of ingredients below is intended to help you through this jungle. It has obviously not been possible to cover every single ingredient, but nevertheless it contains many common foods as well as more unfamiliar items you may come across. Each entry is identified by its common name (in bold type), Latin name where applicable, and finally any alternative names - English and American equivalents are denoted by an oblique stroke, with the English name appearing first. Nutritional information has been included for each entry, except for herbs and spices, where nutrients are minimal. In the case of cereals and cereal products the nutritional information refers to the main entry but where the by-product is particularly important separate information has been added. The bold numbers indicate the position of each ingredient on the appropriate photograph.

Spices, flavourings and seeds

Ajowan (*Carum ajowan*) Bishop's weed **25**
A spice seed that is closely related to caraway and cumin. It contains considerable amounts of thymol or oil of thyme, which means that thyme can often be used as a substitute. Ajowan is used extensively in Indian cookery and is available in shops specializing in Indian products.

Alfalfa (*Medicago sativa*) **12**
A legume, which is most often sprouted, making a savoury and pleasant salad or sandwich filling. The light brown seeds have a delicious nutty flavour and can be sprinkled over savoury dishes, breads and pastries, or added to cakes and desserts.

Allspice (*Pimenta officinalis*) Jamaica pepper, Pimento **17**
The dried berries of the pimento tree combine the flavour of several spices, tasting particularly of nutmeg, cinnamon and cloves. Available whole or powdered, allspice is used in pickles, relishes, pilaus, fruit cakes, mince pies, fruit pies, milk puddings and plum pudding.

Anise (*Pimpinella anisum*) Aniseed, Sweet cumin **42**
These aromatic seeds have the flavour of aniseed and are available whole and powdered. Anise is used in spicy dishes, desserts, cakes and pastries, sweet dishes, creams and confectionery. Use sparingly and add at the beginning of cooking, as over-heating will spoil its flavour. Green anise leaf is used as a flavouring in European and Arab countries.

Caper (*Capparis spinosa*) **3**
These small buds are most usually available pickled, though raw capers may sometimes be bought in Mediterranean country markets. Capers form the basis of caper sauce, and are also used in many other sauces such as ravigote, tartare, vinaigrette and black butter sauce. They are useful additions to salads and hors d'oeuvres and will make an attractive garnish.

Caraway (*Carum carvi*) **44**
Thin crescent-shaped seeds with a strong, characteristic flavour that is not to everyone's taste. Caraway is used in sauerkraut, bread, seed cake, cheese spreads and dips, sweet pickles, biscuits/cookies and buns. It is a popular feature of German and Austrian cooking.

Cardamom (*Elettaria cardamomum*)   **5**
A highly aromatic seed tasting a little like eucalyptus but far richer and sweeter. The small dark brown or black seeds are enclosed inside pods which can be cream, brown, green or white. It is usually the dried seed pods that are sold as cardamom, but the seeds are also sold separately, or ground to a powder. Cardamom is best bought whole, however, as it rapidly loses its flavour when ground. It is used in curries, rice dishes, desserts, cakes, bread, buns, biscuits/cookies and spiced wine.

Carob (*Ceratonia siliqua*) Locust bean   **2**
The dark brown pod of a Mediterranean tree. In recent years it has been acclaimed as a 'health food', and is most commonly used, ground, as a chocolate substitute.

Cassia. See Cinnamon

Cayenne (*Capsicum annuum*)   **13**
Dried pods of a red chilli pepper are ground to produce this hot, pungent spice, though other spices are often added to the powder in its commercial form. It is very hot and should therefore be used sparingly. Cayenne is used in white sauces, soups and stews. It combines well with cooked cheese.

Chilli pepper (*Capsicum annuum*, var. *frutescens*)   **14**
The fruit pod of the capsicum plant, dried and then converted into flakes or powder. Both are popular in Mexican and Indian cooking. Chilli peppers can be either red or green, though some turn brown or even black when ripened and dried. Popular varieties are Cascabel, Guajillo, Guero, Poblana and Serrano. The powder is used in curries, chutneys, sauces, dressings and snacks. It can be hot, so use with discretion.

Cinnamon (*Cinnamomum zeylanicum*)   **28**
The dried aromatic bark of a tree native to India, cinnamon is available in the form of sticks, quills and powder. It is best bought ground in small quantities and constantly replaced, as it quickly becomes stale. It is used in mulled wine, cakes, milk puddings, fruit (particularly apple) pies, curries, pilaus and creams.
Cassia (*Cinnamomum cassia*), or Chinese cinnamon, is similar, but coarser.

Cloves (*Eugenia aromatica*)   **21**
The dried aromatic flower buds of an evergreen tree most commonly found in South-east Asia, their name comes from the Latin *clavus*, meaning 'nail', which the whole buds resemble. Although they are available in powdered form, they should ideally be bought as whole buds, and the central head ground. Cloves are useful ingredients for baking, pickling and spiced drinks. They are also used in apple pies, mincemeat, Christmas pudding, milk puddings, biscuits/cookies, casseroles, and mixed spice. Use sparingly, as they can be very pungent.

Coriander (*Coriandrum sativum*) Dhania   **1**
These spherical seeds can vary when ripe from pale green to cream or brown, but can also be bought ground into a powder. They taste rather like orange peel, and in India tend to be roasted, which brings out a more curry-like flavour. Coriander is a basic spice in Indian curries but is also used for pickles and sweet dishes, including certain types of cake. It is a mild spice and should therefore be used in relatively large quantities.

Cumin (*Cuminum cyminum*)   **20**
Cumin seeds resemble caraway in appearance, but have quite a different flavour, being hot and pungent. They are available in black and white form, and as a powder. One of the main ingredients in commercial curry powder, cumin is also used in Mexican-style rice dishes, dips, yoghurt relishes, soups, salads, pickles and curries. It combines very well with cheese.

Dill seed   **39**. See also Herbs and Flowers   **17**

Dried mango (*Mangifera indica*) Amchoor   **4**
Dried slices of unripe mango (also available in powdered form) are used as a souring and flavouring agent in many vegetarian curries. They are sold in shops specializing in Indian products.

Fennel seed   **29**. See also Herbs and Flowers   **10**

Fenugreek (*Trigonella foenumgraecum*) Methi   **45**
Fenugreek is very important in India, where the seeds are used as a flavouring in curries (and other dishes), and the leaves are used as a vegetable. Both leaf and seed can vary in their aromatic quality. The seeds can be sprouted like mustard and cress, when they will make a tasty addition to salads. They are also available ground.

Five-spice powder/Chinese five-spice powder   **40**
A mixture of star anise, ground anise-pepper, cassia, cloves and fennel, five-spice powder has a faint liquorice taste and is commonly used in Chinese cooking, where it is added to noodles, rice, Chinese-style vegetables and curries. It is usually bought ground. It can be made at home, though the spices are difficult to grind finely.

Garlic (*Allium sativum*) **11**
Probably the most popular flavouring of all, the garlic bulb is sold fresh or dried into flakes and powder. It has a pungent taste and smell and can be used in virtually any savoury dish according to taste. It goes particularly well with parsley and mushrooms and is used in bread, mayonnaise and salt.

Ginger (*Zingiber officinale*) **19**
Available as fresh or dried whole roots or as powder, ginger is widely used in both sweet and savoury dishes. Fresh ginger is less 'spicy' than the dried form. Peeled and ground to a pulp, it is a popular ingredient in many curries; it is also canned, crystallized in sugar, preserved in syrup and used in ginger beer and ginger wine. Dried ginger root must be 'bruised' (i.e. hit with a rolling pin or hammer) before use. This opens the fibres and helps release the hot aromatic flavour. Ground ginger does not give the same flavour to food. It is used mostly in sweet dishes, desserts, creams, sauces, pickles and chutneys. It goes particularly well with melons and peaches.

Gomasio (sometimes known as Sesame salt) **32**
Gomasio is made by grinding roasted sesame seeds very finely and then adding sea salt (5 parts sesame to 1 part salt). It is widely used in Japan and in the macrobiotic diet as an alternative to salt. Its nutty taste makes it a delicious addition to any savoury dish.

Horseradish (*Armoracia rusticana*) **8**
The roots are used, grated, as a flavouring, though most of the pungency is found in the outer part. Although the flavour is very pungent, it is completely destroyed by cooking, and it should therefore never be added to hot dishes. Horseradish is used as a flavouring for mayonnaise or as a cold garnish to salads. It is available dried

and when used in this form must be reconstituted with water. **Wasabi**, or Japanese horseradish, is a hotter version.

Juniper (*Juniperus communis*) **31**
These ripe berries, fresh or dried, are used as a flavouring in sauerkraut and preserves such as pickles and chutneys. They are usually sold dried.

Lemon grass (*Cymbopogon citratus*) Sereh powder **15**
Several species of grass, all possessing the flavour of lemon due to the presence of citric oils. It is available as dried grass or a powder (known as Sereh powder). It is used in South-east Asia.

Linseed **7**
The tiny brown seeds of the flax plant. Although used mainly in the production of linseed oil, their smooth nutty flavour makes them a tasty and crunchy addition to freshly baked bread.

Liquorice (*Glycyrrhiza glabra*) **41**
The root of a small perennial legume, it can be bought simply as the dried root, or as dried slices or as a powder. It is used in soft drinks, ice cream, candy, desserts, cakes and confectionery.

Mace **27**. See Nutmeg

Mustard (*Brassica nigra juncea*; *B. alba*) **34**
The seeds are available in two colours; black (brown, *B. nigra*) or white (yellow, *B. alba*) of which the black is the hotter. The seeds are also available powdered. Mustard is used for a wide range of dishes including curries, cocktail dips, sandwich spreads, relishes, cheese dishes and dressings.

Nutmeg and Mace (*Myristica fragrans*) **26, 27**
Nutmeg is the dried seed of an evergreen tree of the myrtle family; mace is the scarlet web-like cover surrounding it. Both are similar in flavour and aroma. Nutmeg, grated, is used for cakes, custard and in milk puddings, cream soups and hot drinks; mace is used in pickles and preserves, cheese dishes, stewed fruit, and mulled wine. Both are available ground but should be bought whole for the best flavour.

Paprika (*Capsicum tetragonum*) Hungarian pepper **16**
A bright red powder made from the powdered dry flesh of special varieties of capsicum peppers, both sweet and hot varieties are available. Traditionally used in Hungarian goulash, it is also used in cheese dishes, cocktail dips, dressings, sauces and soups, and makes an attractive garnish for eggs.

Pepper (*Piper nigrum*) **18**
The common black pepper we use at the table. It is available as whole green, black or white peppercorns and as black or white powder. The green corns, or berries, are picked from the pepper vine plant, and then sun-dried, which turns them black. The white peppercorns are simply green peppercorns which have been left to ripen fully. Green peppercorns have a fresh and pungent flavour and are usually sold pickled in brine. Black and white pepper are similar in flavour, but the black is the more pungent of the two. Pepper can be used on virtually any savoury dish.

Pomegranate seed (*Punica granatum*) Anardana **24**
The dried seeds of the four varieties of the pomegranate fruit are sprinkled on savoury dishes, such as hummus, in the Middle East. They are also frequently included in parathas and curries.

Spices, flavourings and seeds

1	Coriander	**9**	Szechuan peppers	**17**	Allspice
2	Carob	**10**	Tamarind	**18**	Peppercorns
3	Caper	**11**	Garlic	**19**	Ginger
4	Dried mango	**12**	Alfalfa	**20**	Cumin
5	Cardamom	**13**	Cayenne	**21**	Cloves
6	Vegetable stock/bouillon cubes	**14**	Chilli pepper (and powder)	**22**	Turmeric
7	Linseeds	**15**	Lemon grass	**23**	Pumpkin seed
8	Horseradish	**16**	Paprika	**24**	Pomegranate seeds

25	Ajowan	32	Gomasio/Sesame salt	39	Dill seed
26	Mace	33	Sesame seeds	40	Five-spice powder
27	Nutmeg	34	Mustard	41	Liquorice
28	Cinnamon	35	Vanilla	42	Anise
29	Fennel seed	36	Star anise	43	Sunflower seeds
30	Saffron	37	Salt	44	Caraway
31	Juniper	38	Poppy seeds	45	Fenugreek

Poppy seed (*Papaver somniferum*)   **38**
The seeds of the poppy flower have a pleasantly nutty flavour and aroma. There are two main types: white/yellow and bluish-grey. They are used in salad dressings, pastries, cakes, buns and breads and vegetable and egg dishes, and make an attractive garnish for cheese dishes and snack foods.

Pumpkin seed (*Curcurbita maxima*)   **23**
Pumpkin seeds are mainly used as a source of oil. They can also be deep-fried and toasted, and either eaten as a snack on their own or put on savoury dishes and breads as a nutty garnish.

Saffron (*Crocus sativus*)   **30**
The dried stigmas of the saffron crocus, this is said to be the most expensive spice in the world. Saffron is also available in powdered form, but because it is so expensive, is often adulterated. It is a traditional ingredient of the classic Spanish dish 'paella', and is also used in soups, rice dishes, cakes and biscuits.

Salt   **37**
One of the most traditional of food flavourings, salt is the mineral sodium chloride which is extracted either from the sea or from underground deposits. There are many different types: **table salt** (commercial with added ingredients to stop hardening); **sea salt** (crystals obtained by evaporating sea water); **rock salt** (obtained from underground deposits, and less refined than table salt). **Flavoured salts** such as iodized salt (with added iodine), garlic, onion and celery salts are also available. In recent years, the list has been added to by **low-sodium salt**, which is believed by some to be more beneficial to health.

Sesame seed (*Sesamum indicum*)   **33**
These small flattish seeds can be white, cream, brown, red or black. They have a pleasant nut-like aroma and flavour which is heightened by toasting (as, for example, in gomasio); they can be sprinkled over breads and cakes, and used in salads and biscuits/cookies.

Star anise (*Illicium verum*)   **36**
Dried star-shaped pods containing small oval-shaped seeds. Pods (whole or cracked), and whole or ground seeds are available. Star anise contains the same essential oils as anise. It is much used in Oriental cooking and is one of the ingredients of five-spice powder. It is used in spicy dishes, desserts, cakes, biscuits/cookies and drinks.

Sunflower seed (*Helianthus annuus*)   **43**
The seeds are used for oil but can also be eaten roasted and salted as a snack, and added to bread and cakes.

Szechuan pepper (*Zanthoxyllum piperitum*) Anise pepper, Chinese pepper, Japanese pepper   **9**
These dried red berries have a hot, aromatic flavour and are an ingredient in five-spice powder. Their peppery taste makes them useful additions to soups and sauces.

Tamarind (*Tamarindus indica*) Indian date   **10**
The dried fruit of the tamarind tree. Although it is referred to as 'tamarind seed' it is in fact the pulp around the seeds which is used. Tamarind is used in seasonings, curries and drinks. It has a sour, fruity taste. When bought dried, it is soaked in water and the soaking liquid is used and the seeds discarded.

Turmeric (*Curcuma longa*)   **22**
A rhizome or root stem, which is available whole and dried, or ground into a powder. It has a fragrant and peppery aroma and is one of the basic curry spices. It is also used in grains, beans, chutneys and pickles. Use in small quantities as it can be bitter.

Vanilla (*Vanilla planifolia*)   **35**
The dried fruits of an orchid plant, vanilla pods are at their best when they are dark brown, flexible and covered with a frosting of aromatic vanillin crystals. They can be re-used if washed and dried each time. Vanilla has a wide range of uses in confectionery. It is used as a flavouring in sweet sauces, cakes and desserts, creams, baked goods, ice creams and custards and sugar.

Vegetable stock/bouillon cubes   **6**
Dehydrated vegetable extracts in the form of a cube. They can often contain a multitude of other ingredients, including MSG, herbs and spices, yeast extract, starch, caramel, sugar and fat. However, there are some which are pure reductions of vegetables and herbs and have no added chemical flavourings, so read the label before buying. They are used in savoury dishes and soups.

Herbs and flowers

Basil (*Ocimum basilicum*) Sweet basil   **18**
An annual plant, its aromatic leaves are used fresh and dried. When fresh they smell and taste rather like cloves; dried, they taste more like curry. Fresh leaves should be shredded with the fingers when used, as chopping may spoil their flavour. Basil goes well with eggs, aubergines/eggplants and sweet peppers, but it has a particular affinity with tomatoes, which has made it a popular addition to pasta and pizzas. It is also used in soups, sauces and salads, and forms the basis of the famous Italian sauce, 'pesto' (see page 120).

Bay (*Laurus nobilis*) Laurel, Sweet bay **4**
The leaves of this evergreen tree can be used fresh or dried and are particularly popular in Mediterranean cooking. The fresh leaves are strongly scented and bitter, however, and are not to everyone's taste. They are best left to dry for a few days, although not for too long as old dried leaves will be quite flavourless. Bay is used in stocks, bouquets garnis, milk desserts, soups, sauces, creams and custards.

Chervil (*Anthriscum cerefolium*) **20**
An annual plant with slightly curled leaves which are rather like parsley. Although available dried, for the very best results it should be used fresh - either chopped or in tiny sprigs. It has a delicate taste, somewhere between parsley and anise, should not be boiled, but is best used raw, or added when the dish is almost ready. Chervil makes a tasty addition to salads, soups and garnishes. It is also used in ravigote sauce, vinegars and *fines herbes*.

Chives (*Allium schoenoprasum*) **8**
A member of the onion family. The leafy stems are mostly used fresh (though they are also available dried). Their flavour is unmistakably oniony, but is subtly different. Chives do not benefit from long cooking but should be chopped finely and added to the hot dishes at the last moment. They go well with potatoes, beetroots/beets, eggs, and cream cheese and are used in soups, omelettes, sauces and salads.

Chrysanthemum (Family: Compositae) **3**
A plant which comes in many forms, including the vegetable chrysanthemum greens or shungiku. The flowers make an attractive decoration to salads.

Coriander (*Coriandrum sativum*) Chinese parsley, Cilantro **11**
Often confused with some types of parsley, coriander leaves have a fresh, orangey taste and are an important ingredient of curries. They go especially well with green chilli peppers and form the basis of many Indian chutneys. They must be used fresh. Coriander is also available in seed form (see Spices, flavourings and seeds).

Curry leaf (*Chalcas koenigii*) **14**
Although relatively rare outside India, curry leaves can be bought fresh or dried from shops that specialize in Indian spices. They are a speciality of southern India, where they are used mainly in vegetarian dishes. The dried leaves will often have lost their flavour, and should not be bought unless they smell strongly of curry.

Dill (*Anethum graveolens*) **17, 39**
A plant of the parsley family, of which the leaves and seeds are used. The leaves can be fresh or dried and have a mild, caraway-like flavour. They are commonly used in dill pickles and dill vinegar though they are also used on cooked vegetables and salads, soups, egg dishes and sauces. Dill will lose its aroma and flavour during cooking, and should therefore be added just before the cooked dish is ready. Dill seeds have a slightly sharper, more bitter taste than the leaves. They are used in pickles, cheese dishes, salad dressings and potato salads.

Fennel (*Foeniculum vulgare*) **10, 29**
A perennial plant which looks very much like dill but is quite different in flavour. Both leaves and seeds are used, and the leaves are best used fresh, finely chopped, in mayonnaise, vinaigrette sauces, salads and soups. Fennel seeds have a slight aniseed taste and can be used in a wide range of dishes from apple pies to curries.

Lemon grass **16.** See also Spices, flavourings and seeds **15**

Marigold (*Calendula officinalis*) **21**
A well-known garden flower, its brightly coloured orange-red blooms make an attractive decoration to any dry vegetable dish. The outer petals have a slight aromatic bitterness and have in the past been used for saffron. Today they are used in cakes, salads, cheese and butter. Petals and young leaves can be eaten in salads.

Marjoram (*Origanum majorana*) Sweet marjoram **6**
Not to be confused with wild marjoram or oregano, its flavour is rather like thyme, but is sweeter and more scented. The leaves are used fresh or dried, chopped, crushed or powdered in soups, stuffings, quiches and pies, omelettes, potato dishes and bouquets garnis. Marjoram's delicate flavour is destroyed by cooking, so it is best added just before the dish is ready or used in dishes which only need light cooking.

Mint (*Mentha*, spp.) **2**
There are many varieties including spearmint, peppermint, eau de Cologne mint, Bowles mint, and applemint, of which, from the cook's point of view, spearmint and applemint are most important. Mint leaves can be used fresh or dried (though fresh is better) in salads, sauces, desserts and many drinks. They are a tasty refreshing addition to potatoes, peas, beans, lentils, cucumbers, tomatoes and aubergines/eggplants, and fruits such as gooseberries and apples. They also form the basis of mint sauce, mint jelly and drinks such as mint julep and mint tea.

Herbs and flowers

1	Rose	5	Tarragon	9	Sorrel
2	Mint	6	Marjoram	10	Fennel
3	Chrysanthemum	7	Oregano	11	Coriander
4	Bay	8	Chives	12	Rosemary

13	Thyme	16	Lemon grass	19	Primrose
14	Celery leaf	17	Dill	20	Chervil
15	Parsley	18	Basil	21	Marigold

Oregano (*Origanum vulgare*) Wild marjoram **1**
Closely related to marjoram, but more pungent, it is best known for its use in Italian dishes, especially pizzas. Oregano goes well with tomatoes, aubergines/eggplants, and courgettes/zucchini. Oregano is one of the few herbs that is most frequently used dried.

Parsley (*Petroselinum crispum*) **15**
Probably the most commonly used herb, there are many different varieties, including broad-leaved, curly-leaved, Hamburg and Neapolitan (Italian) parsley. The leaves and stems of the plant are used, of which the stems have the strongest flavour. It is also available in the form of dried flakes, though this is nowhere near as good as the fresh. Parsley is used, chopped, in large quantities to flavour sauces, soups, salads, omelettes and stuffings and can be used as a decorative garnish for virtually any savoury dish. It forms the basis of *fines herbes* and many sauces such as parsley, tartare and ravigote, and *maître d'hôtel* butter. The stems are always included in bouquets garnis.

Primrose (*Calendula* spp.) **19**
Most often used as a garnish in salads, but can be crystallized and used as a cake decoration.

Rose (*Rosa*, spp.) **1**
Not of great culinary importance except in the Middle East, where the crushed aromatic petals are used as a basis for rosewater, which in turn is a widely-used flavouring in many sweet dishes, and (together with rose hips) to make rose petal jam and sherbets. Outside the Middle East, the petals are used for rose-flavoured liqueurs and, when crystallized, make attractive decorations for many desserts.

Rosemary (*Rosmarinus officinalis*) **12**
The bitter-sweet, needle-shaped leaves are used fresh or dried, or in powder form, though when dried they generally lose their strength of flavour. Rosemary is almost always used in the whole sprig and is rarely, if ever, chopped. Used in soups, stews and salads, it is included in bouquets garnis and as a garnish for many vegetable dishes.

Sorrel (*Rumex* spp.) **9**
The leaves have a refreshing, slightly bitter spinach-like taste and can be eaten puréed as a vegetable in their own right, though since they contain oxalic acid should not be eaten in large quantities. Only available fresh, sorrel when used as a herb will make an excellent addition to salads, and can also be used as a flavouring for soups and omelettes and sauces. Sorrel should be cooked for the shortest time possible to preserve its flavour. Don't cook it in an iron pan as this will make it go black.

Tarragon (*Artemisia dracunculus*) **5**
The aromatic leaves have a slight aniseed tang and are used fresh or dried or in powdered form. Tarragon is strongly flavoured and should therefore be used with discretion. It is used in cheese and egg dishes, salad dressings, butters and purées with cream and cream soups. It is also used as a flavouring for vinegar, in tartare and béarnaise sauces, and *fines herbes*.

Thyme (*Thymus vulgaris*) **13**
There are several varieties. Its aromatic and pungent leaves are used fresh and dried equally successfully, although dried leaves should be bought in small quantities and continually renewed, as they will go stale quickly. It goes well with potatoes, tomatoes, courgettes/zucchini and aubergines/eggplants and is used in soups, sauces, stuffings and bouquets garnis.

Vegetables

Artichoke (*Synara scolymus*) Globe artichoke **11**
It is this type of artichoke (as opposed to the Jerusalem artichoke) that is meant when the term 'artichoke' is used on its own. Artichokes can be baked, boiled or stuffed, and can be served with various sauces and dressings. It is the young central bud that is generally eaten. The hairy choke must be discarded. Imported artichokes are available all year round; domestic ones only in the summer. Cut off the stem and trim leaves. Remove the hairy choke after cooking, if you are stuffing the vegetable, or discard it while eating.
• Low-fat. High in calcium, folic acid, biotin and vitamin C.

Asparagus (*Asparagus officinale*) **12**
There are three main types: green, white and (more rarely) purple, each of which comprises many varieties. All are available from spring to early summer. Look for tight, well-formed heads and avoid any that are too thin, or too thick, or those that are wrinkled and woody. Asparagus can be served as an appetizer, hot with butter or with hollandaise sauce, or cold with vinaigrette. It can also be used in soups, quiches, soufflés and garnishes. Break or cut off ends if they are tough, trim to even lengths and tie together for cooking. Steam or boil with the tips facing upwards.
• Low-fat. High in phosphorus, iron, copper, carotene, folic acid, biotin, vitamins B_1, C and E.

Aubergine/Eggplant (*Solanum melongena*) **1**
Aubergines/eggplants come in varying shapes and sizes and two main colours: purple and (more rarely) white. When buying, look for firm, smooth skins. Size will make no difference to flavour.

Aubergines/eggplants are available all year round. They are used in ratatouille and Greek moussaka, and can be stuffed, baked, fried, stewed and pickled. They usually need salting (see page 52) before cooking, to remove moisture and bitterness.
● Low-fat. High in fibre and vitamin C.

Broad/fava bean (*Vicia faba*) Windsor bean, Horse bean   **17**
Available fresh or dried. They are usually shelled, though young pods can sometimes also be eaten if tender enough. Choose small, plump pods. Fresh broad beans can be eaten raw or cooked in salads or as a side vegetable. They are available in the summer.
● Low-fat. High in fibre, phosphorus, magnesium, iron, copper, niacin, pantothenic acid, biotin, vitamins B$_1$ and C.

Celeriac (*Apium graveolens*, spp.)   **35**
A special variety of celery that is cultivated for its tuberous root. A winter vegetable, it should be firm to be at its best. It can be eaten raw in salads, blanched, steamed, boiled, puréed, or stir-fried. Must be peeled. Cut into slices first to peel easily.
● Low-fat. High in fibre, calcium, phosphorus and vitamin C.

Celery (*Apium graveolens*)   **2**
There are two main types: green-ribbed with large green leaves, and blanched white with white ribs and yellow leaves. Celery is available all year round. When buying, choose crisp stalks. Whole heads should have plenty of small inner stalks and 'heart'. Avoid over-large heads as they may be stringy. Celery's crisp and tangy flavour makes it useful in salads, sandwiches and dips.
● Low-fat. High in calcium, biotin and vitamin C.

Chayote (*Sechium edule*) Custard marrow   **4**
The fruits and young shoots and roots of this squash are all used and eaten as a vegetable. The young shoots can be boiled and served as asparagus, but it is the fruits that are mainly used. They can be baked or fried, creamed and eaten in desserts and tarts. The colour of the flesh can vary from creamy white to dark green. Peel before use.
● Low-fat. High in vitamin C.

Chicory/Belgian endive (*Cichorium intybus*) Endive, Witloof   **6**
Available all year round, but best from autumn to spring. Choose compact heads with white leaves and yellow-green edges. Chicory/Belgian endive can be braised or boiled or eaten raw in salads. Leave the head whole or separate each stalk as required.
● Low-fat. High in folic acid.

Chinese greens (*Brassica chinensis*)   **23, 24**
The two main types are Pak-choi (also known as mustard greens or Chinese mustard), which has dark green leaves and broad white stems, and Pe-tsai, which is tall, compact and crisp-leaved. Other varieties are bok-choi, wong-bok and shungiku. Available all year round, they are used in pickles, soups and stir-fries.
● Low-fat. High in magnesium, calcium, iron, copper, carotene, folic acid, vitamins B$_2$ and C.

Daikon. See Radish

Fennel (*Foeniculum vulgare*)   **15**
A bulbous leafstalk with a swollen base and feathery leaves, fennel has a light aniseed-like flavour and is available all year round. It can be chopped and eaten raw in salads, or cooked in the same way as celery. Trim and slice as required.

Green bean (*Phaseolus*, spp.)   **16, 20**
Green beans are grown for their pods and cover many varieties, including thick runner beans and the more slender French/snap beans (now sometimes called Kenya beans). Other varieties are the yellow wax bean, popular in the US, the Indian drumstick bean and garter beans. To be at their best, beans should break with a crisp snap and the insides should be fresh and juicy. Green beans can be boiled, steamed, stir-fried or sautéed. They can be eaten cold in salads or added to savoury dishes and quiches. Runner beans are available from midsummer to autumn; French/snap beans are available all year round but are at their best in early summer and midsummer.
● Low-fat. High in fibre, magnesium, carotene, folic acid, biotin and vitamin C.

Jerusalem artichoke (*Helianthus tuberosus*)   **10**
These can vary in colour from beige to brownish-red. They have a crisp, sweet flesh with a nutty taste, and are cooked in the same way as potatoes. Choose hard artichokes and avoid any with wrinkled skins. Available from autumn to spring, they can be boiled, steamed or fried. The skin can be left on or off as wished. Unpeeled Jerusalem artichokes should be scrubbed thoroughly; peeled ones must be dropped in acidulated water (water with a little lemon juice) to prevent browning.
● Low-fat. High in fibre and vitamin B$_1$.

Kohlrabi (*Brassica oleracea*)   **36**
The thickened stem of a vegetable of the cabbage family, kohlrabi can be either green or purple and is available mainly in the winter. It has a delicate turnip-like taste and can be eaten raw in salads,

Vegetables

1	Aubergine/eggplant	**7**	Mange-tout	**13**	Spinach
2	Celery	**8**	Pea	**14**	Okra
3	Mustard and cress	**9**	Bitter karella	**15**	Fennel
4	Chayote	**10**	Jerusalem artichoke	**16**	French/snap bean
5	Onion	**11**	Artichoke	**17**	Broad/fava bean
6	Chicory/Belgian endive	**12**	Asparagus	**18**	Spring onion/scallion

19	Radish	**25**	Spinach beet	**31**	Winter melon
20	Drumstick bean	**26**	Sweetcorn	**32**	Karella
21	Scorzonera	**27**	Lamb's lettuce	**33**	Tindoori
22	Swiss chard	**28**	Sweet potato	**34**	Daikon radish
23	Chinese cabbage	**29**	Yam (taro)	**35**	Celeriac
24	Shingiken	**30**	Snake gourd	**36**	Kohlrabi

or blanched, steamed, boiled, braised or sautéed. Remove twiggy stems. To eat raw, grate or chop as required.
● Low-fat. High in fibre, calcium, biotin and vitamin C.

Lamb's lettuce (*Valerianella locusta*) Corn salad   **27**
An unusual winter vegetable. The small roundish leaves, when young, have a pleasant, almost primrose-like taste, and will make excellent salads.
● Low-fat. High in iron, carotene, folic acid, biotin and vitamin C.

Mange-tout. See Pea.

Marrow, squashes and gourds (*Cucurbita*, spp.)   **9, 30, 31, 32, 33**
These are all part of a large family which includes courgettes/zucchini, pumpkins and chayotes. All are available in the summer and autumn, though some are only available in winter. They have a rather bland, watery taste and can be stuffed, steamed, sautéed or baked. Other varieties of squash are acorn, spaghetti, snake gourd, butternut, golden nugget, dudi, custard or pattypan, cushaw, karella, winter crookneck, winter melon, bitter gourd, tindoori, wax gourd, sponge gourd and bottle gourd.
● Low-fat. High in biotin and vitamin C.

Mustard and cress (*Lepidium sativum*; *Sinapis alba*)   **3**
Seedlings of cress with mustard, it is used raw in salads and sandwiches and goes particularly well with eggs and cheese. It is available all year round.
● Low-fat. High in fibre, calcium, magnesium, iron, carotene, vitamins C and E.

Okra (*Hibiscus esculenta*) Lady's Finger, Gumbo   **14**
Okra is available all year round. When buying, choose small pods as these will be more tender. Okra can be bought fresh or canned. It is always cooked (sautéed or steamed) and is used to thicken soups and stews as well as being eaten as a side vegetable. It is particularly popular in spicy dishes such as curries. Some people find okra's rather slimy texture unpleasant. This can be removed by salting (see page 52).
● Low-fat. High in fibre, calcium, magnesium, iron, copper, folic acid, vitamins B_1 and C.

Onion (*Allium cepa*)   **5, 18**
There are many varieties of onion. They can be yellow or red, small or large, round or elongated, all varying in pungency. Onions can be eaten raw in salads, baked, boiled, steamed, fried, braised or stuffed, and can be used in most savoury dishes. Spring onions/ scallions are very young, tender onions available from midwinter to midsummer which are eaten, chopped, in salads, or used as a garnish. **Shallots** (*A. ascalonium*) are small, mild varieties of onion which can be used in savoury dishes and stews.
● Low-fat. High in biotin and vitamin C.

Pea (*Pisum sativum*)   **7, 8**
Fresh garden peas are available in the summer months, though frozen and canned varieties are sold. They can be boiled or steamed, puréed, used in soups, salads, savoury dishes and casseroles, and are delicious served with fresh mint. Fresh peas must be used as soon as possible after buying. Choose crisp, young, well-filled pods.

The finest of all are *petits pois* (tiny, sweet, very young and tender). Others are Indian pea, pigeon pea and Mange-tout - which is eaten pod and all.
● Low-fat. High in fibre, magnesium, phosphorus, iron, copper, niacin, biotin, vitamins B_1, B_2 and C.

Pumpkin (*Cucurbita pepo*)
Bright orange in colour, these are particularly noted for their use in American pumpkin pie. They can be boiled, fried, puréed and used in soups, or made into jams.
● Low-fat. High in carotene, biotin and vitamin C.

Radish (*Raphanus*, spp)   **19,31**
The most common variety is the small red radish, but there are many others of varying shapes (both elongated and round) which can be yellow, black or white. One of the more unusual is the daikon or Japanese radish. Radishes are available all year round. Choose firm ones with bright, well defined colours. Radishes can be eaten cooked (usually boiled) in savoury dishes, but are most often sliced or grated and eaten raw. They are also sometimes pickled.
● Low-fat. High in calcium, iron and vitamin C.

Salsify and Scorzonera (*Scorzonera hispanica*) Oyster plant
These long, slightly bitter-tasting roots are white and black versions respectively of the same plant. Both are used in soups, salads and a wide range of savoury dishes. Cut off the top and any roots. Grate and sprinkle with lemon juice to prevent discoloration.
● Low-fat. High in calcium, iron and vitamin C.

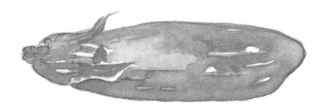

Spinach (*Spinacea oleracea*)   **13**
There are both summer and winter varieties of spinach, of which the summer type is less coarse and bitter tasting, and is so tender that it can be used raw in salads. Otherwise, spinach can be boiled or steamed, used as a stuffing for pancakes and in quiches and other savoury dishes. Be sure to buy it in large quantities as it reduces greatly during cooking.
● Low-fat. High in fibre, calcium, magnesium, phosphorus, iron, copper, carotene, folic acid, biotin, vitamins B_2, B_6, C and E.

Sweetcorn (*Zea mays*) Corn, Maize, Indian corn   **26**
A variety of corn, it is available fresh, frozen or canned, the fresh being available in summer and autumn. When buying fresh sweetcorn, look for creamy-coloured cobs/ears surrounded by green leaves. It is usually boiled and eaten on the cob, but the kernels can be scraped off after cooking and eaten separately. Sweetcorn is also used to make corn bread and hominy.
● Low-fat. High in fibre, magnesium, phosphorus, iron, copper, zinc, niacin, folic acid, vitamins B_1, B_6, C and E.

Sweet potato/Yam (*Ipomoea batata*)   **28**
Despite its name, this is not related to potatoes, even though it is similar in appearance and uses. Sweet potatoes can have white or reddish skins and are available from autumn to early summer. They are a popular feature of Creole cookery, and can be boiled, steamed or baked in casseroles, sweet dishes and pies, or baked in their jackets and eaten as a side vegetable. There's no need to peel them unless the skins are very tough.
● Low-fat. High in carotene, folic acid, pantothenic acid, vitamins B_6, C and E.

Swiss chard (*Beta vulgaris*) Seakale beet   **22, 25**
A handsome-looking vegetable with glossy green leaves, Swiss chard is available from spring to midwinter. The leaves and tender shoots of the plant can be steamed or boiled and are used in the same ways as spinach. There is also a variety called spinach beet. Separate coarse stalks and chop.
● Low-fat. High in calcium and vitamin C.

Yam (*Dioscorea*, spp.) West Indian yam   **29**
A large tuberous root, not to be confused with the American yam, which is just another name for sweet potato. West Indian yams have a thick outer bark which must be peeled off before cooking. They can be boiled, roasted, mashed or fried and have the same uses as potatoes. Common types of yam are elephant's foot or suram, taro or dasheen and the cocoyam. Imported varieties are available all year round.
● Low-fat. High in fibre, carbohydrate, magnesium, copper, vitamins B_1 and C.

Fruit

Apple (*Malus sylvestris*)   **21**
There are over 2000 varieties of apple, both cooking and dessert, so they are available all year round. When buying look for firm, well-coloured fruit with no blemishes. To eat raw, or use in salads, choose a dessert variety; for puréeing, stewing or baking, use one of the larger cooking varieties. Apples can be used in salads, savoury dishes, desserts, cakes, pies, pickles, jams, chutneys and also for their juice. They are also available dried. **Crab apples** are a small very sharp tasting variety, used mainly for making jellies.
● Low-fat. High in biotin and vitamin C.

Banana (*Musa nana*)   **7**
This sweet-tasting fruit is available all year round. Look for firm, evenly yellowed skins with no blackened patches. Bananas can be eaten raw, on their own, or in fruit salads, baked, fried, flambéed with liqueurs, or added to pies, desserts and ice creams, cakes and bread. They are also available dried. Where appearance is important, use immediately or sprinkle with lemon juice to prevent discoloration.
● Low-fat. High in fibre, magnesium, copper, vitamins B_6 and C.

Custard apple (*Anona*, spp.) Cherimoya   **20**
The general name for a number of tropical fruits which come under the same family grouping - they include the sweet sop, sour sop and the cherimoya. They are available in the summer months.
● Low-fat. High in iron and vitamin C.

Fruit

1	Pomelo	6	Ugli fruit	11	Passion fruit
2	Lemon	7	Banana	12	Grapes
3	Grapefruit	8	Pawpaw/papaya	13	Fig
4	Tangelo	9	Plum (*Prunus*, spp.)	14	Tamarillo
5	Lime	10	Ortanique	15	Prickly pear

16	Pomegranate	21	Apple	25	Honeydew melon
17	Mango	22	Ogen melon	26	Watermelon
18	Kiwano	23	Casaba melon	27	Guava
19	Kiwi fruit	24	Cantaloupe melon	28	Persimmon
20	Custard apple				

Fig (*Ficus carica*)   **13**
Available in summer and autumn, figs can be green or purple in colour and bought fresh, dried or canned. Fresh fruits should be evenly coloured and yield evenly under gentle pressure. Ripe figs are delicious eaten on their own, with yoghurt or cream; unripe figs can be stewed, used in cakes, jams and pickles. Peel before use.
• Low-fat. High in fibre and carotene.

Grapefruit (*Citrus paradisi*)   **3**
Grapefruit are available all year round, but are at their best in the winter months. There are several varieties: white, which is best for juicing, pink, which is so sweet it can be eaten like an orange, and red, which is sweeter still. The fruit should be heavy and even-coloured. Most commonly served as a breakfast appetizer, grapefruit is also used to make juice and marmalades, added to fruit salads, ices, cakes and desserts. It can be baked or grilled as well as served raw.
• Low-fat. High in biotin and vitamin C.

Grapes (*Vitis vinifera*)   **12**
Available all year round, grapes can be black (purple), green (white) or red. There are many varieties, of which the tiny seedless grapes are said to be the finest. When buying, choose plump fresh grapes which are firmly attached to their stems. Grapes are used in fruit salads, desserts and pies. They are available dried, in the form of currants, raisins and sultanas/golden raisins.
• Low-fat. High in biotin and vitamin C.

Guava (*Psidium guajava*)   **27**
A tropical fruit, available in the spring and summer. Guavas can be round or pear-shaped and usually have yellow skins with pink flesh. Available fresh or canned, they are delicious in fruit salads, desserts and cakes, and their sharp taste makes them useful for stewing and making tarts and preserves. Cut into quarters, peel and eat the flesh and pips. Use immediately or add lemon juice to prevent discoloration.
• Low-fat. High in fibre, iron and vitamin C.

Kiwano (*Cucumis metuliferus*) Horned melon, African horned cucumber   **18**
A vine fruit originating in tropical Africa, the kiwano is cucumber-like in shape. At its ripest it is orangey-yellow in colour with green pulp. It has a subtle taste of banana and lime and is delicious eaten chilled and raw on its own or added to fruit salad and drinks.

Kiwi fruit (*Actinidia sinensis*) Chinese gooseberry   **19**
Kiwi fruit are available from midsummer to late winter. They can be eaten on their own, sliced and added to salads, desserts, cakes and jams, or used as an attractive garnish for sweet or savoury salads. When buying, look for undamaged fruit which yield evenly to gentle pressure. The hairy skin must be removed before eating.
• Low-fat. High in fibre, vitamins B_1 and C

Lemon (*Citrus limon*)   **2**
The most versatile of citrus fruits, except that they are too sour to be eaten raw, lemons are available all year round. Lemon zest and/or juice will add a wonderful tang to soups, savouries, desserts, cakes, jams and pickles, and slices of lemon will make pretty garnishes for a wide range of sweet and savoury dishes. The ascorbic acid in lemon juice will also prevent fruits like avocados and apples from oxidizing or turning brown when exposed to the air.
• Low-fat. High in fibre, calcium, copper and vitamin C.

Lime (*Citrus aurantifolia*)   **5**
Limes are smaller than lemons, and have a bright green colour. They are available all year round, but in the UK are sometimes difficult to find. Look for firm, heavy fruit and avoid any that look shrivelled or soft. Prepare and use as for lemons.
• Low-fat. High in vitamin C.

Mango (*Mangifera indica*)   **17**
There are over 500 types of mango and they come in varying shapes and sizes: they can be green or yellowish-red, but always have an orange-coloured flesh tasting slightly like peaches but more pungent. Mangoes are available from midwinter to early autumn. Choose firm heavy fruit that yield to pressure and are without blemishes. Mangoes can be eaten on their own or used in fruit salads, cakes, drinks, jams and chutneys. They can be bought fresh or canned and are also available dried, as a flavouring (see page 60). Mangoes can be awkward to handle, as the flesh is very soft. The best way is to cut a thick lengthways slice on either side of the stone, as near to it as possible, then scoop out the flesh.
• Low-fat. High in carotene and vitamin C.

Melon (*Cucumis*, spp.)   **22, 23, 24, 25, 26**
Melons are much prized for their sweet, delicate flavour. There are many different varieties, of which the most common are cantaloupe, charentais, honeydew, Ogen, gallia, tiger and watermelon. The different varieties are available all year round, except for watermelon, which is in season only during the summer and early autumn. A ripe melon should yield slightly when pressed around the stem end. Melons are usually eaten as a starter, but they are also delicious in sweet and savoury salads, preserves, ice creams, sorbets and desserts. They combine well with grapefruit.
• Low-fat. High in carotene, folic acid, pantothenic acid and vitamin C.

Ortanique (*Citrus*, spp.)   **10**
A hybrid citrus fruit, flattened in shape, the ortanique is a cross between a tangerine and an orange. It is very juicy and will make a good substitute for either fruit. It is available mainly in the summer. Avoid bruised fruit and look for smooth, fresh-looking skins. Ortaniques can be eaten on their own, in sweet and savoury salads, ice creams, desserts and cakes.
• Low-fat. High in vitamin C.

Passion fruit (*Passiflora edulis*) Granadilla   **11**
Most readily available in the summer, this knobbly purplish-brown fruit has a strong tangy flavour which makes it particularly useful for fruit salads and drinks. The fruits should be richly purple in colour and firm and heavy with wrinkled skins. They can be used in desserts, sweet and savoury salads, ice creams, sorbets, cakes, juices and jam. Cut in half, scoop out the inside and used as required.
• Low-fat. High in fibre, magnesium, iron, niacin and vitamin C.

Pawpaw/Papaya (*Carica papaya*) Papaw   **8**
Pawpaws/papayas are available in spring and summer. They vary in size and colour, the most common being the yellow-skinned varieties. The flesh is bright pink and contains tiny black seeds which have a peppery flavour. Choose fruit which feels slightly soft to the touch. Pawpaws/papayas have a fairly sweet flavour when ripe (similar to apricots and ginger), and make a good breakfast alternative to grapefruit. They can also be used in sweet and savoury salads, desserts and preserves. Peel and scoop out seeds before eating.
• Low-fat. High in carotene and vitamin C.

Persimmon (*Diospyros kaki*) Sharon fruit, Kaki fruit   **28**
Persimmons look like large orange tomatoes, and have the same succulent flesh. They are available from midsummer to midwinter. Look for heavy bright fruit with no blemishes. They are very unpleasant when underripe, so wait until they are soft before eating. Persimmons are best enjoyed on their own or in a fruit salad, but can be added to puddings and cakes or made into jams and chutneys. Remove the stalk, cut the fruit in half and scoop out the flesh.
• Low-fat. High in carotene and vitamin C.

Plum (*Prunus*, spp.)   **2**
Plums fall into two basic categories: dessert and cooking, though there are many varieties of each. Choose firm, plump fruit that yields evenly to gentle pressure without being oversoft. Avoid shrivelled, split or hard fruit. Different varieties are available from late spring to early autumn. Although both dessert and cooking plums can be cooked, only dessert plums are sweet enough to be eaten raw. Plums can be eaten in pies, puddings, cakes, jams and desserts.

The kernels of the stones will give an almond flavour to any cooked fruit. Among the many varieties of plum are damson, greengage, bullace, cherry and Santa Rosa.
• Low-fat. High in vitamin C.

Pomegranate (*Punica granatum*)   **16**
Pomegranate is available in the autumn months. It is usually eaten as a raw fruit (the deep red pips are sucked of their juice and then usually discarded) though the juice can be used as a flavouring in sweet dishes and drinks. Look for even-coloured, firm fruit with red and juicy-looking seeds. Cut a thin slice off the stem end, cut the fruit into sections, then peel back the skin to free the pips. To release the juice, press the seeds in a sieve over a bowl.
• Low-fat. High in vitamin C.

Pomelo (*Citrus grandis*) Shaddock   **1**
Largest of the citrus fruits, it has a thick skin and a bitter fibrous pulp. It is usually eaten on its own.
• Low-fat. High in vitamin C.

Prickly pear (*Opuntia ficus indica*) Indian fig   **15**
The prickly pear is available from midsummer to midwinter. It can be eaten stewed or raw and is often used in preserves. The fruit has a thorny skin which must be removed before eating.
• Low-fat. High in fibre, calcium, iron and vitamin C.

Tamarillo (*Cyphomandra betacea*) Tree tomato   **14**
A tropical fruit of the same family as the tomato, the tamarillo can be reddish-yellow or purple when ripe. It can be eaten raw, but is usually stewed.

Tangelo (*Citrus*, spp.)   **4**
Tangelos, or Mineola fruit, are tangerine and grapefruit hybrids. Peel and prepare as for oranges.

Legumes and nuts

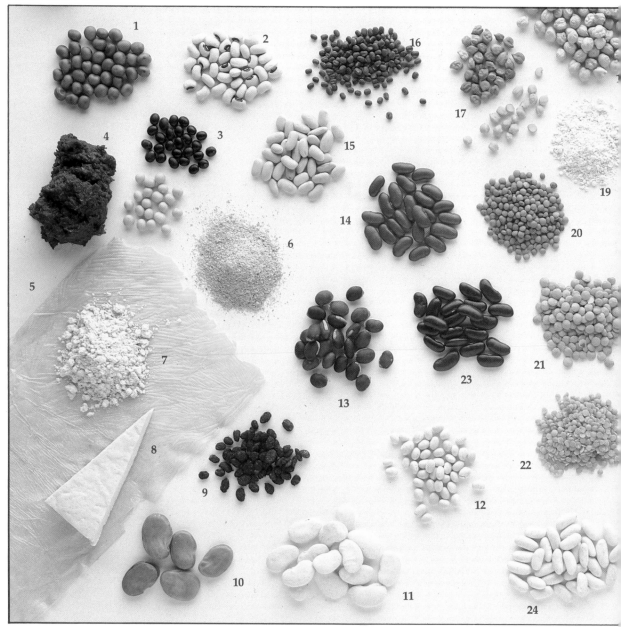

1	Ful medames	9	Fermented soya beans	17	Middle Eastern chick peas
2	Black-eyed beans/peas	10	Broad/fava beans		(channa dal)
3	Soya beans	11	Butter/lima beans	18	European chick peas
4	Miso (soya bean paste)	12	Pearl haricot/navy beans	19	Gram/besan flour (chick-pea
5	Soya bean curd sheet	13	Lablab beans		flour)
6	Soya grits	14	Red kidney beans	20	Brown lentils
7	Soya flour	15	Flageolets	21	Green lentils
8	Tofu (soya bean curd)	16	Urd beans	22	Split orange lentils

23	Black kidney beans	31	Tiger nuts	38	Cashew nuts
24	Haricot/navy beans	32	Aduki beans	39	Brazil nuts
25	Split peas	33	Sprouted mung beans	40	Dried chestnuts
26	Yellow lentils	34	Mung beans	41	Pecan nuts
27	Whole peas	35	Borlotti beans	42	Macadamia nuts
28	Pine nuts	36	Walnuts	43	Peanuts
29	Pistachio nuts	37	Hazelnuts	44	Almonds
30	Coconut				

Ugli fruit (*Citrus*, spp.)   6
A hybrid citrus fruit, the ugli is a cross between the tangerine and the grapefuit. It is more similar to the grapefruit in appearance, except that its skin is thick, knobbly and greenish-yellow. Its sweet pink flesh can be eaten raw, or used in preserves and is also sometimes baked. Prepare and use as for grapefruit.
• Low-fat. High in vitamin C.

Legumes

Aduki bean (*Phaseolus angularis*) Adzuki bean   **32**
Small, reddish-brown beans with a creamy texture and pleasant nutty flavour, they are used in soups, pâtés and sweet and savoury dishes. They are particularly popular in China and Japan, where they are used boiled, mashed and sweetened, as a base for various cakes and sweets. Aduki beans are also available powdered.
• Low-fat. High in carbohydrate, fibre, iron, phosphorus and vitamin B_1.

Broad/Fava bean (*Vicia faba*) Field bean, Horse bean, Windsor bean   **10**
These large pale brown beans are available fresh, dried or canned. They are most often eaten fresh, though the dried beans are very popular in many European countries. In their dried state broad beans need long and slow cooking. They can be eaten on their own, in casseroles and in salads.
• Low-fat. High in fibre, phosphorus, iron, copper, niacin, vitamins B_1 and C.

Butter/Lima bean (*Phaseolus lunatus*) Madagascar bean   **11**
These large creamy-white or pale green beans are available in two sizes, one slightly larger than the other. They have a soft, floury texture and a smooth flavour. Available fresh, dried, canned and frozen they are delicious in salads, pâtés and soups.
• Low-fat. High in fibre, magnesium, phosphorus, iron, copper, zinc, niacin and vitamin B_1.

Chick pea (*Cicer arietinum*) Garbanzo, Ceci   **17, 18, 19**
These large dried peas are usually golden in colour, although there is also a small, dark brown variety known as **channa dal** (used mainly in Middle Eastern cookery). Chick peas have a slightly crunchy and nutty flavour, and can be used in salads, casseroles and other savoury dishes. In the Middle East they are used in the well known dip hummus, and patties (falafel). They are available whole and split and also yield a very good flour called gram or besan. Chick peas are available whole and split. They are very hard and need to be soaked for at least 24 hours before long, slow cooking.
• Low-fat. High in fibre, calcium, magnesium, phosphorus, copper and vitamin B_1.

Ful medames (*Lathyrus sativus*) Foule medames   **1**
This small light brown bean has a white variation called 'ful nabed'. Ful medames give their name to one of Egypt's national dishes and are tasty additions to soups, casseroles, salads and other savoury dishes.
• Low-fat. High in fibre.

Haricot/Navy bean (*Phaseolus vulgaris*) Boston bean   **2, 12, 14, 15, 23, 24, 35**
The term usually refers to the large white haricot, or to its smaller counterpart (pearl haricot) - probably best known for its use in commercial baked beans, but also a traditional ingredient of the French cassoulet. However, the haricot family is very large and includes all the following: **bianco di spagna** - a large white bean popular in Italy (used in soups, salads and savoury dishes); **black-eyed beans/ peas** - similar to small haricot beans, but with a black area on one side (used in pâtés, casseroles and soups); **black beans** - sweet-tasting beans that are very popular in the West Indies. They can be used in soups, salads and savoury dishes; **borlotti beans** - speckled beans in shades varing from cream to pink which cook to a creamy consistency. They are very popular in Italy, as are **cannellini beans** (used particularly with tuna in 'tonno e fagioli'). **Flageolet beans** are a beautiful shade of pale green and are available canned. **Red kidney beans** are used in soups, casseroles and salads, but are best known for their use in Mexican spicy dishes such as chilli con carne. The skins of these beans contain toxins which must be removed after soaking by boiling fast for 10 minutes. **Pinto beans** are speckled and come in various shades of pink or brown. They are often used in Mexican dishes; also in soups, salads and pâtés.
• Low-fat. High in fibre, calcium, magnesium, phosphorus, iron, copper and zinc.

Lablab bean (*Dolichos lablab*) Hyacinth bean, Bonavist bean   **13**
A legume of Asian origin, it is most popular in India and Malaysia where it has the same uses as split pulses (see Pea and Lentil, below) though the raw seeds can cause poisoning. The seeds can be white, reddish, black or mottled.
• Low-fat. High in carbohydrate, fibre, phosphorus, iron and vitamin B_1.

Lentil (*Lens esculenta*) Dahl   **20**, **21**, **22**, **26**
In recent years these have become one of the most popular legumes in Europe and the US. They are available in brown, green, orange, yellow and black, and may be bought whole or split, the latter being quicker to cook. Lentils do not need long soaking - 10 minutes is ideal. The smaller yellow and orange lentils purée very easily, which makes them useful in soups. The others retain their shape well after cooking and can be served as a vegetable, on their own, or in casseroles and in salads. Lentils play a particularly important part in Indian cookery, where they are used in curries and side dishes.
● Low-fat. High in fibre, iron, copper, zinc and vitamin B_1.

Mung bean (*Phaseolus aureus*) Moong dal   **33**, **34**
These small olive green beans are available whole, split and skinless. They are commonly used in stews, or as a vegetable in salads or on their own. In India they are curried, but they are perhaps best known in their sprouted form as 'beansprouts'. They need no soaking before cooking.
● Low-fat. High in fibre, magnesium, phosphorus, iron, copper and vitamin B_1.

Pea (*Pisum sativum*)   **25**, **27**
Dried peas are a useful part of the store cupboard, particularly as fresh ones have such a short season. They are available in various sizes, colours and shapes, being either whole, split, green, yellow or blue. All need to be soaked overnight before cooking. Whole peas can be used as a side vegetable; split varieties will make excellent purées and yield a good flour that flavours and thickens beautifully.
● Low-fat. High in fibre, magnesium, phosphorus, iron, zinc and vitamin B_1.

Soya bean (*Glycine max*) Soybean   **3**, **4**, **5**, **6**, **7**, **8**, **9**
In the Far East soya beans have been regarded as the 'meat of the earth' for thousands of years. They are amazingly versatile, yielding many food products, and are unique among beans in containing the eight essential amino acids, thus providing complete protein. The beans themselves can be yellow or black, and are available whole, dried and fermented. They can be cooked in stews, but are probably best known for their by-products, which include soy sauce, tofu (bean curd), miso (fermented bean paste), tempeh (fermented bean cake), soya grits, soya flakes, dried bean curd sheets and textured vegetable protein (TVP).
● Low-fat. High in fibre, calcium, magnesium, iron, folic acid and vitamin B_1.

Urd bean (*Phaseolus mungo*) Urd dahl, Black gram   **16**
Available whole, split and skinless, urd beans, when whole, look like mung beans. Like other legumes, they can be used whole as a side vegetable, or puréed and used in soups.
● Low-fat. High in fibre, calcium, magnesium, iron, folic acid and vitamin B_1.

Nuts

Almond (*Prunus dulcis*)   **44**
There are bitter and sweet varieties, both of which have a bitter green skin inside which must be removed before using. Bitter almonds must be roasted to drive off their acid content. They are sometimes used in jams and liqueurs. Sweet almonds are added to anything from ice cream to trout. They are widely used in confectionery and are also made into drinks and liqueurs. They combine successfully with cheese and vegetables to make a good stuffing, and may be added raw to salads. An interesting dish called 'nougarda' is made from puréed almonds mixed with lemon, garlic and parsley. Use almonds whole, blanched (skinned), flaked/slivered or toasted.
● High in fibre, protein, calcium, magnesium, phosphorus, iron, zinc, niacin, folic acid, vitamins B_1, B_2 and E.

Brazil nut (*Bertholletia excelsa*)   **39**
Brazil nuts are very oily, but have a distinctive flavour. They keep best in the shell, and so should be bought fresh whenever possible. Available whole and shelled, they can be eaten raw as snacks, toasted and used in cakes, or, alternatively, ground in a food processor or blender and used in stuffings, vinaigrettes and soups.
● High in fibre, protein, calcium, magnesium, phosphorus, iron, copper, zinc, niacin, vitamins B_1, B_6 and E.

Cashew nut (*Anacardium occidentale*)   **38**
Cashew nuts are usually sold shelled and salted. They can be eaten as a cocktail nut, in baking and to flavour butter. They also make excellent purées.
● High in fibre, protein, carbohydrate, magnesium, iron, niacin, vitamins B_1 and B_2.

Chestnut (*Castanea sativa*) Sweet chestnut   **40**
Chestnuts can be eaten whole, either roasted, boiled or steamed. They are available fresh, canned and dried, and are best if cooked and eaten fresh. (Boil them whole for 40 minutes, then slice and extract the kernels.) Chestnuts can be used chopped in stuffings, sprinkled over vegetables, or puréed in soups. The dried variety are a useful standby. They need to be soaked for about one hour before use. Once shelled,

Cereals and cereal by-products 1

1	Chinese black glutinous rice	**6**	Wheatgerm
2	Rice flakes	**7**	Cous cous
3	Semolina (unrefined)	**8**	Italian short-grain brown rice
4	Matzoh meal	**9**	Corn kernels
5	Wheat flakes		

10	Bulgar
11	Wild rice
12	Corn meal
13	Cracked maize

14	Oats	18	Buckwheat	22	Barley flakes
15	Oat groats	19	Roasted buckwheat (kasha)	23	Soya flour
16	Rye flakes	20	Oat flakes	24	Millet flakes
17	Rye grain	21	Pot barley	25	Millet

chestnuts are preserved in sugar or syrup as marrons glacés. They are also available in the form of chestnut purée, which can be used in soups, desserts, crêpes and cakes.
• High in fibre, carbohydrate, magnesium, copper, biotin, vitamins B_1, B_2 and B_6.

Coconut (*Cocos nucifera*) **30**
Especially useful in Indonesian and West Indian dishes, coconut is available fresh and whole or in slices, or dried and flaked. The milk is extracted and the flesh may be pounded to a cream, or processed and desiccated/shredded. It can add a delectable flavour to food, but is high in saturated fats.
• High in fibre, magnesium, phosphorus, iron and copper.

Hazelnut (*Corylus avellana*) and **Filbert** (*Corylus maxima*)**37**
These are varieties of the same nut. Both are rich in oil and used in butters, confections and desserts. They are used mainly in chocolates and ice cream. In France they are pounded into butter to make 'beurre de noisettes', a garnish for hors d'oeuvres. In Spain they are used in a dish called 'calcotada' where the nuts are roasted with spring onions/scallions over vine clippings. Their most famous use is in 'salsa romesco' (see page 246).
• High in fibre, magnesium, phosphorus, iron, copper, zinc, folic acid, pantothenic acid, vitamins B_1, B_6 and E.

Macadamia nut (*Macadamia ternifolia*) Queensland nut **42**
Native to Australia, these nuts are usually only available shelled and roasted outside their native country. They are mainly eaten as cocktail nibbles, but are also occasionally used in confectionery.
• High in fibre, calcium, phosphorus, iron and vitamin B_1.

Peanut (*Arachis hypogaea*) Groundnut, Monkeynut **43**
Technically a legume rather than a nut, the peanut can be eaten raw or roasted and is used mainly for peanut butter and peanut oil. In Indonesia and many African countries, they are often used as the basis of sauces and stews, and can also be used in any of the way suggested with other nuts. They are available whole and shelled.
• High in fibre, protein, iron, magnesium, phosphorus, copper, zinc, niacin, folic acid, pantothenic acid, vitamins B_1, B_6 and E.

Pecan nut (*Carya illinoensis*) **41**
Similar in flavour and appearance to walnuts, but oilier. Their shells are a smooth, shiny red and much easier to crack. Pecan nuts are popular in the US, where they are used to make the famous pecan pie. They are also used in stuffings, nutbreads, ice creams and savoury vegetable dishes. They are available whole and shelled.
• High in fibre, protein, calcium, iron, niacin, vitamins B_1 and E.

Pine nut (*Pinus pinea*) Indian nut **28**
Small, soft nuts that can be eaten raw or roasted and salted like peanuts. They can be chopped finely and used in soups and sauces. They are probably best known for their use in the famous Italian sauce 'pesto' in which they are pounded in a pestle and mortar with fresh basil leaves. They are also delicious when added to rice and aubergine/eggplant dishes. When fresh, pine nuts may smell quite strongly of turpentine, which is a product of some pine trees. This smell fades during storage. Pine nuts are usually only sold shelled.
• High in protein, phosphorus, iron, niacin, vitamins B_1 and B_2.

Pistachio nut (*Pistacia vera*) **29**
Available whole or shelled, pistachio nuts are delicious green nuts which may be roasted, salted and eaten as a snack, or used to flavour and colour ice cream, Turkish delight and halva. They are also delicious in salads and stuffings, either coarsely chopped, pounded to a paste, or both. They are sold with dyed red shells or their natural tan ones.
• High in fibre, protein, iron, calcium, niacin, vitamins B_1 and B_2.

Tiger nut (*Cyperus esculenta*) Chufa nut **31**
Although always referred to as nuts these are in fact the rhizomes of a plant. Usually sold dried, they have an almondy taste and can be eaten on their own, like peanuts. When ground they are used in the Spanish drink 'horchata de chufa'.
• High in fibre and protein.

Walnut (*Juglana regia*) **36**
There are many varieties of this nut, which is sold whole, shelled, ground and chopped, fresh, dried or pickled. They are extremely versatile and may be used at different stages of their growth. (The moister the walnut, the fresher it will be.) Green walnuts, which have not yet developed a hard shell, are picked in summer to make pickles, ketchups and chutneys. Wet walnuts, picked around early autumn, have moist kernels with a hard outer shell. They have a delicious and fragrant flavour which is marvellous in savoury dishes. Dried walnuts, the type most often eaten, are simply an older version of wet walnuts from which the moisture has been allowed to evaporate. They can be added to salads, savoury dishes, cakes and breads. Walnut oil is cold pressed from ripe nuts and makes a subtle and delicious salad dressing.
• High in fibre, protein, magnesium, phosphorus, iron, copper, zinc, niacin, folic acid, pantothenic acid, biotin, vitamins B_1, B_6 and E.

Cereals and cereal by-products

Barley **21**, **22**

In ancient times, barley was often used to make bread. Nowadays it is more often used for thickening soups and stews. Cooked on its own it will make a pleasant alternative to potatoes, rice or pasta. Barley is available in many forms. **Barley flakes** are made from the whole grains which are processed and then dried. They can be eaten raw in muesli or cooked to make a variety of porridge **Pearl barley** is a refined version of pot barley, and is therefore far less nutritious. It takes only 15 minutes to cook and is used in soups and stews. **Pot barley** is the whole grain, which has had only the hard outer husk removed, so it is rich in protein. It takes a good 30 minutes to cook and is used on its own or added to soups and stews.

● Low-fat. High in fibre, iron, carbohydrate, magnesium, niacin and vitamin B_1.

Buckwheat (also known as beechwheat or saracen corn) **18**, **19**, **55**

Despite its name, buckwheat is not actually a cereal, but a member of the rhubarb family. It is available in the form of unroasted and roasted grains. The unroasted grains are a greenish colour and are best cooked with other ingredients, as in a casserole. The brown roasted grains are used to make a flour which can be used for pancakes, crisp thin cakes, and Japanese noodles called soba. It makes an excellent substitute for rice and various risotto-like dishes can be made from it. **Buckwheat flour** is beautifully light and used on its own or mixed with wheat flour, makes delicious crêpes. It is also used in the traditional Russian dish called 'blinis'.

● Low-fat. High in fibre, protein, carbohydrate, iron, niacin, phosphorus, vitamins B_1 and B_2.

Bulgar (also known as bulgur, burghul, bourgouri, pourgouri) **10**

Although this is often referred to as 'cracked wheat' it is in fact a more refined version, which has been steamed and dried before being cracked. When cooked, bulgar swells to a fluffy texture similar in appearance to cous cous. Bulgar can be cooked as a pilaf or soaked and served raw in a salad. It is the main ingredient of the Lebanese dish tabbouleh (see page 123).

● Low-fat. High in fibre, protein, calcium, phosphorus, iron, niacin and vitamin B_1.

Corn/Maize **9**, **12**, **13**, **52**, **53**

An extremely versatile grain that yields many useful products. Available as whole or cracked grains, it comes in many varieties and has several by-products: **flint corn** is used as animal feed; **dent corn**, a hard variety, is ground into meal and flour; **popcorn** has a hard outer covering which stores water (it is this which pops when heated); **flour corn** has a thin outer layer to its seeds from which cornflour/cornstarch is made. It is low in nutrients, but a good thickening agent. **Cornflour/cornstarch** is a finely ground form of corn meal used mainly for sauces and thickening soups and stews. When mixed into a cream and boiled it will form a clear jelly. **Corn meal** when ground to a powder can be made into porridge, or used in cakes, desserts and pancakes. **Polenta** is similar to cornmeal, but has a fine, granular texture that is more like semolina. In Italy the name is also given to the dish made form it. It can be served as a vegetable accompaniment, fried or grilled, or, alternatively with any sauce. **Sweetcorn** is used as a vegetable (see page 73). **Wholemeal corn** has a low gluten content, so it will not leaven bread. It can be used for sprinkling over bread before baking, or scattered on the greased surface of the loaf tin or baking sheet, to aid removal.

● Low-fat. High in fibre, carbohydrate, protein, iron, niacin and vitamin B_1.

Gram/Chick pea flour (also known as besan flour) **63**

Gram flour is made from ground chick peas. A popular feature of Indian cookery, it has a good flavour and creamy texture. It forms a batter when mixed with water that is much used in India for coating foods for frying, and is also used for various sweetmeats. It is very useful for making soups and sauces; as it is additive-free it must be stirred vigorously to eradicate all the lumps.

● Low-fat. High in fibre, calcium, magnesium, phosphorus, copper and vitamin B_1.

Millet **24**, **25**, **50**

Yellow seeds with a pleasant nutty taste. In Third World countries millet is ground, boiled and made into porridge or unleavened bread. In India it is used, together with black beans to make pancakes called 'ragi dosas'. Although in the West it was traditionally thought of as bird food, it can now be found in many health food shope and makes a very good substitute for rice. Millet is available as whole grains or flakes (which can be cooked into a porridge or eaten raw as part of a meal). **Millet flour** is low in gluten, and therefore will not make leavened bread. However, it thickens soups and stews beautifully, adding flavour and nutrition.

● Low-fat. High in carbohydrate, niacin, protein, phosphorus, iron and vitamin B_1.

26	Ruoti (wheels)	33	Spaghetti (wholewheat and	38	Penne
27	Farfallini (small bows)		plain)	39	Japanese transparent noodles
28	Farfalle (large bows)	34	Green lasagne	40	Fusilli bucati
29	Tortellini	35	Tagliatella (green,	41	Cannelloni
30	Rice sticks		wholewheat, plain)	42	Ditalini
31	Egg noodles	36	Pastina	43	Somen (Japanese white wheat
32	Rice noodles	37	Macaroni and wholewheat		noodles)
			elbow macaroni		

44	Soba (Japanese buckwheat noodles)	50	Millet flour	57	Chinese transparent noodles
45	Capelletti	51	Rye flour	58	Potato flour/starch
46	Conchiglie (shells)	52	Polenta	59	Lumache (snails)
47	Fusilli	53	Cornflour/cornstarch	60	Gnocchi
48	Spirale	54	Split pea flour	61	Capellini
49	Refined semolina	55	Buckwheat flour	62	Rice flour
		56	Wholewheat flour	63	Gram/besan (chick pea flour)

Noodles   30, 31, 32, 39, 43, 44, 57
Noodles are sold dried. They are
usually made from wheat flour, and
may or may not contain eggs (unlike
commercially made Italian pasta, which
never contains eggs). They are a
particularly popular feature of Oriental
cookery, where they are probably best
known for their use in *chow mein* dishes.
Usually, noodles are made from wheat
flour and eggs, but they can also be
made from rice flour, buckwheat (as in
the Japanese soba noodles), soya beans
(Japanese harusame noodles), and all
manner of starchy substances such as
arrowroot. They can also be made from
mung beans, in which case they will
need soaking before cooking, and will
have a gelatinous texture when cooked.
● Low-fat. High in protein, fibre,
magnesium, iron, copper, zinc, niacin
and vitamin B_1.

Oats   14, 15, 20
Oats are probably best known for their
use in the Scottish breakfast dish,
porridge - known as oatmeal in the US.
In the UK, 'oatmeal' refers to the milled
oat grains (which come in varying
degrees of coarseness) as opposed to
rolled oats or oat flakes which are the
whole flattened grains. **Oat groats** are
whole oat kernels. They are high in fibre
and nutritional content. Oats can be
used in oat cakes, haggis, granola bars,
muesli products, rissoles and
croquettes.
● Low-fat. High in fibre, carbohydrate,
calcium, magnesium, phosphorus, iron,
copper, zinc, folic acid, pantothenic
acid, biotin, vitamins B_1 and E.

Pasta   26, 27, 28, 29, 33, 34, 36, 37, 38,
41, 45, 46, 47, 47, 48
The word 'pasta' literally means
'dough'. There are many different
types. Pasta is actually sold in two main
forms: the factory made dried pasta, or

pasta secca (made from flour and water),
that is commonly available in packets;
and the homemade fresh pasta or *pasta
all'uovo* (made from flour and eggs) that
is increasingly available in
delicatessens. Although, strictly
speaking, all pasta should be made from
semolina flour milled from durum
wheat, ordinary plain/all-purpose flour
can also be used successfully. There was
a time when only pasta made from
unrefined semolina was available in a
wide variety of shapes. In recent years,
pasta-makers have also produced pastas
in a wide range of colours, such as
green (coloured with spinach purée)
and pink (coloured with tomato purée).
    Fresh and dry pasta can also be
divided further, according to use. There
is *pasta ripiene*, or 'stuffed pasta', which
applies to pasta such as lasagne,
tortellini, tortelloni and cannelloni,
which can be stuffed with a variety of
fillings; *pasta in brodo*, or *pastina* (tiny
pasta shapes, used mainly in soups),
and *pasta asciutta* (probably the most
common form of pasta, covering
spaghetti, tagliatelle, macaroni and all
the various pasta shapes). Pasta has
endless uses. It can be combined with
any vegetable, cheese, seafood or meat;
boiled and added to vegetables and
sauces, stuffed, baked, or used in soups
and salads. There are even some
desserts made from pasta. In Italy, it is a
staple, replacing potatoes and rice.
Some of the more popular pasta shapes
include spaghetti, tagliatelle, ruoti,
tagliolini, ziti, ditali and ditalini,
macaroni, bucatini, farfalle, and
farfallini, anelli, tortellini and capellini.
Finally, there is an interesting variety
known as gnocchi, that is made from
potato flour (see page 166).
● Low-fat. High in protein,
magnesium, phosphorus, iron, zinc,
niacin, biotin and vitamin B_1.

Potato flour/starch (also known as
fecule)   58
This is made from cooked potatoes,
dried and ground. It is often used for
thickening and adds a subtle flavour to
cakes and biscuits where a delicate
starch is needed.
● High in carbohydrate and iron.

Rice   1, 2, 8, 62
The staple grain of over half the world's
population, there are hundreds of
varieties, though these basically fall into
two main types: long grain and short
grain. Long grain rice has dry, separate
grains when cooked and is often used in
Indian cookery; short grain tends to
have a stickier, softer texture and is a
popular feature of Oriental cookery.
Rice can be used in a wide range of
savoury dishes, either as part of the
dish itself, or as an accompaniment. It
can also be used in desserts and salads.
In the West, it is mainly white, refined
rice that is eaten, though this is the least
nutritious of all. Other varieties of rice
include brown rice, Basmati (long
grain), Italian or arborio (short grain)
and pudding rice (mainly used in China
and Japan), which can be either black or
white. When boiled, it becomes sticky
and sweet and is therefore used mainly
in baking and confectionery. Apart from
the whole grain, rice is also available in
the form of flakes (made from either
brown or white rice). These can be used
to make a variety of muesli and also a
rice porridge. **Rice flour** is a gluten-free
flour made from both brown and white
rice. It is used mainly in Oriental
cookery for making noodles, cakes and
biscuits. It is also used as a thickening
agent. See also Wild rice.
● Low-fat. High in fibre, carbohydrate,
magnesium, copper, niacin, zinc, folic
acid and vitamin B_1.

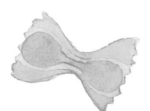

Rye   16, 17, 51

A strong-flavoured grain, it is used mainly for animal fodder, but is also used in rye bread the well-known Scandinavian crsipbread and in drinks such as whisky, gin and beer. Rye is available as the whole or cracked grain (used mainly for coarse rye breads) and rye flakes (whole rye grains that have been flattened and lightly toasted. **Rye flour** is the main ingredient in black bread, pumpernickel and some crispbreads. It also makes excellent pancakes and is often used to make leavened bread, though since it has no gluten, it will have to be mixed with two-thirds wheat flour when used in this way.

● Low-fat. High in fibre, magnesium, iron, copper, zinc, folic acid, pantothenic acid, biotin, vitamins B_1, B_2, B_6 and E.

Soya flour   23

Made from dried soya beans, this is used as a nutritious supplement to soups, cakes and bread. It is not used as a conventional flour.

● High in fibre, protein, calcium, magnesium, phosphorus, iron, niacin, pantothenic acid, vitamins B_1, B_2 and B_6.

Split pea flour

Made from dried and ground yellow/split peas, this cannot be used as a flour in the conventional sense, but makes a good thickener for soups or stews.

Wheat   3, 4, 5, 6, 7, 49, 60

Probably the most important grain of all, there are two basic types: common or bread wheat, and durum wheat.

Common wheat is used mainly for flour to be used in bread and cakes. There are two types: hard wheat (best for milling and bread making) and soft wheat (starchier, with fluffier grains; it is best for cakes, desserts and sauces). Wheat is available in many forms. **Cracked wheat** consists of whole wheat grains that are cracked open by machine (to make cooking easier and quicker). Boiled or baked, they make an excellent substitute for rice. **Wheat flakes** are flattened and usually toasted. They can be eaten raw as part of a breakfast cereal or cooked, like rolled oats, into a coarse porridge. **Wheat bran** and **wheat germ** can both be used as cereal ingredients.

● Low-fat. High in fibre, protein, carbohydrate, magnesium, phosphorus, iron, copper, zinc, niacin, folic acid, biotin, vitamins B_1, B_6 and E.

Wheat flours are available in many forms, most of which are high in gluten and excellent for bread-making and baking. **Granary flour** is a blend of wholewheat and rye flours with malted grains and caramel. As its constituents suggest, it has a slightly sweet, malted flavour and makes excellent bread and pastry (see page 40). **Matzoh meal** is made by grinding matzohs (Jewish unleavened crispbreads made of wheat flour and water). It can be medium or fine, and is used mainly in Jewish cookery in Passover cakes and to thicken soups. **Plain/All-purpose flour** is white flour that is used for general cooking and baking. It may include a number of additives, such as emulsifiers, colours, flavourings, preservatives and anti-oxidants, to prolong shelf life. Check before you buy. **Self-raising flour** is a fine, white flour with added baking powder to act as a leavening agent. It should be used soon after purchase as its potency declines, especially in damp conditions. **Strong/all-purpose flour** is white but unbleached, and has had the bran and wheatgerm removed. It makes good bread that rises easily.

Wheat flour of 81% extraction (until recently known as wheatmeal) is available in the UK. It has up to 20% of its coarser elements removed during milling. It makes good tasty loaves, and is suitable for thickening some soups and stews, without making them gritty or stodgy. **Wholemeal flour** is the British name for *any* flour made from the whole grain. Bread and flour manufacturers have created much confusion by using 'wholemeal' to mean 'wholewheat', but labelling laws are gradually changing, so any confusion should be ironed out. **Wholewheat flour** (sometimes known in the US as graham flour) is brown in colour and coarse in texture, containing all the bran and wheatgerm. It makes delicious if somewhat densely-textured bread, which takes longer to rise than the white variety. For baking purposes it should be sifted to get air into it. Be sure to return all the bran from the sieve to the mixing bowl - its fibre content is particularly valuable. Sometimes wholewheat flour may be labelled 'stoneground'. This simply means that it has been ground, in the traditional way, between two huge stones. Although it has its advocates, it is virtually impossible to discern any difference in flavour from wholewheat flour milled by modern technology. Low-fat. High in fibre, protein, carbohydrate, magnesium, iron, phosphorus, copper, zinc, niacin, biotin, folic acid, vitamins B_1, B_6 and E. Durum wheat in the form of semolina, is used to make pasta (see above) and cous cous. **Cous cous** is the steamed, dried and cracked grains of durum wheat. It is similar to bulgar, but is more refined, with a paler, creamier colour before cooking and a lighter texture when cooked. It is the main ingredient

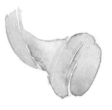

Unusual foods

1	Vine/grape leaves	**9**	Chinese shiitake mushrooms (dried and reconstituted)	**14**	Wakame seaweed
2	Smetana/low-fat sour cream			**15**	Mousserons mushroom (dried and reconstituted)
3	Hiziki seaweed	**10**	Morel mushroom (reconstituted)		
4	Yeast extract			**16**	Pink champagne mushrooms (reconstituted)
5	Carrageen seaweed	**11**	Chanterelle/Girolle mushrooms		
6	Agar agar (Chinese grass)			**17**	Dried boletus mushroom (reconstituted)
7	Tahini	**12**	Arame seaweed		
8	Oyster mushrooms	**13**	Canned Chinese grass jelly	**18**	Cornes d'abondance mushrooms (dried and reconstituted)

19	Wood ear mushrooms (Chinese black fungus, dried and reconstituted)	25	Textured vegetable protein (TVP)	31	Dulse seaweed
20	Yuba (bean curd strips)	26	Soya milk	32	Quark
21	Miso paste	27	Olives	33	Kuzu flour
22	Soya bean curd (tofu)	28	Carob powder	34	Malt extract
23	Fermented bean curd	29	Kombu seaweed	35	Umeboshi plums
24	Soya sauce	30	Shiofuki (prepared kombu kelp)	36	Dried gourd strips
				37	Fructose crystals

of the North African dish of the same name, but it is also delicious served with vegetable stew, or made into desserts and cakes. Low-fat. High in carbohydrate, iron and vitamin B_1.
Semolina is produced from the starchy part (endosperm) of durum wheat grain, it is sometimes used to make pasta, but is also used in gnocchi and in desserts. It is available refined and unrefined. Low-fat. High in protein, carbohydrate, magnesium, phosphorus, iron and vitamin B_1.

Wild rice   11
Despite its name, this is not really rice at all, but a wild grass. Despite its costliness, its pleasant nutty flavour makes it an attractive alternative to rice in savoury dishes. It is cooked in the same way as ordinary rice, and is thought to be particularly nutritious.
● Low-fat. High in fibre, phosphorus, iron, niacin, vitamins B_1 and B_2.

Unusual foods

Agar agar (also known as Chinese grass, Ceylon moss and Kanten)   6
A thickening agent obtained from various Far Eastern seaweeds, agar agar is available as a powder, sticks and flakes. It is used mainly to make jellies and gelatine-like desserts.
● Low-fat. High in carbohydrate, calcium and iron.

Carob powder   28
A flavouring made from the pulp of the dried carob bean. It is used in the soft drinks industry and in confectionery as a chocolate substitute.
● Low-fat. High in fibre, calcium, phosphorus and carbohydrate.

Dried gourd strips   36
These are used mainly in Chinese and Japanese cooking, where they are reconstituted or cooked in liquid, in soups and stews. They are useful for tying up roulades that have to be poached.
● High in fibre, phosphorus and iron.

Fructose (also known as fruit sugar)   37
A sugar that is found in fruit juices, honey and flower nectar. In recent years it has become available in the form of white powder, which can be used interchangeably with ordinary sugar. It is the only sugar which is believed to have nutritional benefits, and as such is recommended by health experts.
● High in carbohydrate.

Grass jelly   13
A black jelly made with seaweed. It is sold canned in shops which specialize in Chinese foods. It is used in sweet dishes in China and parts of South-east Asia.

Kuzu   33
Made from the boiled and mashed roots of a Japanese vine, kuzu is used as a thickener in much the same way as cornflour, for sauces and gravies, or as a glaze for desserts and puddings.

Malt extract   34
The soluble part of the malted grain (usually barley) is extracted and boiled. It is usually sold in jars and is available from chemists or health food shops, or from shops that specialize in materials for homemade beers and wines. Malt extract is used in hot or cold milky drinks and also, sometimes, for baking.
● Low-fat. High in carbohydrate.

Mushrooms, truffles and fungi   8, 9, 10, 11, 15, 16, 17, 18, 19
Apart from the common button and field mushrooms we are all familiar with, there are many other, more unusual varieties, which in recent years have gained popularity. The most common examples are varieties of Chinese and Japanese mushrooms, which are usually sold dried and must be reconstituted with water before use. Some of the most popular of these are Chinese mushrooms (shiitake), wood ears (Chinese black fungus) and the Japanese Matsutake. Unusual European varieties include oyster mushrooms, pink champagne mushrooms, the brown, sponge-like morel (available dried and canned), the boletus, the Corne d'abondance (or Horn of Plenty), chanterelle or girolle, and the tiny mousserons (all available dried).
● Low-fat. High in protein, carbohydrate, fibre, calcium, phosphorus, iron, niacin, vitamins B_1 and B_2.

Olives   27
The fruits of a Mediterranean tree, these are only ever sold pickled, the fresh ones being used mainly for the production of olive oil. They can be green or black and are sold whole, stoned or stuffed with red pepper or almonds. Olives are used mainly as finger foods, but can also be used in pizzas, salads and cooked savoury dishes.
● High in fibre, iron and copper.

Quark   33
Low-fat curd cheese which in recent years in the UK has become increasingly popular as a health food because of its low saturated fat content. A medium-fat version is also available.
● Low-fat. High in protein, calcium, phosphorus and vitamin $B_1$2.

Sea vegetables   3, 5, 12, 14, 29, 30, 31
The use of sea vegetables, or seaweeds, as foods was originally confined mostly to Oriental cookery. They have now, however, become acceptable in the West, and are gaining in popularity all the time. Depending on the variety, they can be grilled/broiled until crisp, cut and added to soups, stews and salads, stir-fried or cooked to soften and wrapped round moulds. They expand considerably when soaked, so only a little is needed. Varieties include: **arame** and **hiziki** (thin, shredded-looking variety used as vegetables in Japanese cooking); **carrageen** (a European variety that is cooked to eat like a vegetable); **dulse** (a coarse Northern variety which is usually sun-dried; it can be cooked like spinach); **kombu** (a Japanese kelp seaweed, with broad, blackish-grey ribbons; **wakame** (a long variety with thin ribbon-like strands, used in soups and salads) which is used to flavour the Japanese stock *dashi*, and can also be soaked and cut in strips for wrapping up pieces of raw fish to make *sushi*. It is also available shredded, in a ready-to-eat form as *shiofuki*).
● Low-fat. High in protein, carbohydrate, fibre, calcium, iron, phosphorus, and niacin.

Smetana   2
Low-fat sour cream which can be used as a healthy cream or sour cream substitute in savoury dishes.
● Low-fat. High in protein, calcium, phosphorus and vitamin B_{12}.

Soya products   21, 22, 23, 24, 25, 26
Soya beans are used far more in the form of by-products than as the beans themselves. **Miso** (fermented soya bean paste) is used as a flavouring for soups, sauces and stews. Low-fat. High in protein, carbohydrate, calcium, phosphorus and iron. **Soya milk** is available in liquid or dried form. It has a nutty taste and can add flavour to soups but is not very successful in tea or coffee. Mixed with yoghurt, it makes a splendidly refreshing lassi. Carob-flavoured varieties are also available. Low-fat. High in protein. **Soy sauce** is an essential ingredient of Oriental cookery, in which it is used to enhance virtually any savoury dish - usually sauces, rice, stews and soups. High in calcium, iron and vitamin B_1. **Tofu** (soya bean curd) is available both fermented and unfermented. In recent years it has been acclaimed as *the* high-protein food. It has a rather bland flavour but is palatable when fried or mixed with other vegetables. Low-fat. High in protein, calcium, iron and copper. **TVP**, or textured vegetable protein, is made from processed soya beans. It resembles meat in texture and appearance and is therefore used as as meat substitute. High in protein, calcium, magnesium, phosphorus, iron, niacin, pantothenic acid, vitamins B_1, B_2 and B_6. **Yuba** (dried bean curd strips) must be soaked before use. They make an unusual addition to braised vegetables.

Tahini (sesame spread)   7
An oily paste made from sesame seeds. It is sometimes added to hummus (see page 188) and may also be mixed with miso (see page 138). It is highly nutritious.

Umeboshi plums   35
Japanese salted and pickled plums that are available whole or puréed. They are used as a flavouring in savoury drinks and vinegar. The puréed plums and the vinegar can be used in stir-fry dishes. The whole plums can be boiled with rice or sliced into stir-fried vegetables.
● Low-fat. High in vitamin C.

Vine/Grape leaves   1
These are very popular in Turkish, Greek and Middle Eastern cookery. They are probably best known in the form of *dolmades*, vine leaves stuffed with minced/ground meat and rice (see page 148), but can also be fried in batter or cut up and used in salads.

Yeast extracts
Yeast extracts are very nutritious. They are used mostly in sandwich spreads, or hot savoury drinks, but are also used to flavour soups and stews.
● Low-fat. High in protein, folic acid, vitamins B_1, B_6 and B_{12}.
Low-fat. High in protein, carbohydrate, calcium, phosphorus and iron.

CHAPTER 4

The Vegetarian Feast

One of the great blessings of the vegetarian diet is that it can free you from conformist eating patterns - 'meat and two veg', three-course meal and three solid meals a day regime. A spread of ten vegetarian cereals can become lunches, salads, breakfasts or light dishes and tempt the appetite and satisfy hunger at any time of day.

As we are all individuals, our dietary needs are never the same. Some of us may only be able to work efficiently in the morning if we breakfast well. Others, like myself, find anything solid at that hour induces sluggishness. The nutritionists exhort us to all have a sensible breakfast, but I know my body better than they do.

However, there are vegetarian breakfasts to tempt the most austere of diners: a salad of soft summer fruits eaten in the garden and accompanied by peppermint tea, homemade muffins with quince jam for a nippy autumn morning, or a Sunday morning brunch of curried eggs, Spanish omelette, wholewheat toast, cornbread, Caesar salad, fresh fruit juices, kir and champagne. Such feasts should, I believe, be rare. Too much food, too often, can blunt the perceptions and damage health.

I would proselytize always for a light lunch on work days - say a good vegetable and bean soup in winter, and a salad in summer. But on special days and holidays, the sky's the limit and vegetarian feasts can be more elaborate than many others.

When planning a more ambitious meal of three or four courses, try alternating between cold courses and hot, raw foods and cooked, fruits and vegetables, or fiery hot spices and cooling yoghurt sauces. The motif of acid and sweet is in nature itself and every good cook will use it to advantage. This is all part of the balance in a meal: the food to crunch, bite and chew against the foods which are smooth and velvety. Eat hummus with a celery stick and you will experience the sensation. These combinations are basic: a buckwheat and brown rice rissole spiced with cumin, fenugreek and asafoetida, has the perfect foil in a strong, smooth lemon and tomato sauce; a grainy tabbouleh salad flavoured with mint and onion is served and eaten with a crisp cos/romaine lettuce; a crunchy gratin of potato, ginger and pumpkin is eaten with a smooth, layered vegetable timbale.

For the single person or the single parent, tired and probably eating alone, the evening meal need not mean opening a can of baked beans. Quick, simple, delicious meals can be contrived in a second: half an avocado sliced into scrambled eggs, an omelette spiced with green peppercorns, melted cheese with homemade chutneys, a wholewheat sandwich of alfalfa and cucumber, an Italian-style fried sandwich with Mozzarella, a bowl of fromage frais or soft cheese with dried fruits and nuts are just a few of the possibilities. There are many ideas in the following pages.

Note: The preparation time for each recipe is given in minutes after each title. It does not include any time for such things as pre-soaking beans or allowing dough to rise. Weights and measures are given in metric/imperial/American throughout. Be sure to use only one of these systems when making recipes.
The symbols following the preparation times are:
$\boxed{V}$ *Vegan* $\boxed{P}$ *Complete protein* $\boxed{F}$ *Suitable for freezing.*

Clockwise from top left: Walnut and cabbage mould, Pasta with green sauce, Fresh peach salad, Sicilian orange salad (see pages 162), 193, 125 and 120).

Breakfasts and Breads

It is easy to get into the habit of starting the day with something which is only an addictive drug and not a healthy drink or meal. Breakfasts can be a highly imaginative beginning to the day, giving us a positive stimulus to extract the maximum amount of enjoyment from the hours ahead. Nutritionists believe that breakfasts are important, but I tend to think that we know how our bodies work best.

Some people will luxuriate on quite a large breakfast, while others merely want a refreshing drink. There is a huge difference between the breakfasts you trouble to make yourself out of fresh ingredients and the ones you get out of a carton or packet. This is true even of fruit juice. A juice made of whole apples two minutes before it is drunk is a revelation in taste experience. I say this even though you can now buy excellent natural fruit juices without additives. If you can afford it, it is worthwhile investing in a good juice extractor which will make excellent juices from beetroots/beets and carrots, as well as apples and pears. Do not use them for citrus fruits because the taste of the whole peel is not pleasant.

In the following pages, there are recipes for muesli and other grain dishes, but even the most simple combination of, say, oats and bulgar wheat, soaked overnight in apple juice and then topped with pumpkin and sunflower seeds is a superb way of starting the day. And there can be endless variations on this combination of soaked grains with the addition of nuts or seeds. All you need is a little foresight the night before.

Many of the recipes for breads can be eaten with some of the spreads - often without butter, if you are concerned with the amount of saturated fat in your diet. But on weekends and holidays, we quite often want to make more of breakfast and indulge ourselves. It is pleasant then to enjoy more substantial dishes of pancakes, baked eggs, brioches, or sour dough breads, with yoghurt and fruit. One of the most pleasant experiences in the world is to have a hearty and late breakfast outside in the garden on a summer's day and to wash it down with a mixture of fruit juice and champagne, or iced herb teas. One can then skip lunch altogether.

In the winter, on weekends and holidays, try toasting the breads and adding devilled mushrooms, smoked tofu, cheeses and vegetable pâtés, with maybe grilled tomatoes and coddled eggs. Enjoy breakfast and there is every chance that you'll go on enjoying the rest of the day.

Porridge/Oatmeal ② Ⓥ Ⓟ

*The best porridge is made from whole oats or,
as it is often called in wholefood shops, oat
groats (not 'quick' oats). This is the whole oat
kernel, which has all the flavour and
nourishment.*

Variation
● *The next best porridge is made from jumbo
oatflakes. To make enough for one, cover
75 g/3 oz/1 cup of oats with boiling water and
leave overnight. In the morning, add more
water or milk and simmer for 15 minutes.*

225 g/8 oz/2 cups whole oats
1 teaspoon salt
1.7 litres/3 pints/7½ cups boiling water

Place the oats in a large casserole. Add the salt and water.
Cover and leave in the oven overnight at 120°C/250°F/Gas
mark ½. In the morning you will have a creamy porridge to
which you can add honey, dried or fresh fruit, nuts, cream,
buttermilk or yoghurt. This is a thoroughly excellent
breakfast for cold winter mornings.

Muesli ② Ⓥ Ⓟ

*This is a basic mixture which can be stored in
an airtight container and will keep happily for
a few months. It is excellent with fresh fruit
juice instead of milk. This mixture has no
sugar, as that is a matter of personal taste.*

225 g/8 oz/2¼ cups rolled oats
50 g/2 oz/2 cups each wheat flakes and rye flakes
50 g/2 oz/1 cup bran
225 g/8 oz mixed dried fruits
100 g/4 oz/generous cup mixed chopped nuts

Mix all the ingredients together and serve with the topping
of your choice: yoghurt, Smetana/low-fat sour cream, milk,
honey, fruit juices or fresh fruit.

Granola ⑳ Ⓥ Ⓟ

*This is a deservedly popular breakfast dish
which can be made in bulk and stored in an
airtight container. It has a satisfying crunchy
texture and will keep happily for a month.*

450 g/1 lb/4½-5 cups rolled oats
100 g/4 oz/1 cup each blanched almonds, chopped
hazelnuts,
unroasted cashews and chopped walnuts
25 g/1 oz/2 tablespoons each sesame seeds and sunflower
seeds, roasted
8 tablespoons clear honey
2 tablespoons sunflower oil

Pre-heat the oven to 180°C/350°F/Gas Mark 4. Mix all the dry
ingredients together, then stir in the honey and oil. Mix
thoroughly and spread the mixture out on an oiled baking
sheet. Bake for about 20 minutes, then take it out, turn the
mixture over and break it up slightly. Bake for a further 40
minutes, ensuring that it browns evenly. Break into chunks
again while still warm.

Homemade yoghurt ⑩ P

This is surprisingly easy and satisfying to make. Use a yoghurt starter, which is a culture you can buy from health shops, or add a portion of good commercial live yoghurt. A starter is best, as it yields a thicker yoghurt.

Variation

● *Fruit flavourings can be added to the yoghurt after it has set. The addition of a fresh fruit purée (see page 198) makes a refreshing breakfast.*

1 litre/1¾ pints/1 quart milk
yoghurt culture: either purchased starter *or*
150 ml/5 fl oz/⅔ cup of plain, live yoghurt

Bring the milk to the boil and then let it cool. Use a thermometer to test the temperature and when the milk is lukewarm (approximately 41°C/106°F), add some of it to the yoghurt culture and mix thoroughly. Then combine with the rest of the milk. Mix well and either pour into a yoghurt maker, or a large bowl and leave for 12 hours, or overnight, in a warm place. When it has set, transfer to the refrigerator. Keep 2 tablespoons of the mixture to make the next batch and refrigerate until needed. After about five or six batches, the yoghurt will get thinner, so use a fresh starter. A few tablespoons of skimmed milk powder may be stirred into the milk to enrich it; you will then have a thicker yoghurt.

Whole fruit compote ⑩ V F

Fruit is particularly good for breakfast; its clean taste freshens the palate. A compote is traditionally stewed fruit preserved in syrup. However, most fruits are naturally sweet enough without added sugar. If not, add some dried fruits where the fructose (the natural sugars) is intensified by the shrinking and drying of the fruit. The following recipe is a mixture of wild and cultivated fruits.

100 g/¼ lb Hunza apricots
600 ml/1 pint/2½ cups apple juice
225 g/½ lb damsons/prune plums
225 g/½ lb dessert plums
100 g/¼ lb wild plums (bullace, Oregon, Texan or peach)
600 ml/1 pint/2½ cups water
2 tablespoons honey
mint leaves for garnish

Soak the apricots in the apple juice overnight. Wash the damsons and plums, and place in a saucepan. Add the water and honey and bring to the boil. Remove from the heat, cover and leave to cool. Stir in the apricots and their juice. Turn out into a glass dish. Garnish with mint leaves before serving.

*Gram flour crêpes filled with chestnut purée and a
mixture of fresh figs, apples, dried apricots and
raisins (see page 100).*

Gram flour crêpes ⑤ Ⓥ Ⓕ

Pancakes made from gram/chick pea flour are so light, they seem like crêpes. The flour has a subtle flavour and, with a filling or a sauce, one of these pancakes is a meal in itself. Eat them with some of the curried vegetable dishes (see page 154), or with a curry sauce and jajiki (see page 190), or omit the spices and eat them with fruit for a special breakfast.

100 g/4 oz/1 cup gram/chick pea flour
½ teaspoon salt
½ teaspoon turmeric
pinch of cayenne pepper
350 ml/12 fl oz/1½ cups iced water
corn oil for frying

Mix the flour, salt and spices together. Gradually add the iced water until you get a smooth batter. Heat a little oil in a pan and tilt it to cover the inside. Add a quarter of the batter and cook until the edges are brown and crisp, and the top has dried out. Slide it on to a plate and keep warm. Make the other three crêpes, oiling the pan each time.

Griddle cakes ⑧

These American-style pancakes have a slight crunch to them and are splendid for brunch or the more ambitious weekend breakfast. They are excellent with summer soft fruits, and go well with butter, honey, maple syrup and sour cream. This recipe makes about 10 pancakes 10 cm/4 inches in diameter.

4 tablespoons butter
100 g/4 oz/2 cups fresh white breadcrumbs, toasted (see page 48)
1 egg
65 g/2½ oz/⅔ cup plain/all-purpose flour
150 ml/5 fl oz/⅔ cup sour cream
150 ml/5 fl oz/⅔ cup milk
½ teaspoon baking powder
seasoning to taste

Melt the butter in a frying pan, mix in the breadcrumbs and stir for a moment. Mix the egg and flour together, then add the sour cream, milk and baking powder. Fold in the breadcrumbs and season. Oil or butter a hot frying pan or skillet and fry spoonfuls of the mixture, turning them over when the surface of each is marked with bubbles.

Devilled mushrooms ⑤ Ⓥ

Most people assume devilled dishes include mustard, as this has long been a quick way of pepping up yesterday's leftovers. The heat in this recipe comes from chillies, and it is a delicious way of preparing cultivated mushrooms. Eat them on toast, or as an accompaniment to such tarts as fresh pea and courgette/zucchini, or potato, marrow/squash and lemon (see pages 177 and 178).

Variation
● *Add a little plain yoghurt to the mixture to make it milder.*

2-3 tablespoons olive oil
1 tablespoon each cider vinegar and Worcestershire sauce (see page 41)
1 teaspoon onion, finely chopped
1 garlic clove, finely chopped
3 dried red chillies, broken open
freshly ground black pepper
100 g/¼ lb mushrooms

Mix all the ingredients together, then marinate the mushrooms in it for 2-3 hours. Grill/broil the mushrooms on toast, or bake in a hot oven for about 5 minutes.

Israeli fruit salad ⑤ Ⓥ Ⓕ

Some of the most delicious fruit salads can be made from dried fruits soaked in apple juice. No extra sugar is needed. In this recipe, the fresh eating apples and nuts add crunch and texture. Always use best quality dried fruit.

Variations
Soak the dried fruit in any of the following, instead of the apple juice:

- *6 tablespoons eau de vie mixed with 200 ml/7 fl oz/1 scant cup apple juice.*

- *150 ml/5 fl oz/⅔ cup wine mixed with 150 ml/5 fl oz/⅔ cup apple juice.*

100 g/4 oz/⅔ cup dried apricots
50 g/2 oz dried figs
50 g/2 oz/½ cup raisins
80 ml/10 fl oz/1¼ cups apple juice
2 eating apples
50 g/2 oz/½ cup flaked/slivered almonds, toasted (see page 56)

Soak the dried fruits overnight in the apple juice, then cut into bite-sized pieces. Slice the apples thinly and add them to the mixture. Toss well and sprinkle with the almonds.

Carob milkshake ① Ⓥ

Delicious either hot or cold, this drink needs very little carob to flavour it. Add it carefully to suit your taste.

300 ml/10 fl oz/1¼ cups soya milk
2 teaspoons carob powder, or to taste
1 teaspoon honey
dash of vanilla essence/extract
½ teaspoon cinnamon

Mix all the ingredients together thoroughly in a blender and drink at any time of the day.

High protein drink ② Ⓟ

This is an excellent tonic for slow mornings. As wheatgerm does not integrate easily, I use wheatgerm oil. This gives the same nutritional content without the grittiness.

Variation
- *If you prefer, substitute skimmed milk powder or soya milk for the fruit juice.*

150 ml/5 fl oz/⅔ cup fresh orange or grapefruit juice
juice of 1 lemon
1 egg, beaten
1 tablespoon wheatgerm oil
1 teaspoon brewer's yeast powder (optional)
2 tablespoons skimmed milk powder
honey to taste (optional)

Thoroughly mix all the ingredients in a blender. Cool in the refrigerator and stir well before drinking.

Breads

The smell of homemade bread is one of the most inviting aromas in the world. Even if you have an excellent bakery near where you live, it is still far more fulfilling to make your own: you know exactly what goes into your own bread and it is cheaper on the pocket.

Baking bread at home is now a somewhat easier task as there is a new type of yeast available which does not have to be activated in warm water first. It can be mixed with the dry ingredients and only becomes active when warm water is added. It is known as micronized yeast in the UK, and active dry yeast in the US, and may be bought under several different brand names. Bread made with this yeast needs only one rising, though there are respected authorities who maintain that bread is infinitely better if it is allowed to rise twice. It is very much up to personal taste. Try both methods and decide. Micronized/active dry yeast can be purchased in small sachets, usually sufficient for a 450g/1 lb loaf, from good shops and supermarkets.

There is a belief that yeast needs sugar to work, but you can make perfectly good bread without it. For everyday bread and rolls, I would omit the sugar altogether. Prolonged contact between sugar and yeast can destroy the yeast cells.

The main secret of successful bread-making is to knead the dough for a good length of time: 8-10 minutes by hand, less if done in a food processor with dough hooks. The kneading distributes the yeast cells and helps to break down the flour molecules so that the yeast begins to generate gas, which aerates the bread and makes it rise.

After kneading, the dough must be put in a warm place, covered and left to rise. It should triple its bulk within 1 hour, but this depends on the type of flour used. A white loaf, which has no wheatgerm or bran, is lighter and will rise more quickly than a wholewheat loaf. If the wholewheat flour has additional grains and seeds, the bread will be heavier still and take longer to rise.

Most bread recipes instruct the cook to place the dough in loaf pans, but I prefer to place the dough on a baking sheet, cover it with a large mixing bowl while it rises, and then cook the loaf in the oven on its sheet. This method creates a round loaf with a good crust all over. The second method is to use two large earthenware oven dishes which can be fitted one on top of the other. Place the dough in the smaller one to rise, then bake it in the oven with the larger dish still on top. A good crust can be made if the top dish is taken off the bread ten minutes before the end of baking.

When you think the bread is done, turn it on to a cooling rack and gently tap the bottom of the loaf. If it sounds hollow, the bread is done. If not, simply place the bread on a baking sheet and put it back in the oven for another 5 minutes.

To make loaves and rolls look more appealing, brush the tops with a little beaten egg after rising, and strew them with salt, poppy seeds or cracked wheat.

*Sweet brioche served with spiced orange
butter balls (see pages 109 and 141).*

103

Basic wholewheat loaf ⑮ V F

*The dense, moist texture of this loaf means
that it keeps very well and is the perfect
accompaniment to soups, pâtés and cheese.
Note: Use a 450 g/1 lb (13 x 8 x 5 cm/5 x 3 x 2
inch) loaf pan for all the bread recipes. The
weight refers to the amount of flour used.*

450 g/1 lb/4 cups wholewheat flour
1 teaspoon sea salt
2 tablespoons olive oil
1 sachet micronized/active dry yeast (see page 41)
scant 300 ml/10 fl oz/1¼ cups warm water

Pre-heat the oven to 220°C/425°/Gas mark 7. Mix all the dry
ingredients together, add the water and knead the dough for
at least 6 minutes if using dough hooks, and 10 if by hand. If
using a loaf pan, grease it liberally and place the dough in it.
Cover with a cloth or plastic wrap and leave in a warm place
until it has filled the pan (about 1 hour). If you are not using
a loaf pan, simply place the dough on a baking sheet and
cover with a bowl. Bake for 45 minutes.

Variations

Wholewheat and rye loaf   *Rye flour
makes a darker, nuttier-tasting loaf, but as it
has no gluten content it will not rise. Use a
little to give flavour to other loaves.*

For this loaf, substitute 75 g/3 oz/¾ cup of the wholewheat
flour with the same amount of rye flour and then proceed as
for the basic loaf.

Wholewheat and granary loaf   *This is a
popular loaf with a malt flavour. (See notes on
granary flour, page 40.)*

Follow the recipe for the basic loaf, but use 225 g/½ lb/2 cups
of granary flour to 225 g/½ lb/2 cups of wholewheat.

High protein loaf   *This loaf takes longer to
rise and will probably only just double its
bulk. Though it is a heavy loaf, it tastes
delicious and makes good crunchy toast for
breakfast.*

Follow the recipe for the basic loaf, but add 1 tablespoonful
each of bran, soya flour, wheatgerm, linseeds, sesame seeds
and dried milk powder.

Wholewheat herb loaf   *This will give you
a beautifully flavoured loaf which is excellent
with cheese, but also toasts well.*

Follow the basic loaf recipe, but add 1 teaspoon each of your
three favourite herbs. Any of the following used alone or in
combination are suitable: ground sage, thyme, rosemary,
dill seed, marjoram, oregano, celery seed and celery salt.

Light wheat loaf   *This will give you a loaf
which rises quickly, but still has plenty of
flavour.*

Follow the basic loaf recipe, but substitute half the
wholewheat flour with 225 g/½ lb/2 cups of unbleached
strong white/all-purpose flour.

White granary loaf *Lovely loaves can be made out of granary flour alone, and from strong white/all-purpose flour. Both these loaves will rise easily.*

White herb loaf *This makes an excellent bread to have with cheese.*

Rolls *All of the bread doughs can be made into rolls. Obviously heavier doughs take longer to rise and the rolls will be correspondingly heavier. A rye bread dough I made hardly rose at all and each roll felt as heavy as a cricket ball, but they were still eaten by my lunch guests because the flavour was so striking - so what you lose on the swings, you sometimes gain on the roundabouts. The white herb dough makes excellent rolls.*

For a light loaf with plenty of flavour follow the basic loaf recipe, but substitute the wholewheat flour with 225 g/½ lb 2 cups granary flour (see page 40) mixed with 225 g/½ lb 2 cups strong white unbleached/all-purpose flour.

Follow the basic loaf recipe, but substitute unbleached strong white/all-purpose flour and add 1 teaspoon each of sage, thyme, dill seed, celery seed and celery salt.

After the dough has been kneaded, slice it into four and then into eight and roll each piece into a ball. Thoroughly grease a bun tin/muffin pan and place a roll in each space. Cover and leave in a warm place until the rolls have doubled in size. Bake for about 35 minutes at 220°C/425°F/Gas mark 7.

Sour dough wholewheat loaf ⑳ Ⅴ F

The original method of making bread was to keep a piece of dough back from the day's baking, moisten it with water and then use it for the following day's baking, much as a portion of yoghurt is used to make a fresh batch. The sour flavour of this bread is popular in the US, especially when made with rye flour.

Variations

Rye sour dough
Use the sour dough starter when it smells sour, usually after 24 hours. Mix it with 225 g/8 oz/2 cups rye flour, 225 g/8 oz/2 cups strong white/all-purpose flour and 1 teaspoon each of caraway and fennel seeds. Then follow the basic loaf method on page 104.

Granary sour dough
Mix the sour dough starter with the wholewheat granary recipe on page 104.

Sour dough pancakes
Add the sour dough starter to the pancake batter recipe on page 183.

Sour dough starter
125 g/5 oz/1¼ cups strong white/all-purpose flour
150 ml/5 fl oz/⅔-¾ cup water
1 tablespoon sugar
Loaf
450 g/1 lb/4 cups wholewheat flour
1 teaspoon sea salt
1 sachet micronized/active dry yeast (see page 41)
2 tablespoons olive oil
scant 150 ml/5 fl oz/generous ½ cup warm water

Two days before making the bread, blend all the ingredients in the sour dough starter and leave in a warm place to ferment. After one day it should appear frothy and smell sour. On the second day it will look smoother, with only a few bubbles. Check it from time to time to see that it is working. Transfer to the refrigerator until needed. Following the basic loaf method on page 104, combine the loaf ingredients with the starter, but do not add the water until they are well mixed. Knead well and bake as before.

Soda bread ⑤ Ⓟ Ⓕ

Soda bread has become linked in our minds with Ireland, for it is almost a national dish there. It is made with baking powder rather than yeast and is best if eaten soon after baking. Excellent soda breads can also be made with buttermilk, sour milk or a mixture of yoghurt and water to moisten the dough.

450 g/1 lb/4 cups wholewheat flour
1 teaspoon bicarbonate of soda/baking soda
2 teaspoons sea salt
150 ml/5 fl oz/⅔-¾ cup milk
150 ml/5 fl oz/⅔ cup plain yoghurt

Pre-heat the oven to 220°C/425°F/Gas mark 7. Mix all the ingredients together well. Form the dough into a cake-shape and place in a well-buttered oven dish. Cover with another oven dish and bake for 30 minutes. Remove the top dish 10 minutes before the end so the loaf forms a brown crust.

Spoon bread ⑮ Ⓟ

This is a breakfast bread eaten in the US, but to non-Americans it seems more like a heavy soufflé. If eaten hot, it can be spooned out. If eaten cold, turn it out and slice like a cake. Either way, it's delicious.

600 ml/1 pint/2½ cups milk
1½ teaspoons sea salt
100 g/4 oz/1 cup corn meal
5 eggs, separated

Pre-heat the oven to 200°C/400°F/Gas mark 6. Scald the milk, then pour in the salt and corn meal. Stir continuously to get a smooth mixture and simmer for 5 minutes until it thickens. Allow to cool. Stir the egg yolks into the mixture. Whip the egg whites until stiff and fold them in. Pour into a 1.75-litre/3-pint/2-quart soufflé dish and bake for 45 minutes, or until the mixture is well risen and nicely brown.

Walnut and carrot bread ⑳

A delicious moist bread to have with a first course. Its nutty texture is a good accompaniment to cheese. Be careful when adding water to the dough. The amount needed depends on the juiciness of the carrot and the absorption of the flour.

450 g/1 lb/4 cups wholewheat flour
1 sachet micronized/active dry (see page 41) yeast
1 teaspoon salt
100 g/4 oz carrot, grated
75 g/3 oz/¾ cup Cheddar cheese, grated
50 g/2 oz/scant ½ cup walnuts, chopped
1 tablespoon walnut oil
1 egg, beaten
scant 300 ml/10 fl oz/1¼ cups warm water

Mix together the yeast and all the dry ingredients, reserving a little of the cheese. Add the oil and most of the egg, then add the water gradually until the dough binds. Knead for 5 minutes. Grease a loaf pan and place the dough in it. Leave to rise for 1 hour. Pre-heat the oven to 200°C/400°F/Gas mark 6. Glaze the loaf with the remaining egg and cheese. Place in the oven and bake for 30 minutes. Transfer to a baking sheet for another 10 minutes.

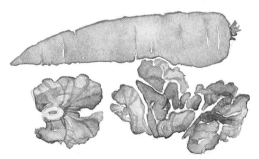

Fruit loaf ⑩ P F

This is a typical English fruit bread, excellent for breakfast, tea or snacks. It is equally good toasted. This recipe can be further enriched by doubling the amount of dried fruit.

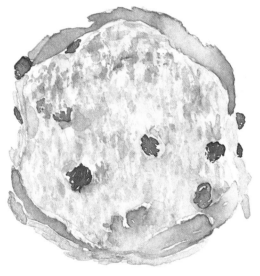

100 g/4 oz/²⁄₃ cup currants
50 g/2 oz/4 tablespoons butter
150 ml/5 fl oz/²⁄₃ cup milk
350 g/12 oz/3 cups wholewheat flour
1 sachet micronized/active dry yeast (see page 41)
25 g/1 oz/2 tablespoons soft brown sugar
1 teaspoon salt
2 teaspoons each powdered cinnamon, mace, allspice, nutmeg and cloves, mixed
1 egg, beaten
Glaze
1 tablespoon caster/superfine sugar
1 tablespoon milk

Place the currants and butter in the milk and warm a little. Mix the flour, yeast, sugar, salt and spices together. Add the milk mixture and the egg. Stir well and knead for 5 minutes. Butter a 450 g/l lb (13 x 8 x 5 cm/5 x 3 x 2 inch) loaf pan, put the dough in it then cover and leave for 1 hour in a warm place. Pre-heat the oven to 220°C/425°F/Gas mark 7. When the bread has risen to the top of the pan, place in the oven for 15 minutes, then reduce the heat to 190°C/375°F/Gas mark 5 for another 15 minutes. Dissolve the sugar in the milk and use to glaze the loaf straight from the oven. Leave for 2 minutes before turning it out to cool.

Bara brith ⑩

This is a speckled fruit bread from Wales, which is far richer than the English variety. Eat it hot, cold or toasted for a wonderful treat at any time.

75 g/3 oz/¹⁄₂ cup each currants and raisins
300 ml/10 fl oz/1¹⁄₄ cups milk
25 g/1 oz/3 tablespoons candied peel, chopped
50 g/2 oz/¹⁄₃ cup soft brown sugar
75 g/3 oz/6 tablespoons butter
450 g/1 lb/4 cups wholewheat flour
1 sachet micronized/active dry yeast (see page 41)
1 teaspoon each salt and mixed/apple pie spice

Soak the dried fruit in the milk overnight. Drain and reserve the milk. Mix the dried fruit, peel and sugar together and place in a warm oven for a few minutes. Heat the butter and milk until the butter has melted. Leave to cool until lukewarm. Mix all the dry ingredients together, then add the milk. Knead for 5 minutes. Butter a 450 g/l lb loaf pan and place the dough in it. Cover and leave to rise for 1 hour. Pre-heat the oven to 200°C/400°F/Gas mark 6. Bake the loaf for 30 minutes, protecting the top with buttered paper for the last 10 minutes.

Cheese brioche stuffed with leek purée ⑳ P

Brioches are easy to make, and are a luxurious breakfast or lunch, being rich in butter and eggs. In their sponge-like texture, they are similar to cold spoon bread and, if they are stuffed, they are particularly enticing.

Variations

● *If you make the brioche dough without cheese, you can use a sweet filling, such as 100 g/4 oz/½ cup apricot purée or canned chestnut purée, or raisins and currants pre-soaked in apple juice. This makes a breakfast treat, especially if served hot with spiced butter (see page 141).*

● *If you prefer, the quantity given can be used to make about 8 individual brioches, which need only 15 minutes to bake. When done, they can be turned out, glazed with beaten egg and briefly returned to the oven to give them a lovely, shiny finish.*

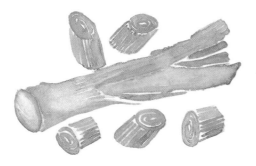

300 g/10 oz/2½ cups strong white/all-purpose flour
100 g/4 oz/½ cup butter, diced
1 teaspoon salt
100 g/4 oz/1 cup Cheddar cheese, grated
3 eggs, beaten
2 tablespoons milk
1 sachet micronized/active dry yeast (see page 41)
Stuffing
200 g/7 oz leeks
25 g/1 oz/2 tablespoons butter
pinch of sea salt
50 g/2 oz/½ cup Cheddar cheese, grated

Mix the flour, butter, salt and cheese together. Add the eggs, milk and yeast and knead for 5 minutes. As the dough is very sticky, it is best done with dough hooks, but if doing it by hand, work quickly to prevent the butter melting and be sure to flour your hands and the work surface. Leave it to rise in a warm place for 1 hour. Meanwhile, make the stuffing. Trim and clean the leeks, and slice them finely. Melt the butter in a pan and cook the leeks gently with a pinch of salt. Simmer for 3 to 5 minutes or until tender. When cool, add the cheese. When the dough has risen, keep about a third of it to one side. Butter a brioche or loaf pan and place the bulk of the dough in it. Make a hole in the centre at the top and fill with the stuffing. (The stuffing will sink a little, so it is best to place it near the top.) Cover with the remaining dough, which will expand to cover the top. Leave to prove for 30 minutes or until the dough has risen to the top of the pan. Bake in a pre-heated oven at 190°C/375°F/Gas mark 5 for 20 to 25 minutes. Turn out on to a wire rack.

Wholewheat muffins ⑤ P F

The following two recipes are traditional American ones that incorporate wholewheat flour and baking powder, so the resulting muffins will not rise a great deal. If you want a lighter muffin, substitute half a sachet of micronized/active dry yeast (see page 41) for the baking powder. These muffins make an excellent breakfast with savoury spreads or preserves, and toast well for a teatime snack.

225 g/½ lb/2 cups wholewheat flour
2 tablespoons wheatgerm
1 tablespoon baking powder
1 teaspoon sea salt
350 ml/12 fl oz/1½ cups milk
3 tablespoons olive oil
1 egg
4 tablespoons honey

Pre-heat the oven to 220°C/425°F/Gas mark 7. Mix all the dry ingredients together thoroughly. Then add the rest and whisk or beat vigorously for a few minutes. Grease a bun tin or muffin pan and pour the batter into each space. Bake for 20 minutes. Turn on to a rack and leave to cool.

Corn muffins ⑤ P F

125 g/5 oz/1¼ cups corn meal
75 g/3 oz/¾ cup wholewheat flour
1 tablespoon baking powder
1 tablespoon brown sugar
1 teaspoon sea salt
1 egg
250 ml/8 fl oz/1 cup milk
2 tablespoons corn oil
2 tablespoons sesame seeds, toasted (see page 56)

Pre-heat the oven to 220°C/425°F/Gas mark 7. Mix the two flours together with the baking powder, sugar and salt. Then break in the egg and add the milk and oil to make a batter. Beat thoroughly using a whisk or an electric beater. Grease a bun tray or muffin pan and pour the batter into each space. Sprinkle with the sesame seeds and bake for 20 minutes, or until the muffins have risen and browned. Turn on to a rack and leave to cool.

Blueberry muffins ⑩

These delicious muffins have a lovely speckled appearance. They are a good accompaniment to savoury dishes, such as spiced bean casserole (see page 152), but also make a satisfying breakfast or snack. You can substitute cranberries, if you wish, but avoid very soft fruits, such as blackberries and redcurrants as they will disintegrate when baked. Dried fruit also works very well. Try a mixture of raisins, sultanas/golden raisins and currants, pre-soaked in apple juice, or use pre-soaked apricots chopped very finely.

100 g/4 oz/1 cup strong white/all-purpose flour
100 g/4 oz/1 cup wholewheat flour
1 teaspoon baking powder
pinch of sea salt
75 g/3 oz/6 tablespoons butter, grated
1 egg, beaten
1 tablespoon honey
225 g/½ lb blueberries
1 tablespoon milk, if needed

Pre-heat the oven to 180°C/350°F/Gas mark 4. Mix the flours, baking powder and salt together, then rub in the butter until the mixture resembles small breadcrumbs. Add the egg, honey and blueberries. You should now have a paste. If it won't bind, add the milk. See that the blueberries are nicely scattered through the dough. Grease a bun tin or muffin pan and spoon in portions of the dough. Bake for 30 minutes, or until a toothpick inserted in a muffin comes out clean.

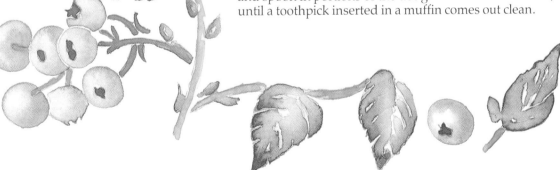

Soups, Salads and Light Dishes

Homemade soups are probably the easiest of dishes to make, and infinitely preferable to manufactured soups, which often contain many preservatives and additives, and frequently too much salt. Compared with packets and cans, homemade soups are highly nutritious and economical, and they need not take long to make. An electric blender or food processor is immensely useful, but some cooks prefer to use a mouli-legumes/food press as it gives a grainier texture. There are certain soups, of course, that need no blending at all. These often tend to be the heartier soups we eat in the winter. There are an infinite number of these made from legumes, but they are usually improved if only half the amount of beans is blended to thicken the soup. Remember - most legumes need to be soaked before cooking. See page 51 for details.

There has long been a school of thought which believes that good soups cannot be made without meat stock. This is nonsense. As long as soups are initially flavoured with herbs and spices, and a good vegetable stock is used, vegetarian soups are just as good, if not better. Purists will want to use a homemade stock, so I give a recipe below.

But when time is tight, vegetable stock/ bouillon cubes and soya cubes are a useful standby. When buying, be sure to check that they contain no additives. There are some soups where water can easily be substituted for stock, as the ingredients themselves are strong enough in flavour.

There are certain basic points to remember in the making of soups. First of all the vegetables must be sautéed in good olive oil or butter. Then sweat the herbs and spices to release their oils. These techniques are explained on page 52 and will give you essential flavour. Be careful not to drown the soup with too much liquid. If it appears too thick at the end of its cooking, stock or water can always be added then. To give additional flavour, experiment with different flours as thickening agents (see page 85).

As cow's milk is high in saturated fats, use either skimmed milk or soya milk. The latter has many advantages in that its slightly nutty flavour helps some soups immensely. Avoiding full fat milk allows you to go to town and use cream and butter for flavour. If this seems a mad hatter policy my reason is that milk in itself is a dull ingredient, while butter and cream can, at times, be a huge boost to the final flavour of a dish.

Basic vegetable stock ⑩ Ⓥ Ⓕ

Do not expect this to taste delicious in itself; it adds a subliminal flavour to any soup or stew and is an additional source of nutrition. It will keep happily for a couple of weeks, or may be frozen for up to 3 months.

2 heads of celery
2 large onions
2 carrots
bunch of parsley stalks
2.25 litres/4 pints/10 cups water

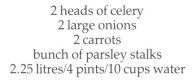

Clean and prepare the vegetables, chop coarsely and boil in the water for 30 minutes. Leave to cool, then purée the mixture and pass it though a sieve. Discard the vegetable debris and store the stock in a sealed container in the refrigerator.

*Warming soups for a cold winter's day:
Danish apple soup (left), Spinach and
sage soup (right), served with wholewheat
and rye bread (see pages 113, 115 and 104).*

Clear celestial soup ⑩ Ⓥ Ⓕ

The Chinese are particularly good at making clear soups. They are usually strongly-flavoured stocks with a few well-manicured vegetables floating in them - more refreshing than sustaining. Serve this soup before a substantial main course, such as Hoppin' John (see page 153).

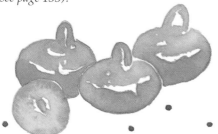

2 tablespoons toasted sesame oil
25 g/1 oz ginger root, peeled and sliced
3 garlic cloves, thinly sliced
3 spring onions/scallions, sliced
2.25 litres/4 pints/10 cups vegetable stock (see page 110)
2 pieces kombu seaweed, soaked and thinly sliced
5 water chestnuts, thinly sliced
2 tablespoons soy sauce
seasoning to taste

Heat the oil in a large pan and cook the ginger and garlic for a moment, then add the spring onions/scallions. Cook for another minute before adding the vegetable stock which has been heated to simmering point. Add the rest of the ingredients. Cook for a moment more before serving.

Garlic and potato soup ⑩ Ⓟ Ⓕ

Garlic is a marvellous plant. It adds a savoury hotness to this great soup, which is especially good on a cold winter's day. Eat with wholewheat herb bread (see page 104).
Variation
• *Add 50 g/2 oz/½ cup grated Cheddar cheese with the potatoes and saffron.*

3 heads of garlic, peeled (see page 52)
6 tablespoons olive oil
675 g/1½ lb floury/baking potatoes, peeled and chopped
pinch of saffron
seasoning to taste
1.2 litres/2 pints/5 cups water
300 ml/10 fl oz/1¼ cups single/light cream
2 tablespoons parsley, finely chopped

Roughly chop the garlic and sauté it in the oil for 3 to 4 minutes until soft but not brown. Add the potatoes, saffron, seasoning and water. Simmer for 30 minutes, then cool and purée. Reheat gently and add the cream and parsley.

Cream of artichoke soup ⑩ Ⓟ Ⓕ

A velvety smooth soup that is quite delicious. Unfortunately, it can provoke flatulence in a lot of people, so try it in private before serving it in public. Garnish with garlic croûtons (see page 48) and a little parsley.

450 g/1 lb Jerusalem artichokes
25 g/1 oz/2 tablespoons butter
1 onion, thinly sliced
1.2 litres/2 pints/5 cups vegetable stock (see page 110)
300 g/10 oz/1¼ cups Quark or puréed cottage cheese
seasoning to taste

Clean the artichokes, but do not peel them. Chop coarsely and cook in the butter with the onion for a moment or two, before adding the stock. Simmer for 20 minutes. Leave to cool, then blend to a purée. Pour back into the pan and reheat gently, adding the cheese and seasoning.

Onion soup ⑩ P F

This classic dish cannot be made quickly. In traditional French farmhouses it simmers on the hob all day. One of the most important things to remember is not to brown the onions; they should remain translucent throughout.

50 g/2 oz/4 tablespoons butter
2 tablespoons olive oil
900 g/2 lb onions, thinly sliced
pinch of brown sugar
25 g/1 oz/2 tablespoons flour
2.25 litres/4 pints/2½ quarts boiling water
300 ml/10 fl oz/1¼ cups dry vermouth, sherry
or white wine
seasoning to taste
1 tablespoon brandy
1 tablespoon Worcestershire sauce (optional)
dash of Tabasco
slices of French bread, toasted
225 g/8 oz/2 cups Parmesan cheese, grated

Heat the butter and oil in a saucepan and gently soften the onions for about 15 minutes. Add the seasoning and sugar, and leave to cook for 30 minutes. Then add the flour and stir continuously for another few minutes. Add the boiling water and vermouth. Cover and simmer for 45 minutes. Taste and correct the seasoning. Before serving, add the brandy, Worcestershire sauce and Tabasco, then pour the soup into individual bowls. Top each serving with a piece of toast and cover with Parmesan.

Danish apple soup ⑤

A great soup for using up windfalls in the autumn. It makes a good first course to precede a spicy main dish (see page 154).

50 g/2 oz/4 tablespoons butter
450 g/1 lb Cox's or Newtown Pippin apples, peeled, cored
and chopped
1.2 litres/2 pints/5 cups vegetable stock (see page 110)
zest and juice of 1 lemon
8 tablespoons dry white wine
50 g/2 oz creamy blue cheese
seasoning to taste
Garnish
1 Cox's or Newtown Pippin apple, cored but not peeled
few sprigs of chervil

Melt the butter in a pan. Add the apples and cook for 2 minutes before adding the stock, lemon juice and zest, and wine. Simmer gently for about 20 minutes. Remove from the heat and break up the apple pieces by beating with a whisk. Add the cheese and reheat gently, allowing the cheese to melt. Season carefully. Slice the cored apples and fry the rings in the remaining butter until soft. Use to garnish the soup, and top with sprigs of chervil.

Avocado and green pepper soup ⑮ F

This is a good winter soup, though its shades of green are reminiscent of spring. Eat with walnut and carrot bread (see page 106).

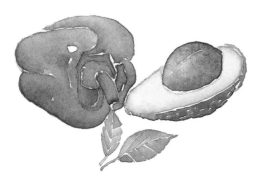

3 green peppers
50 g/2 oz/4 tablespoons butter
1.2 litres/2 pints/5 cups vegetable stock (see page 110)
seasoning to taste
3 small or 2 large ripe avocados
squeeze of lemon juice
chopped mint for garnish

Chop the green peppers, discarding the central core and seeds. Melt the butter in a pan and cook them gently for 5 minutes. Add the stock and seasoning and cook for a further 10 minutes. Peel and stone the avocados and blend to a purée with the pepper stock. Add the lemon juice and reheat gently; *the avocado must not boil*. Serve with a garnish of chopped mint.

Curried cream of lentil soup ⑤ F

I always find lentils comforting and earthy, and they go very well with all the curry spices. A 10-minute soak helps to shorten the cooking time, but is not essential. This soup is good in winter and never fails to please. Serve with wholewheat and rye bread (see page 104).

25 g/1 oz/2 tablespoons butter
2 garlic cloves, crushed
1½ tablespoons curry powder (see page 42)
100 g/4 oz/½ cup dried yellow lentils (see page 51)
1.7 litres/3 pints/7½ cups water
300 ml/10 fl oz/1¼ cups single/light cream
seasoning to taste

Melt the butter and cook the garlic and curry powder for a moment. Add the lentils, stir well and pour in the water. Simmer for 20 minutes or until the lentils resemble a purée. Add the cream and seasoning, and reheat gently.

Andalusian white bean soup ⑤

The Spanish use almonds in a multitude of ways, and this soup is a perfect example. The flavours of the beans and nuts fuse splendidly and the resulting soup is thick and creamy. Serve with homemade bread and garnish with a few flaked/slivered almonds.

100 g/4 oz/½ cup haricot/navy beans,
pre-soaked (see page 51)
150 ml/5 fl oz/⅔ cup olive oil
1.2 litres/2 pints/5 cups water
100 g/4 oz/¾ cup blanched almonds (see page 52)
4 or 5 garlic cloves, crushed
seasoning to taste

Drain the beans. Heat the oil in a pan, add the beans and cook for a moment before adding the water. Simmer for 1 hour or until the beans are tender. Pound or grind the almonds to a powder and add to the beans with the garlic. Cook for 5 minutes, add the seasoning and then purée.

Spinach and sage soup ⑧

The beautiful flavours of spinach and sage are made for each other. Eat with corn muffins (see page 109) for an excellent winter lunch. The soup needs no garnish as the spinach speckles it beautifully.

675 g/1½ lb spinach
50 g/2 oz/4 tablespoons butter
1 tablespoon sage, chopped
2 tablespoons gram/chick pea or plain/all-purpose flour
1.7 litres/3 pints/7½ cups hot skimmed milk (not boiled)
100 g/4 oz/1 cup Sage Derby or hard white cheese, grated
seasoning to taste

Wash the spinach and drain well. Melt the butter, add the spinach and sage and simmer very gently, stirring frequently until cooked. Stir in the flour. Remove from the heat and gradually add the hot milk, stirring all the time to prevent lumps forming. Bring to the boil and simmer gently for a few minutes. Purée the mixture. Add the cheese and reheat gently, allowing the cheese to melt. Taste and adjust seasoning.

Borscht ⑩ [F]

The beautiful colour of this soup is much enhanced by suspending some raw grated beet in it after cooking. It is a classic cold soup, but in some countries it is served hot to departing guests to keep out the cold. Eat it with wholewheat sour dough (see page 105).

450 g/1 lb raw beetroots/beets
2 large onions, sliced
2 large carrots, sliced
2 bay leaves
2 tablespoons olive oil
25 g/1 oz/2 tablespoons butter
1.5 litres/2½ pints/6 cups boiling water
juice of 1 lemon
seasoning to taste
1 raw beetroot/beet, grated
sour cream or yoghurt for garnish

Peel the beetroots/beets and cut into small dice. Place them with the other sliced vegetables in a large saucepan with the bay leaves, olive oil and butter. Add a pinch of salt and sauté them over a low heat for 10 minutes. Add the boiling water then cover and simmer for about 2 hours, or until all the vegetables are tender. Add the lemon juice and a little black pepper; leave to cool. Remove the bay leaves and blend the soup to a purée. If it is too thick, add a little vegetable stock. Take the soup off the heat, place the raw beetroot/beet in a muslin/cheesecloth bag and suspend it in the soup. Remove after a few hours and stir the soup well. Reheat it gently, or serve chilled with yoghurt, or swirls of sour cream.

Chilled avocado lemon soup ⑤ P F

A smashing soup. I personally think the combination of avocado and soya is excellent, but if you don't like the nutty taste of soya milk, use skimmed milk instead. The perfect accompaniment to this soup is the cheese and leek brioche (see page 108).

flesh from 3 small or 2 large, ripe avocados
juice and zest from 2 lemons
seasoning to taste
1.7 litres/3 pints/7½ cups soya milk (unsweetened)
150 ml/5 fl oz/⅔ cup sour cream or fromage blanc/cream cheese

Blend the avocados with the zest and juice from 1 lemon, the seasoning and soya milk. Pour the sour cream into a separate bowl and mix in the zest and juice of the other lemon. Chill the soup for 2 hours. Serve with the sour cream mixture.

Gazpacho ㉟ V F

This is a summer soup that demands superb tomatoes; tomato juice is no substitute and should only be used in emergencies. Serve chilled and float a few ice cubes on top. Spoon bread (see page 106) goes well with this soup.

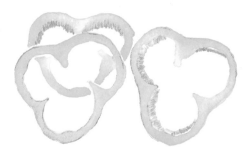

1 cucumber
1 onion
900 g /2 lb ripe, juicy tomatoes, peeled (see page 52)
1 green pepper
1 red pepper
2 garlic cloves, crushed
2 tablespoons parsley, chopped
150 ml/5 fl oz/⅔ cup olive oil
juice and zest of 2 lemons
1.2 litres/2 pints/5 cups vegetable stock (see page 110)
pinch of cayenne pepper
1 teaspoon paprika
seasoning to taste

Grate the cucumber and onion into a bowl. Chop up the rest of the vegetables finely, or purée them with the rest of the ingredients in a blender.

Tomato and fresh basil soup ⑳

It is essential to use fresh basil in this soup - do not even think of using dried! If fresh basil is unavailable, pesto sauce may be used instead; this will give a muddier colour and a stronger tasting soup, but it will still be delicious. Garnish with a few basil leaves and serve either hot or cold with granary bread (see page 104).

2 tablespoons olive oil
1.5 kg/3 lb tomatoes, chopped
3 garlic cloves, crushed
seasoning to taste
300 ml/10 fl oz/1¼ cups good Burgundy
generous handful of fresh basil leaves, chopped

Place the oil, tomatoes, garlic, seasoning and wine in a saucepan. Bring to the boil over a low heat. Simmer for 10 minutes until the tomatoes have become pulp, then add the basil. Cook for another 2 minutes, then cool. Purée and then put through a sieve. Discard the skin and seeds and reheat the soup gently.

Soupe au pistou ⑳

Similar to minestrone in having pasta and vegetables in it, this soup also has the delicious flavour of pesto. Wholewheat bread is the ideal accompaniment. This recipe makes enough for ten, but it's so good, you'll be happy to eat it for a few days. It is a meal in itself.

100 g/4 oz/1½ cups haricot/navy beans, pre-soaked (see page 51)
2 litres/3½ pints/2 quarts water
3 medium carrots, diced
3 medium potatoes, diced
3 medium courgettes/zucchini, chopped
2 leeks, chopped
450 g/l lb tomatoes, peeled
100 g/¼ lb French/snap beans, chopped
bouquet garni (see page 56)
65 g/2½ oz/⅔ cup small noodles, uncooked
seasoning to taste
Pistou sauce
20 basil leaves
3 garlic cloves, crushed
100 g/4 oz/1 cup Parmesan cheese, freshly grated
6 tablespoons olive oil
seasoning to taste

Drain the beans and boil in fresh water for 1 hour. Add the vegetables and bouquet garni and simmer for 45 minutes. Add the noodles and cook for a further 10 minutes. Taste and season. Discard the bouquet garni. Transfer the soup to a large serving dish. Swirl in the pistou sauce. Serve with freshly grated Parmesan.
Pistou sauce Blend the basil and garlic with the oil to a thin purée. Add the seasoning and cheese to make a thick sauce.

Corn chowder ⑮ Ⓟ Ⓕ

Chowder originated in Brittany, coming from the expression 'faire la chaudière', which means to make a soup from oddments of fish and biscuit. Breton fishermen took the dish to Newfoundland and from there it spread down the Atlantic coast to New England, which has now become famous for it. Serve it with corn muffins (see page 109).

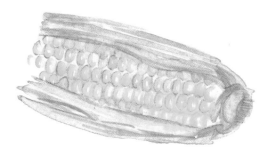

4 cobs of corn
2 onions, thinly sliced
3 garlic cloves, crushed
225 g/½ lb mushrooms, thinly sliced
100 g/4 oz/½ cup butter
225 g/½ lb each fresh garden peas, fresh broad/fava beans and fresh French/snap beans
seasoning to taste
900 ml/1½ pints/3¾ cups milk
3 tablespoons corn meal

Boil the corn in plenty of water for about 8 minutes. Drain and keep the water. Cut all the corn off the cobs (see page 137). Soften the onions, garlic and mushrooms in half the butter. Add the peas and both kinds of beans. Season well, add the reserved corn water, and simmer for 15 minutes. Add the corn and milk, then mix the remaining butter with the corn meal to form a paste. Stir this into the soup bit by bit until it is thick and creamy. Taste and check the seasoning.

Salads

The more raw, fresh foods we eat the better our diet. Indeed, on nutritional grounds alone (see page 14), a good part of our diet should be raw. We should certainly all eat a salad a day.

Almost any vegetable (except potato) can be eaten raw if you prepare it in the proper manner. Obviously, root vegetables have to be grated to be digestible, but the flavour of raw beetroot/beet, for example, is a different experience than the same vegetable cooked. Vegetables eaten raw must be very fresh indeed, and in prime condition; flavour, vitamin and mineral content decline the longer they stay out of the earth, so do not experiment with jaded vegetables.

There is an endless variety of salads, beginning with the one we all know, the green salad. This simple classic can be transformed with the use of different leaves, some of which grow wild in gardens and countryside. Use a crisp lettuce whenever possible and, depending on where you live,

try mixing it with dandelion, wild sorrel, claytonia and many more.

But salads are not just composed of 'greens'. In the following pages you will find salads made from beans, sprouting seeds, grains, avocado, nuts and fruit - the permutations are endless. It is easy to sprout beans and grains (see page 56). Try a mixture of sprouts from aduki, fenugreek and lentil tossed in a light lemon and oil dressing.

It has long been a vegetarian habit (perhaps because of anxiety about consuming enough protein) to add nuts and dried fruits to salads. If used, these must be added with caution; a salad is intended to refresh the palate.

Salads need not be cold; surprisingly, there are many delicious warm salads, such as cous cous and roast pepper salad. These Mediterranean dishes come from a cuisine rich in interesting salads, while the less familiar styles of the Middle and Far East offer yet more ideas to whet the palate.

Caesar salad ⑤ P̄

The delight of this salad lies in the method as much as the ingredients. It was created by Caesar Cardini during the Prohibition years when he had a restaurant in Tijuana, Mexico, but there are many variations. Most versions include anchovies and a blue cheese, like Roquefort, but the original omitted these and made the salad as shown below. Traditionally this salad was eaten with the hands, using the lettuce leaves to scoop up the sauce and croûtons. The eggs create a very light mayonnaise dressing.

2 cos/romaine lettuces
2 eggs
6 tablespoons olive oil
3 garlic cloves, crushed
seasoning to taste
1 teaspoon Worcestershire sauce (see page 41)
juice and zest of 1 lemon
25 g/1 oz/¼ cup Parmesan cheese, freshly grated
50 g/2 oz/1 cup wholewheat garlic croûtons (see page 48)

Break the lettuce leaves from the central stalk, wash and refrigerate in a plastic bag for 1 hour. Boil the eggs for 1 minute exactly, then plunge into cold water to stop them cooking. Have the rest of the ingredients to hand. Pour the oil into a large salad bowl, add the lettuce and toss well. Add the garlic, seasoning, Worcestershire sauce, lemon juice and zest and then the peeled eggs, ensuring that you scoop out the thin layer of cooked white near the shell. Toss again, then sprinkle with Parmesan and croûtons.

Two elegant salads, easily made: Pear and pistachio, and Avocado and quail's egg (see pages 124 and 125).

Tomatoes with pesto ⑮

For people who love the herb basil, pesto sauce is the most delicious creation and has long been the classic complement to tomatoes, especially in northern Italy and southern France. If basil is unobtainable, try using parsley and/or coriander. It won't be pesto, but it will still taste good!

900 g/2 lb fresh tomatoes
For the pesto
generous handful of basil leaves
300 ml/10 fl oz/1¼ cups olive oil
juice and zest of 1 lemon
3 garlic cloves, crushed
40 g/1½ oz/⅓ cup Parmesan cheese, finely grated
40 g/1½ oz/⅓ cup pine nuts
seasoning to taste

First make the sauce by chopping all the basil leaves and placing them in a blender. Add the rest of the ingredients, but go easy on the salt as the Parmesan may be salty enough. Blend to a thick purée. Slice the tomatoes thinly and lay them on a platter. Drip the sauce over the tomatoes so that each piece is covered and serve immediately.

Sicilian orange salad ⑮

I was first given this when living in Sicily, but I have since discovered that variations of this salad crop up all over the coast of North Africa. Serve with cabbage and coriander pâté, or any pasta dish (see pages 138 and 165).

Variation
• *Use pink grapefruit instead of the oranges.*

1 oak leaf lettuce or cos/romaine lettuce
3 oranges
10 or 12 black olives
Dressing
5 tablespoons olive oil
juice and zest of 1 lemon
seasoning to taste
3 tablespoons fresh mint, chopped (optional)

Arrange the lettuce on a platter. Peel the oranges, divide into segments and remove the pith and membranes. Arrange the segments and olives on top of the lettuce. Mix all the dressing ingredients together and spoon over the salad just before serving. Garnish with the mint.

Avocado stuffed with courgettes/zucchini and pistachio ⑤

The nutty flavour of raw courgettes/zucchini complements the luxurious blandness of the avocado. This is a pretty salad in shades of cream and green. Serve as a first course or a light lunch with soda bread (see page 106).

50 g/2 oz/⅓ cup unsalted pistachio nuts, shelled
2 tablespoons olive oil
2 small courgettes/zucchini, grated and salted (see page 52)
1 teaspoon lemon juice
seasoning to taste
2 or 3 avocados, stoned

Pound or grind half the pistachio nuts to a powder. Add to the oil and lemon juice. Squeeze out all the moisture from the courgettes/zucchini and add them to the sauce. Season and mix thoroughly. Pile into the cavities of the avocados and decorate with the rest of the pistachio nuts.

Fasoulia ⑮ V P F

In Greece this salad is made from a variety of kidney bean which is allowed to grow large in the pod, and then picked, dried and used immediately. This means that they are never tough, and do not need to cook as long as shop-bought dried beans. As these are difficult to get outside Greece, use any sized haricot/ dried white bean. Fasoulia is another salad that may be eaten warm. Spoon it into crisp lettuce leaves for a pretty effect. In the summer eat it with crudités and other appetizers, such as tapenade and jajiki (see pages 186 and 190).

450 g/1 lb/2 cups large haricot/navy beans,
pre-soaked (see page 51)
150 ml/5 fl oz/⅔ cup olive oil
4 garlic cloves, chopped
2 bay leaves
1 teaspoon oregano
sprig of rosemary
4 tablespoons tomato purée/paste
juice from 1 lemon
seasoning to taste
1 large onion, thinly sliced

Drain the beans and fast-boil in fresh water for 10 minutes. Pour the olive oil into an earthenware crock, marmite or saucepan, add the garlic, bay leaves, oregano, rosemary and drained beans. Heat and simmer for a few minutes. Pour in enough water to cover the beans by about 1 inch, then add the tomato purée/paste and lemon juice. Cover and cook in a low oven at 145°C/290°F/Gas mark 1. Alternatively, cook the fasoulia in a saucepan over a low flame for 2 hours. Inspect the dish from time to time to see that the beans are not sticking. When they are soft and gooey, remove the dish from the heat, season to taste and add the onion. The onion will soften off the heat if the dish is kept covered.

Salade Niçoise ⑩ P

This famous salad from Provence is generally made with tuna fish, anchovies, green beans and potatoes. There are many variations. Mine is relatively light.

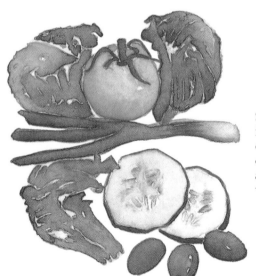

1 iceberg or Webb's wonder/romaine lettuce
bunch of spring onions/scallions
225 g/½ lb tomatoes
15 black and green olives, stoned
1 small cucumber, scored and sliced
50 g/2 oz/½ cup Gruyère cheese, diced
2 hard-boiled eggs, chopped
1 tablespoon capers
50 g/2 oz/1 cup garlic croûtons (see page 48)
parsley for garnish
sauce vinaigrette to taste (see page 128)

Separate the lettuce leaves, wash and dry them and arrange in a large bowl. Chop the onions/scallions, tomatoes and olives and scatter them over the lettuce leaves. Arrange the cucumber, cheese and eggs on top. Sprinkle with the capers and croûtons. Garnish with the parsley and then toss in the vinaigrette at the table.

Greek salad ⑤ P

This wonderful salad appears at every meal in Greece, but wherever it is eaten, it always evokes Mediterranean sun and sea. Feta, a strong-tasting cheese made from ewe's or goat's milk, can be bought in sealed packets and will keep in the refrigerator for weeks. As this salad is such a lively combination of colours, it is a nice idea to make it on individual plates.

1 cucumber, sliced fairly thinly
2 large marmande/beefsteak tomatoes, sliced
100 g/¼ lb Feta cheese
generous handful of oregano leaves
12 black olives, stoned

Arrange the cucumber on individual plates. Add the tomatoes and then crumble the Feta and oregano on top. Garnish with the olives. Allow your guests to dress their own salads with oil and vinegar so the multi-coloured pyramids remain intact for them to admire.

Salade mimosa ⑩

This is a classic French salad which is particularly good as a light lunch dish. Serve with stuffed sweet potatoes (see page 150).

3 hard-boiled egg yolks
1 cos/romaine lettuce
2 or 3 heads of endive
a generous handful of parsley, finely chopped
2 tablespoons mint, finely chopped
8 tablespoons sauce vinaigrette (see page 128)

Hard boil the eggs using the method on page 54 and push the yolks through a fine sieve. Clean and trim the lettuce and endive and arrange on a large platter. Scatter with the chopped parsley and mint, then sprinkle with the sieved egg yolks. Toss with the vinaigrette at the table.

Walnut and buckwheat salad ⑫ V P

This is a light and fluffy grain salad made up of shades of beige, amber and gold. The combination of apricots and walnuts gives it superb texture and flavour. Serve with dry green curry (see page 157).

50 g/2 oz/½ cup dried apricots, pre-soaked
juice and zest from 2 lemons
2 garlic cloves, crushed
100 g/4 oz/1 cup buckwheat
1 bunch spring onions/scallions
100 g/4 oz/1 generous cup broken walnuts
150 ml/5 fl oz/⅔ cup sauce vinaigrette with
lemon and Meaux/wholegrain mustard (see page 128)
2 tablespoons mint, finely chopped

Drain and finely chop the apricots. Place them in a large bowl with the lemon juice, zest and garlic. Cook the buckwheat in boiling, salted water for 10 minutes, then drain well, squeezing out all excess water. Add to the apricot mixture. Chop the spring onions/scallions and add to the salad with the walnuts. Stir in the vinaigrette. Add the mint just before serving.

Cous cous ㉔ Ⓥ

This is a grain product of semolina and is most famous in North Africa, where the cereal is steamed over a mutton and vegetable stew. Cous cous is readily available in wholefood shops and needs very little preparation. It has a slightly nutty flavour and a satisfying grainy texture. It is an excellent complement to a range of vegetable and spiced bean dishes, but it is equally good as a cold salad.

Variation
● *Cous cous is delicious with chopped fresh herbs, garlic and butter.*

225 g/8 oz/1 cup cous cous
150 ml/5 fl oz/⅓ cup vegetable stock (see page 110),
or equal parts of water mixed with wine or soy sauce for
steaming

Pour the cous cous into a bowl. Cover with cold water and strain immediately through a wire sieve. Leave in the sieve for 15 to 20 minutes, raking the grains with your fingers to break up the lumps as the grains swell. Steam over your chosen liquid. You can also steam the grain over any of the vegetable or bean stews (see pages 151-153).

Tabbouleh ⑤ Ⓥ

This salad has become more popular in the last few years, as its main ingredient, bulgar or partially cooked cracked wheat, is now widely available. The salad itself was probably first introduced to British cooks in the late 1960s when Claudia Roden's marvellous book of Middle Eastern food was first published. The predominant flavours should be mint, garlic and lemon. This is a very refreshing salad, especially served with crisp cos/romaine lettuce leaves, which can be used to scoop it up. Serve with a stew like the spiced bean casserole on page 152.

175 g/6 oz/1 cup bulgar wheat
juice and zest from 2 lemons
150 ml/5 fl oz/⅔ cup olive oil
5 garlic cloves, crushed
2 bunches of spring onions/scallions
generous handful of fresh mint, finely chopped
generous handful of fresh parsley, finely chopped
seasoning to taste

Soak the bulgar in cold water for 20 minutes. Then place it in a sieve or colander and press out all the water. Mix up the rest of the ingredients in a large salad bowl. Stir in the bulgar and leave to stand for 2 hours before serving.

Rice and almond salad ⑩ Ⓟ

Similar to a pilaf, in that it contains a variety of vegetables, this is a satisfying crunchy salad with the delicious taste of toasted almonds.

100 g/4 oz/½ cup Patna/long grain rice
50 g/2 oz/½ cup flaked/slivered almonds,
toasted (see page 56)
2 peppers, cored, seeded and chopped
4 sticks of celery, chopped
1 bunch of spring onions/scallions, chopped
2 hard-boiled eggs, peeled and diced
150 ml/5 fl oz/⅔ cup chilli vinaigrette (see page 128)
4 tablespoons mint, finely chopped

Cook the rice (see page 50), and dry it out in a warm oven. Combine the rice, almonds, vegetables and eggs in a large bowl. Mix thoroughly and pour in the vinaigrette. Let the salad settle for 1 hour before garnishing with the mint and serving.

Russian salad ⑮

This salad is well known in Britain, perhaps because it is available in cans and is so often seen swimming in pink sauce on the salad counters of wine bars. This is enough to put us all off the salad for life. However, the homemade version can be quite delicious and makes an excellent summer lunch with a simple green salad. The amounts I give serve 12, but it keeps beautifully in the refrigerator.

450 g/l lb cooked new potatoes, diced
225 g/½ lb cooked French/snap beans, sliced
6 cooked baby carrots, sliced
100 g/4 oz/½ cup cooked haricot/navy beans
1 tablespoon white wine vinegar
3 tablespoons olive oil
seasoning to taste
3 hard-boiled eggs
2 tablespoons capers
2 tablespoons gherkins, chopped
2 tablespoons parsley, finely chopped
2 tablespoons mint, finely chopped
aïoli mayonnaise to taste (see page 129)

Mix all the vegetables together in a large bowl with the oil, vinegar and seasoning. Chill for 2 hours. Before serving, chop the hard-boiled eggs and add them to the salad with the pickles and herbs. Finally, fold in the mayonnaise.

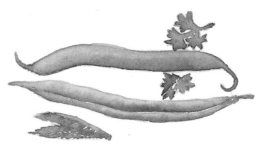

Pear and pistachio salad ⑮ Ⅴ

This recipe combines the various shades of pistachio, grape and pear, and sets them off with the crimson of the radicchio. It makes a first course which seduces both the eye and the palate. Serve with a honey and walnut oil vinaigrette (see page 128).
Note: If you want to prepare the pears some time in advance, dip the pear slices in lemon juice to prevent discoloration.

Variation
• *Substitute blue cheese for the pistachios and grapes.*

4 pears, preferably Comice or similar shape
175 g/6 oz grapes, seeded and coarsely chopped
50 g/2 oz/½ cup pistachio nuts, shelled and chopped
1 raddichio lettuce

With each pear in turn, cut off the top, leaving the stalk intact and reserve. Core each pear and then cut into horizontal slices about 5 mm/¼ inch thick. Reassemble the slices into the original pear shape. Mix one-third of the grapes with the pistachios and fill the pear with the mixture. Replace the top. Stand each pear on a raddichio leaf and surround with the remaining grapes.

Celeriac remoulade ⑩

This beautiful vegetable is gaining in popularity and becoming more widely available when it comes into season in the autumn. Its flavour is similar to the hard core of celery. Buy celeriac when it is roughly the size of a tennis ball; bigger ones tend to be too fibrous.

Variation
• *Lovage is a herb which goes particularly well with celery and celeriac. Chopped finely and added to this recipe, it makes an unusual and radical difference.*

3 or 4 small celeriac
juice of 1 lemon
300 ml/10 fl oz/1¼ cups remoulade
mayonnaise (see page 129)

Peel and grate the celeriac. Toss well in the lemon juice, then add to the mayonnaise. This creates a delicious nutty-tasting salad. Serve on a bed of radicchio.

Avocado and quail's egg salad ⑮

This is a highly sophisticated version of a Mexican salad. The quail's eggs are left unshelled because their aesthetic appeal is so great. This makes an excellent first course and I would be tempted to have a little bowl of sesame salt and celery seed to dip the eggs into. Serve with a vinaigrette or mayonnaise of your choice (see pages 128-129).

½ head curly endive
4 thin spring onions/scallions, finely sliced
12-16 quail's eggs
12 very small new potatoes, boiled and cooled
flesh of 2 large avocados, scooped into small balls
juice of 1 lemon
1 tablespoon each fresh thyme, oregano and basil, finely chopped

Arrange the endive either on individual plates or a large single platter and sprinkle with the onions/scallions. Boil the quail's eggs for 3 minutes only, drain and leave in their shells. Arrange the new potatoes in an attractive pattern on top of the endive. Dip the avocado balls in the lemon juice to prevent discoloration and arrange between the eggs and potatoes. Sprinkle with the fresh herbs.

Fresh peach salad ⑤

The celery and yoghurt in this recipe cut across the intense fruitiness of the peaches to make a highly refreshing summer salad.

Variations
• *To make a more substantial version of this salad, add 350 g/12 oz/1½ cups of cottage cheese.*

• *Try a mixture of fresh and dried fruits, for example, 3 fresh sliced peaches, 3 fresh sliced pears, 50 g/2 oz/½ cup dried apricots, and 2 tablespoons of raisins. Soak the dried fruit in apple juice overnight. Drain and save the juice for drinking. Arrange all the fruits on a bed of lettuce leaves. Pour over the dressing.*

5 ripe peaches
2 or 3 tender celery stalks
3 tablespoons plain yoghurt
1 tablespoon honey
juice and zest of 1 lemon
seasoning to taste
2 tablespoons chopped almonds

Stone and slice the peaches in crescent shapes, chop the celery and put both in a large bowl. Mix together the yoghurt, honey, lemon juice and seasoning and pour over the peaches. Sprinkle with the chopped almonds.

Salad Dressings

Most salad dressings are based on oil and vinegar, or oil and the juice from a citrus fruit. They depend for their perfection on the quality of the oil and the acidity. A dressing made from blended vegetable oil and malt vinegar would be unspeakably disgusting and render any salad inedible. It is best to use olive oil, preferably the first pressing, which is labelled as extra virgin; this has the maximum amount of flavour from the olives. Other good oils that can be added to olive oil, or used alone, are walnut, hazelnut and toasted sesame, which will perfume and flavour a salad magnificently.

Red and white cider or wine vinegar are both suitable for dressings, but there are many other flavoured vinegars available - raspberry, basil, tarragon, shallot and garlic, to name only a few. Herb vinegars can be made very cheaply at home (see page 37). There are also excellent vinegars from China and Japan and, for certain salads, these have a sensational effect. Japan produces umeboshi vinegar, and China makes various vinegars from rice wine and black beans. Keep a variety of vinegars so that you can experiment with flavours.

Lemon juice is a common alternative to vinegar, but in order to get the essential lemon oil flavour, it is best to add the zest. A sharp dressing can be made from the juice and zest of Seville oranges, and a beautifully fragrant dressing can be made from limes. Alternatively, a mixture of fruits, such as lemon juice and raspberry vinegar, can make a very successful dressing.

A mayonnaise is an emulsion formed by egg yolks fusing with oil. There is a common belief that mayonnaise is difficult to make. This is nonsense, if a few simple rules are remembered and adhered to.

● Both oil and egg yolks should be at room temperature, as should the utensils that the mayonnaise is made in. A mayonnaise will fail if the eggs are used straight from the refrigerator or a cool larder, though the ironic thing is that cold egg yolks whip harder and more easily.

● The oil must initially be added to the egg yolks drop by drop.

I prefer to make mayonnaise in a pudding basin with a wooden spoon, rather than an electric blender, and I find it a particularly satisfying task. It cannot be hurried and it has an ancient alchemy in its creation - the fusion of the two ingredients leading to something quite different in character.

If the worst happens, and your mayonnaise curdles, start again in a clean bowl with a fresh yolk. When it has amalgamated with the first drop of oil, gradually add the curdled mayonnaise, followed by the rest of the oil.

It is best to flavour the mayonnaise after it has been made, though there are different schools of thought on this. I favour the French method of making mayonnaise, which involves adding a little powdered mustard to the egg yolks at the beginning.

Clockwise from top left: Green peppercorn vinaigrette, Fresh mayonnaise served in a hollowed pepper, and a salad of edible flowers (see pages 128 and 129).

Basic sauce vinaigrette ② Ⅴ

Variations

The oil and vinegar mixture may be enriched and flavoured in a number of ways.

● *Add one crushed garlic clove and ½ teaspoon of Dijon mustard.*

● *Add 4 or 5 crushed garlic cloves and 1 tablespoon of capers.*

● *Add 1 tablespoon of green peppercorns and 1 tablespoon of finely chopped parsley.*

● *Use 2 tablespoons of walnut oil and 3 tablespoons of olive oil, and 1 tablespoon of lemon juice instead of vinegar. Stir in 1 tablespoon of freshly ground walnuts.*

● *Add 1 tablespoon of tahini and 2 crushed garlic cloves to the wine vinegar at the beginning. A similar dressing can be made with peanut butter, but this tends to be rather heavy so the amount should be watched carefully.*

● *Add 2 dried red chillies and let them marinate for 2 hours. Take out the chillies and stir in a tablespoon of finely chopped shallots.*

● *Substitute lemon juice for the wine vinegar, and stir in 1 tablespoon of sour cream and 1 tablespoon of chopped chives. As an alternative to sour cream, use mashed tofu, curd/small curd cheese or double/heavy cream.*

● *Use lemon juice instead of vinegar, and stir in 2 egg yolks and 2 teaspoons of Meaux/ wholegrain mustard. Then proceed as for the basic dressing.*

● *Add 40 g/1½ oz/⅓ cup Roquefort cheese, diced and crumbled, to the wine vinegar before adding the rest of the ingredients.*

● *Use walnut oil, and the juice and zest of 1 lemon instead of the vinegar. Add 1 crushed garlic clove and 1 teaspoon of honey. Mix together with the seasoning.*

5 tablespoons olive oil to 1 tablespoon red or white wine vinegar
½ teaspoon sea salt
a generous grinding of fresh black pepper

Combine all the ingredients together and mix energetically.

Basic mayonnaise ⑤

Variations
Once you have made the basic mayonnaise it can be flavoured in the following ways.

Rouille
Add a good pinch of cayenne pepper or a half teaspoon of Tabasco sauce. For colour, add a tablespoon of tomato purée/paste and a teaspoon of paprika.

Verte
Add a tablespoon each of blanched and finely chopped spinach leaves, sorrel and watercress.

Remoulade
Add one cooked egg yolk, well pounded, to the egg yolks in the basic recipe. When the yolks have soaked up the olive oil, add one teaspoon each of finely chopped capers, chives, rocket/ aragula, parsley and tarragon.

Mayonnaise Escoffier
Add a tablespoon of freshly grated horseradish and two teaspoons each of finely chopped shallots and parsley. Creamed/prepared horseradish may be substituted for fresh, but it will be less hot. I have also experimented with Japanese horseradish, called Wasabi; half a teaspoon added to the mayonnaise creates a sensational flavour.

Tartare
Add half a teaspoon each of finely chopped capers, chives, gherkins, green olives and parsley.

Aïoli
Add five crushed garlic cloves.

Scandinavian mayonnaise
Add two tablespoons of Dijon mustard and 1 tablespoon of dill weed.

Avocado mayonnaise
Add the puréed flesh of one ripe avocado.

Mayonnaise mousseline
Fold in two stiffly beaten egg whites.

2 egg yolks
½ teaspoon mustard powder
300 ml/10 fl oz/1¼ cups olive oil
1 tablespoon lemon juice or white wine vinegar
2 teaspoons water (optional)
seasoning to taste

Beat the egg yolks and mustard together to make a paste. Add the olive oil drop by drop, stirring constantly to ensure that it successfully amalgamates with the egg yolks. As the sauce becomes thicker and creamy, the oil can be added in a single steady stream. When all the oil has been added you should have a very thick, rather gummy sauce. This can be thinned with the lemon juice or wine vinegar. (The lemon juice will bleach the deep yellow of the mayonnaise to a paler colour.) You may also need to add a little water to get the right consistency. Only trial and error informs you. Finally, add the seasoning.

Vegetable Side Dishes

In cookery books, one often states the obvious. To get the finest flavours from vegetables, they ought to be freshly picked and in prime condition. Then, they should be briefly cooked and eaten with the simplest of accompaniments like sea salt and good farm butter. On pages 52-53 of this book, I talk about various ways of briefly cooking vegetables - steaming, poaching, stir-frying and so on.

When vegetables are plucked straight from the garden, they are best cooked in the simplest of manners. However, it is rare for us to be fortunate enough to eat as well as this for most of the time. For vegetables just off the peak of perfection, we have contrived limitless ways of treating them with various flavours, sauces, herbs, spices and dairy products. The whole tradition of international cuisine has an infinite number of vegetable dishes. In this section, I briefly touch upon the range. Hopefully, it will encourage you to have your own imaginative ideas. Do not be afraid to try unexpected combinations; for example, nut spreads mixed with miso can be used as a sauce. Both yoghurt and garlic are indispensable as sauces and background flavours.

Though these recipes are side dishes, they can be used as first courses, light lunches or snacks in the evening. The good thing about a vegetarian diet is that it is completely flexible. You are free to compose meals of many small dishes if you wish and enjoy them in any order which appetite dictates.

The term vegetable savouries can cover a multitude of dishes. I use it to describe 'finger foods' - versatile snacks which can be eaten at any time of day, made in quantity for parties, served as first courses, or eaten as a side dish with a main meal.

Creamed salsify ⑤ P

The flavour of salsify defies definition. It hovers between asparagus and artichoke, with a hint of oyster. It is perfect with any of the savoury pies or tarts, and also goes well with egg dishes (see pages 173 and 142).

675 g/1½ lb salsify
300 ml/10 fl oz/1¼ cups vegetable stock (see page 110)
25 g/1 oz/2 tablespoons butter
25 g/1 oz/2 tablespoons plain/all-purpose flour
300 g/10 oz/1¼ cups Smetana/low-fat sour cream
seasoning to taste

Trim and peel the salsify. If it is very thin, scrape the dirt and blemishes off rather than peeling it. Wash under running water and then simmer in the vegetable stock for 10 minutes, or until just tender. Raise the heat in the last few minutes so that the stock reduces by half. Remove the vegetable and make a paste with the butter and flour and add a little of it to the stock. Season and then add the Smetana/low-fat sour cream. Put the vegetable back in when the sauce is complete. Watch that the sauce is not too thick and that it does not taste floury - you may not need all the flour and butter to get the right consistency.

Spinach moulds, beautifully layered with
soft cheese purée and served with beurre
blanc and saffron sauce (see pages 143
and 190).

Brussels sprouts with almonds ⑤

This is a very successful combination, as Brussels sprouts go well with all kinds of nuts. Serve with two-artichoke pie (see page 180), or any other pastry-based dish.

Variation

• *Any steamed root vegetable can be substituted for the sprouts. Top with nuts and bake in the oven for 5 minutes.*

675 g/1½ lb Brussels sprouts
25 g/1 oz/2 tablespoons butter
25 g/1 oz/¼ cup flaked/slivered almonds,
toasted (see page 56)
seasoning to taste

Trim and prepare the Brussels sprouts and boil in a little salted water for about 5 minutes. Melt the butter in a pan and add the almonds, the drained sprouts and the seasoning. Stir-fry vigorously for a moment, then transfer to a serving dish.

Parsnips in a spiced tomato sauce ⑩ Ⅴ Ｆ

Parsnips are naturally sweet and can stand a strong, spicy sauce like the one given here. Serve with falafel or croquettes (see page 168), or with one or two other side dishes to make a complete meal.

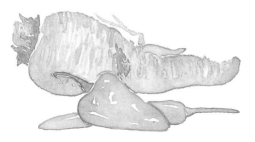

4-6 parsnips
For the sauce
900 g/2 lb tomatoes, halved
2 dried red chillies
5 garlic cloves, crushed
2 tablespoons olive oil
150 ml/5 fl oz/⅔ cup dry red wine
seasoning to taste

Make the sauce first. Place the tomatoes in a pan with the rest of the ingredients. Cook over a low heat for 10 to 15 minutes, then push the ingredients through a sieve and discard the vegetable debris. Trim, scrub and chop the parsnips, and boil or steam until tender. Drain and place them in a gratin dish. Pour the hot tomato sauce over them and serve.

Broad/fava beans in garlic sauce ⑩

Good as broad beans are, they can occasionally be dry. However, this delicious garlic sauce counteracts that problem. If the broad beans are not young and small, they should be peeled individually. They will need to simmer for only 2 or 3 minutes in the garlic sauce. Frozen broad/fava beans are an acceptable substitute for fresh. Serve with a leek timbale (see page 142), or any of the savoury pastries.

Variation

• *This recipe also works with breadfruit, plantain and yam.*

6 tablespoons olive oil
1 head of garlic, peeled (see page 52)
300 ml/10 fl oz/1¼ cups vegetable stock (see page 110)
seasoning to taste
900 g/2 lb fresh broad/fava beans, shelled
3 tablespoons Greek yoghurt (see page 45)
parsley for garnish

Sauté the garlic in the olive oil for a few moments. Add the stock and seasoning and cook for 20 minutes. Purée half the stock and garlic in a blender. Pour back into the pan, add the beans and cook for 10-12 minutes. Add the yoghurt in the last 2 minutes of cooking. Garnish with finely chopped parsley.

Sukha bundhgobi ⑩ V

The exotic name of this recipe simply means 'side dish of cabbage'. It goes well with mild pâtés and eggs (see pages 138-145).

Variation
• *Cook the cabbage in 8 tablespoons ghee with chilli pepper, mustard seed and 2 tablespoons of coconut milk.*

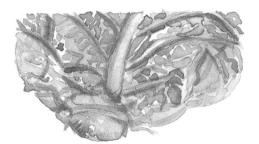

1 medium white/tight-head green cabbage
2 large potatoes
150 ml/5 fl oz/⅔ cup olive oil
1 tablespoon mustard seed
2 teaspoons each cumin, coriander and fenugreek seeds
12 garlic cloves, peeled (see page 52)
1 onion, sliced
seasoning to taste
1 tablespoon lemon juice

Slice the cabbage thinly and dice the potatoes. Heat the oil in a large frying pan and cook the spices until the mustard seeds stop popping. Add the garlic, onion and potato and cook for a further 3 minutes. Now add the cabbage and seasoning, cover the pan and cook for another 15 minutes. When the potato is fully cooked, add the lemon juice. Stir briskly and serve.

Breadfruit with ginger and green pepper sauce ⑫

Breadfruit is a large green fruit with a yellowish flesh which is inedible unless cooked. Similar in texture to potato, it can be substituted for any starchy vegetable and makes a good accompaniment to a main dish, such as buckwheat pilaf (see page 173), particularly with this piquant sauce.

Variation
• *This sauce is also good with steamed sweet potatoes, carrots and yams.*

1 breadfruit, about 450 g/1 lb in weight
2 large green peppers, skinned (see page 52)
2 tablespoons olive oil
5 cm/2 inches root ginger, peeled and grated
3 green cardamoms, crushed
1 teaspoon each asafoetida and fenugreek, ground
1 large green cooking apple, cored and sliced
2 teaspoons peanut butter
1 tablespoon dry sherry
seasoning to taste

Peel and core the breadfruit. Cut into smallish chunks and steam for about 30 minutes or until just tender. Seed and chop the peppers. Heat the oil with the ginger and spices. Add the peppers and apple and simmer until soft. Place everything but the breadfruit in a blender with the peanut butter and sherry and blend until smooth. Season to taste. Transfer the breadfruit to a serving dish and cover with the sauce.

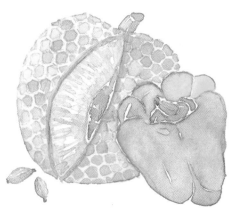

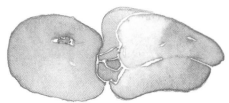

Cauliflower in tahini sauce ⑤

Tahini is a purée of roasted sesame seeds which, like this recipe, originated in the Middle East. Serve with rice, cous cous or croquettes (see pages 123 and 167).

Variation

● *The cauliflower may be coated with tempura batter (see page 136) and fried. Serve the tahini separately for dipping.*

1 large cauliflower, broken into florets
3 garlic cloves, crushed
1 heaped tablespoon tahini
juice and zest from 1 lemon
300 ml/10 fl oz/1¼ cups water
seasoning to taste
1 tablespoon sesame seeds, roasted (see page 56)

Steam the cauliflower briefly, or boil in a little salted water until just tender, but al dente. Meanwhile, make the sauce. Crush the garlic into the tahini and add the lemon juice, zest, water and seasoning. Stir until you have a thick sauce. Drain the cauliflower carefully, arrange in a serving dish and pour the sauce on top. Sprinkle with sesame seeds.

Buttered lettuce ②

Although it is advisable to cut down on saturated fats wherever possible, this is one recipe that must *use butter. Not many people realize how good cooked lettuce can be. It is important to use a crisp variety; although it reduces a vast amount, it does retain a little bite in the stalk. Serve with a baked curry or pie (see pages 157 and 180), or as a hot side salad.*

1 large cos/romaine lettuce
40 g/1½ oz/3 tablespoons butter
1 teaspoon celery salt
seasoning to taste
6 tablespoons dry sherry
1 teaspoon celery seed

Break the lettuce into individual leaves, tearing the larger ones into two or three pieces. Wash and dry well. Melt the butter in a large pan and add the lettuce. Sprinkle with the celery salt and seasoning, stir and then cover the pan for up to 5 minutes. Pour in the sherry and raise the heat, stirring vigorously for another minute. Turn out into a serving dish with any sauce left in the pan and sprinkle with the celery seed and perhaps some chopped chives.

Mushrooms in red wine and mustard sauce ③ 🄵

It is easy to find a wide variety of dried mushrooms nowadays, and it is well worth experimenting with them. Although, on the face of it, they seem expensive, they grow like 'triffids' when soaked and have an intense flavour. Serve with a cheese soufflé or gratin dauphinois (see pages 145 and 158).

Variations

● *Try soaking the mushrooms in the wine, adding just enough water to cover them.*

● *This dish can also be made with 675 g/1½ lb of fresh mushrooms, sliced in half.*

50 g/2 oz dried mushrooms
seasoning to taste
50 g/2 oz/4 tablespoons butter
150 ml/5 fl oz/⅔ cup dry red wine
1 tablespoon each of Meaux/wholegrain mustard and Dijon mustard
25 g/1 oz/2 tablespoons plain/all-purpose flour

Cover the mushrooms with water and soak for 5-6 hours. Drain and cook whole with the seasoning and half the butter until soft. Add the wine and mustard, stir well and cook for a minute. Mix the rest of the butter with the flour and add it in pellets until the sauce has thickened.

Cabbage with coriander ③

This is a classic combination of flavours that goes well with tomato and pumpkin quiche (see page 179). A side salad is a crisp accompaniment.

50 g/2 oz/4 tablespoons butter
1 teaspoon coriander seeds, crushed
a pinch each of ground cumin and caraway
1 medium white/tight-head green cabbage, thinly sliced
seasoning to taste
150 ml/5 fl oz/⅔ cup sour cream
1 teaspoon paprika

Melt the butter in a pan and briefly fry the coriander, cumin and caraway. Add the cabbage and stir briskly. Season, cover and cook over a low heat for 4 to 5 minutes. Stir vigorously. If the cabbage has halved its bulk and is just tender, but still al dente, it is done. Pour in the sour cream, stir and check the seasoning, then pour into a serving dish and sprinkle with the paprika.

Gingered pumpkin ⑫ Ⅴ

Pumpkin is a very versatile vegetable that deserves to be used more often. In this recipe it has a sweet, caramelized flavour and is an excellent accompaniment to curries. Eaten cold, it goes well with jajiki, onions and relishes (see pages 190 and 195).
Variation
● *This recipe works well with plantain, yam and any root vegetable except beetroot/beet.*

3 tablespoons olive oil
450 g/1 lb/4 cups pumpkin flesh, cut into small dice
40 g/1½ oz root ginger, peeled and grated
1 teaspoon caraway seeds
1 tablespoon honey
seasoning to taste
chopped spring onion/scallion tops for garnish

Heat the oil in a pan and fry the ginger and pumpkin over a fairly high heat until the pumpkin is crisp and brown on the outside and fairly soft in the centre. Pour in the caraway seeds, honey and seasoning and cook for a moment or two more. Serve at once garnished with the onion tops.

Vegetable spaghetti/spaghetti squash ②

This is the most flavoursome member of the squash family, but it has a tendency to be watery. To offset this, serve it with a sauce or top with a mixture of Quark or puréed cottage cheese and sour cream. Note: If your vegetable is too big to fit any of your pans, cut it in half, butter the cut end, wrap it in foil and boil or bake for half the recommended time.
Variation
● *Make a hole in the top of the vegetable, cover it with foil and place in a dish containing a little water. Bake in a hot oven for about 40 minutes, or in a pressure cooker for about 25 minutes.*

Make a hole in the top of the vegetable and simmer in boiling salted water for about 40 minutes. Remove and slice in two. The seeds have a pleasant flavour when soft, but discard them if they are still hard. Then remove the strands of flesh and mix with butter, salt and pepper, or serve with a sauce such as salsa romesco (see page 246).

Blue cheese savouries ㉚ F

The addition of blue cheese to these potato savouries gives them an interesting flavour. They make an unusual party snack, or a good light lunch with a simple green salad.

225 g/½ lb blue cheese
450 g/1 lb potatoes, boiled and mashed
seasoning to taste
2 eggs, beaten
white breadcrumbs, toasted (see page 48)
oil for frying

Grate the cheese into the mashed potatoes, add the seasoning and mix thoroughly. Use a little of the egg to bind the mixture, then form into balls or sausage shapes, dip them in the remaining egg, then roll them in the breadcrumbs. Fry in a little oil until golden brown.

Tempura ⑤ P

The Japanese fry slices of vegetables covered in featherlight batter, making a delicious feast (often cooked at table) called tempura. Choose fresh vegetables in peak condition: courgettes/ zucchini, cauliflower, fennel, peppers, green beans, artichoke hearts, mushrooms, aubergines/eggplants, onions, leeks or radishes. They must be sliced thinly, but not so that they break or bend. Serve with soy sauce to dip them in.

100 g/4 oz/1 cup plain/all-purpose flour
1 egg, beaten
150 ml/5 fl oz/⅔-¾ cup iced water

Stir the flour into the beaten egg and add the iced water slowly until you have a smooth, runny paste. Dip your sliced vegetables into the batter and fry immediately. They should cook instantaneously to a light brown colour.

Pakoras or bhajis ⑤ V

These are the Indian version of tempura. The batter is made from gram/chick pea flour and spices, and may be used in the same way and with the same vegetables as tempura.
Variation
● *Baigan pakora is a classic Indian dish. Slice and salt 1 large aubergine/eggplant (see page 52). Batter and fry the slices until golden brown. Serve with jajiki and a selection of chutneys (see pages 190 and 195).*

175 g/6 oz/1½ cups gram/chick pea flour
½ teaspoon each salt, baking powder, turmeric, cumin, coriander and black pepper
300 ml/10 fl oz/1¼ cups iced water

Mix the dry ingredients together, ensuring there are no lumps in the flour. Gradually add the water to form a paste and then a batter, beating continuously with a fork.

Sweetcorn fritters ⑮ Ⓟ Ⓕ

It may seem a chore to cut corn from the cob, but it is so much better than the canned or frozen variety that it is worth the effort. To make it easier to remove, run the blade of a knife down between the rows of kernels. These fritters make a good first course served with a tomato sauce (see page 192), and an interesting side dish to any of the curries.

6 cobs of corn, boiled for 8 minutes and drained
For the batter
50 g/2 oz/½ cup wholewheat flour
25 g/1 oz/¼ cup plain/all-purpose flour
pinch of salt
1 egg
150 ml/5 fl oz/⅔-¾ cup milk
olive oil for frying

Mix all the batter ingredients together and leave to rest for 1 hour. Cut the kernels from the cobs and mix with the batter. Heat the oil and shallow-fry spoonfuls of the mixture until brown and crisp, turning them once only.

Tortillas ⑩ Ⓥ Ⓕ

Tortillas are Mexican pancakes made from very fine corn meal called 'masa harina'. They are light and tasty, and when filled with the traditional bean stuffing, are known as 'tacos'. They also taste great with a filling of Ricotta, chopped spring onions/scallions and herbs. It is possible to buy tortillas ready-made, but it is more satisfying to make your own.

225 g/8 oz/2 cups corn meal
50 g/2 oz/½ cup wholewheat flour
1 teaspoon sea salt
165 ml/6 fl oz/¾-1 cup water

Mix all the dry ingredients together and add enough water to make a dough. Knead for about 5 minutes, then refrigerate it for 30 minutes. Divide it into 12 and roll each piece into a ball. Flour your hands and the working surface with more corn meal and roll out each ball to a flat disc. Cook until pale brown on an ungreased skillet or griddle, turning once only.

Tacos ⑮ Ⓟ Ⓕ

This famous Mexican dish consists of a spicy stuffing inside a corn meal pancake called a tortilla. Tacos always make a successful beginning to a meal, but they are also excellent party food. Try them with sliced spring onions/scallions and a creamy herb sauce (see page 193).

2 onions, diced
2 green chillies, chopped
corn oil for frying
225 g/8 oz/1 cup pinto beans, cooked and mashed (see page 51)
100 g/4 oz/½ cup cottage cheese
100 g/4 oz/1 cup potato, cooked and diced
½ teaspoon cumin
seasoning to taste
12 tortillas
2 eggs, beaten

Soften the onions and chillies in a little oil. Mix the beans with these and the rest of the filling ingredients. Dip each tortilla in the beaten eggs, place 2 tablespoons of filling in the centre, fold over and press down lightly. Fry until crisp.

Pâtés, Spreads and Herb Butters

The dishes in this section are part of the classic repertoire of the vegetarian cook. Pâtés can be used as first courses or light lunch dishes, and are the basic material for the more ambitious layered terrines (see page 163). The spreads are useful for sandwiches and stuffings.

The herb butters are particularly delicious with plain steamed or boiled vegetables. They can also be stirred into grain dishes, or eaten simply with homemade bread. Spiced butters can add a very luxurious feeling to the most simple meal. Eat them with brioches or a plain slice of toast.

Cabbage and coriander pâté ③⓪ P F

I think this is a very good combination of flavours. Serve with toast as a starter, or eat as a main course with baked potatoes, and spicy soy and ginger sauce (see page 191).

1 medium sized savoy cabbage
25 g/1 oz/2 tablespoons butter
1 teaspoon ground coriander
2 eggs
300 g/10 oz/1¼ cups Quark or puréed cottage cheese
100 g/4 oz/½ cup Ricotta cheese (see page 55)
seasoning to taste

Pre-heat the oven to 220°C/425°F/Gas mark 7. Trim and slice the cabbage into very small pieces. Melt the butter in a saucepan and sweat the coriander for a moment or two (see page 52). Add the cabbage and cook it over a very low heat for about 5 minutes, or until just soft. Let it cool. Generously butter a 450 g/1 lb (13 x 8 x 5 cm/5 x 3 x 2 inch) terrine or loaf pan. Pour the cabbage and its juices into a blender and reduce to a thick purée. Add the eggs, cheeses and seasoning, and blend again. Pour into the terrine, cover the top with greaseproof or waxed paper and bake in a bain marie (see page 53) for 40-45 minutes. Test by piercing the centre with a knife; if it comes out clean, it is cooked through. Wait 10 minutes before turning it out on to a platter. (Do not let it get cold before turning out because it will stick.) Serve chilled.

Miso and tahini spread ②

This is one of the easiest spreads to make, and is also highly nutritious and delicious. Simply mix 1 part of miso paste to 2 parts of tahini. Store in a screw-top jar and keep in the refrigerator. This is a marvellous spread for sandwiches and biscuits/crackers.

Carrot and apricot pâté ⑳ Ⓟ Ⓕ

*This pâté is lovely with sweet and sour sauce,
beurre blanc or curry sauce (see pages 190 and
194). Serve with toast or biscuits/crackers.*

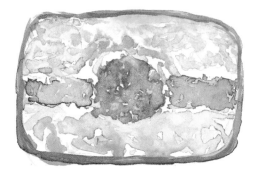

450 g/1 lb carrots
75 g/2 oz/½ cup dried apricots, pre-soaked
2 garlic cloves, crushed
50 g/2 oz/4 tablespoons butter
50 g/2 oz/½ cup Gruyère cheese, freshly grated
300 g/10 oz/1¼ cups Quark or puréed cottage cheese
2 eggs
seasoning to taste

Dice the carrots and apricots and cook in a little boiling
salted water for about 20 minutes, or until tender. Drain and
purée with the garlic and butter. Add the cheeses, eggs and
seasoning. Blend again. Generously butter a 450 g/1 lb (13 x 8
x 5 cm/5 x 3 x 2 inch) terrine or loaf pan and cook as cabbage
and coriander pâté.

Leek and parsley pâté ⑳ Ⓟ Ⓕ

*This pâté goes well with peanut sauce or
tomato and malt whisky sauce (see pages 194
and 192).*

675 g/1½ lb leeks
50 g/2 oz/4 tablespoons butter
a generous handful of chopped parsley
50 g/2 oz/½ cup Gruyère cheese, grated
50 g/2 oz/½ cup Parmesan cheese, grated
300 g/10 oz/1¼ cups Quark or puréed cottage cheese
2 eggs
seasoning to taste

Slice the leeks thinly and cook in the butter until soft. Leave
to cool, then blend with the rest of the ingredients. Butter a
450 g/1 lb (13 x 8 x 5 cm/5 x 3 x 2 inch) terrine or loaf pan, and
bake as cabbage and coriander pâté.

Mung bean pâté ⑭ Ⓟ Ⓕ

*This is a fairly smooth pâté which can be eaten
as a first course, or as a light lunch with a
salad. Eat with wholewheat bread or toast for
complementary protein.*

Variation
● *This recipe can also be served as a salad if
you leave the beans whole rather than puréed.*

225 g/8 oz/1½ cups mung beans, pre-soaked (see page 51)
600 ml/1 pint/2½ cups water
4 tablespoons olive oil
2 onions and 1 garlic clove, peeled and chopped
juice and zest of 1 lemon
2 tablespoons capers, chopped
4 tablespoons parsley
100 g/4 oz/½ cup Ricotta cheese (see page 55)

Bring the beans to the boil in the water and simmer for 40
minutes. Heat the oil and cook the onions and garlic until
soft. Stir in the beans, lemon juice and zest and blend to a
rough purée. Stir in the capers, parsley and Ricotta. Place in
a mould and chill for several hours. Turn out and serve.

Caribbean bean pâté ⑳ P F

This is a pleasant, strong and spicy pâté, excellent on oatmeal biscuits/crackers or rye bread, and even better as a sandwich with plenty of crunchy salad.

225 g/8 oz/1 cup pinto beans, pre-soaked (see page 51)
75 g/3 oz/¾ cup Feta cheese
75 g/3 oz/¾ cup Ricotta or curd/cottage cheese
½ teaspoon curry powder (see page 42)
½ teaspoon each oregano and chilli powder
2 garlic cloves, crushed
1 small onion, finely chopped
1 teaspoon each coriander and cumin, ground
2 tablespoons lemon or lime juice
1 tablespoon tomato purée/paste
seasoning to taste

Drain the beans, then bring to the boil in fresh water and boil for 1 hour, or until soft. Drain, but reserve the water. Blend everything together, adding enough bean water to make a thick purée. Pile into a mould and refrigerate for several hours. Unmould on to a plate and garnish with a spray or two of coriander leaves.

Nut and mushroom pâté ⑩ P F

An easy pâté to make, and a delicious one when eaten with wholewheat toast or oatmeal biscuits/crackers. It is the nearest thing I have made to that millstone around the vegetarian's neck, the nut loaf, but I must admit this is particularly good.

Variation
• *To make a herb pâté, follow the above recipe, but add a good handful of fresh mixed herbs when blending the ingredients.*

2 tablespoons olive oil
450 g/1 lb mushrooms, finely sliced
2 onions, chopped
2 garlic cloves, crushed
100 g/4 oz/1 scant cup walnuts
2 eggs, hard-boiled and finely mashed
seasoning to taste

Heat the oil and cook the mushrooms, onion and garlic until soft. Blend to a rough purée. Pour into a mixing bowl and add the rest of the ingredients. Press down in a dish and refrigerate for a few hours. Garnish with watercress.

Soft cheese spread ⑤ P F

Offer this at the end of a meal on the cheese board, or keep in the refrigerator for snacks.

100 g/4 oz/½ cup curd/small curd cottage cheese
100 g/4 oz/½ cup Quark or puréed cottage cheese
1 tablespoon each of chopped parsley, chives, chervil and basil
50 g/2 oz/4 tablespoons softened butter
seasoning to taste
toasted sesame seeds for garnish (see page 56)

Mix everything together thoroughly. Chill and serve.

Potted cheese ⑤ P F

*This is a useful spread to have in the
refrigerator. It makes a tasty snack, or can be
served with toast as a first course.*

Variation

Sage cheese   *Finely chop a good handful of
sage leaves and grate 450 g/1 lb of hard British
cheese. Mix the two together with 225 g/
8 oz/1 cup butter and pot as above.*

450 g/1 lb Cheddar, or any hard cheese
8 tablespoons brown ale/dark beer
225 g/8 oz/1 cup butter
2 tablespoons allspice, ground

Grate the cheese, then add the beer, butter and allspice. Mix
together thoroughly (in a food processor, if you have one)
then pack it into a screwtop pot (a large jam jar will do) and
refrigerate. To serve, dig spoonfuls from the pot or remove
the whole cheese and cut slices from it.

Spiced orange butter balls ⑩ F

*Butter shaped into balls or curls makes any
meal seem more festive. This particular
variety is delicious served with brioches.*

Variation

● *While the butter is pliable, place it on a
sheet of foil and twist the ends to enclose it.
Roll it into a sausage shape and chill well. Roll
in grated orange rind and cinnamon, and cut
into thin circles before serving.*

225 g/8 oz/1 cup butter, slightly salted
juice of 1 large orange
finely grated rind of 1 large orange
½ teaspoon ground cinnamon
½ teaspoon ground mixed/apple pie spice
2 teaspoons light brown sugar or honey

Blend all the ingredients together, then pack the mixture
tightly into a container, cover and chill thoroughly. Shape
the butter into balls using a small ball scoop. If you wish, the
balls may be rolled in grated orange rind and sprinkled with
cinnamon.

Parsley butter ⑤ F

*Herb butters are a luxurious addition to
breakfast breads and rolls, but they are also
particularly good with steamed root
vegetables.*

Variations

● *Add any of the following fresh herbs, finely
chopped: chives, fennel, mint, tarragon and
watercress. For more unusual flavours, try
adding a tablespoon of alcohol: Pernod goes
well with fennel, brandy with mustard, and
whisky with tarragon.*

● *Spiced butters can be made by adding
garlic, shallots, curry powder (see page 42),
mustard and chillies. These flavourings also
combine well with herbs.*

225 g/8 oz/1 cup butter
generous handful of parsley, finely chopped
1 tablespoon lemon juice

Soften the butter to room temperature and beat the herbs
and lemon juice into it. Then fashion it into a roll, wrap with
either greaseproof/waxed paper or plastic wrap and freeze.

Eggs

Oeufs à la Crècy ⑮ P

The aroma of rose water and the colour of the carrots make this classic dish a real beauty.

Variation
● *Substitute hard-boiled eggs, sliced in half lengthways. Arrange in a buttered oven dish and cover with onion sauce (see page 191).*

450 g/1 lb carrots, thinly sliced
1 teaspoon rose water
seasoning to taste
25 g/1 oz/2 tablespoons butter
25 g/1 oz/2 tablespoons flour
150 ml/5 fl oz/⅔ cup milk
150 g/5 oz/⅔ cup Quark or puréed cottage cheese
4 soft-boiled eggs, peeled (see page 54)

Boil the carrots in a little salted water until tender. Drain well and purée with the rose water and seasoning. Make a béchamel sauce from the butter, flour, milk and cheese (see page 191). Add the carrot purée and stir thoroughly. Butter a shallow oven dish, arrange the eggs in it and pour the carrot sauce over them. Place in a hot oven for 2 or 3 minutes only.

Leek timbale ⑮ P

Timbales are related to soufflés and make a very good main course dish, or can be eaten cold for a light summer lunch. They are, in essence, a flavoured egg custard and can be cooked in a soufflé dish or any decorative ovenproof dish from which the contents can be easily unmoulded. Timbales should be eaten with a sauce (see pages 190-194).

Variation
● *Substitute the leek purée with the same amount of spinach, mushroom, celeriac, tomato or pepper purée.*

450 g/1 lb leeks, trimmed and cleaned
50 g/2 oz/4 tablespoons butter and
fine breadcrumbs for coating mould
50 g/2 oz/½ cup Gruyère cheese, grated
seasoning to taste
5 eggs, beaten
300 ml/10 fl oz/1¼ cups milk
pinch of nutmeg

Slice the leeks thinly and cook gently in the butter until just soft. Liberally butter a 1.5-litre/2½-pint/1½-quart mould or soufflé dish and coat the inside with the breadcrumbs. Pour the leeks and juices into a bowl and add the cheese, seasoning and beaten eggs. Mix thoroughly to distribute the leeks evenly. Heat the milk with the nutmeg until just simmering. Pre-heat the oven to 180°C/350°F/Gas mark 4. Pour the milk carefully on to the leek mixture, stirring thoroughly. Then pour into the buttered dish. Place in a bain marie (see page 53) and bake for 45 minutes. When cooked, it should look like a soufflé. Allow the dish to rest for 5 minutes then turn out on to a large platter.

Spinach moulds ⑳ Ⓟ

Individual moulds make a spectacular start to a dinner party. Place a herb leaf or prettily trimmed piece of vegetable in the bottom of each ramekin; this will decorate the top of the mould when you turn it out. Serve with beurre blanc and saffron sauce (see page 190).

10 g/½ oz/1 tablespoon butter
675 g/1½ lb spinach leaves
225 g/8 oz/1 cup Ricotta cheese (see page 55)
25 g/1 oz/¼ cup Gruyère cheese, freshly grated
25 g/1 oz/¼ cup Parmesan cheese, freshly grated
2 eggs
4 tablespoons single/light cream
pinch of nutmeg
seasoning to taste

Butter four to six individual ramekins. Blanch about ten of the largest spinach leaves (see page 52). Drain well and arrange in the ramekins to cover the bottom and sides, and generously overlap the edges. Blanch the remaining spinach for about 2 minutes, then chop finely. Heat the oven to 200°C/400°F/Gas mark 6. Combine the rest of the ingredients in a bowl. Fill each ramekin with alternate layers of the cheese mixture and chopped spinach, then fold over the spinach leaves. Put a knob of butter on each ramekin and bake in a bain marie (see page 53) for 25-30 minutes. Unmould when they have rested for a few minutes.

Oeufs Florentines ⑮ Ⓟ

This is one of the great classic Italian dishes that must be perfectly timed. You can poach the eggs or bake them, but the yolks should always be runny.

25 g/1 oz/2 tablespoons butter
900 g/2 lb spinach leaves, washed and drained
4 eggs
300 ml/10 fl oz/1¼ cups cheese sauce (see page 191)
pinch of nutmeg
seasoning to taste

Melt the butter in a large pan and pack in the spinach. Cover and simmer over a low flame for 5 minutes. Stir and simmer again for another 5 minutes. If the spinach is tender and has reduced by two-thirds, it is done. Chop it coarsely and drain off all the liquid; reserve this for the sauce. Butter a shallow oven dish and spread the spinach out in it. Make four deep indentations and keep warm in the oven. Poach, bake or steam the eggs until the whites are just cooked and the yolks runny (see page 54). Make a cheese sauce adding the spinach liquid, nutmeg and seasoning. Place the eggs in the spinach, cover with the sauce and brown under a hot grill/broiler. (If the dish is browned in the oven, the yolks harden.)

Piperade ⑮ P

This dish is an old favourite of mine. I first cooked it in my early twenties and it never failed to please. Piperade can be eaten hot or cold and is delicious as part of a summer lunch. It can also be eaten as part of a layered salad, or puréed to make a dip.

Variation
Chakchouka *This is a dish eaten in North Africa and the Middle East, and must either be a cousin of piperade, or the original recipe. The ingredients are the same but the eggs are broken in whole and cooked in the vegetable mixture.*

6 tablespoons olive oil
2 or 3 peppers, cored, seeded and sliced
3 garlic cloves, crushed
2 onions, sliced
450 g/1 lb tomatoes, peeled and sliced (see page 52)
seasoning to taste
5 eggs, lightly beaten

Heat the oil and gently cook the peppers, garlic and onions until soft, stirring occasionally to create a rough purée. Add the tomatoes and cook for a further 5 minutes. If it seems too liquid, do not worry - it is supposed to be that way. Add the seasoning and eggs, stirring briskly to scramble them. Serve at once.

Basic omelette ⑤ P

The classic French omelette is not a difficult dish to make if a few rules are followed: do not attempt to make an omelette with more than 3 eggs; use a small omelette pan with sloping sides so that the omelette can be rolled out on to the plate; use only a small knob of butter.

Variations
• *Add 1 tablespoon freshly grated cheese. When it is just beginning to melt, fold the sides in and slide the omelette out.*

• *Add about 1 tablespoon finely chopped parsley, chives, chervil, mint or tarragon.*

2 eggs
seasoning to taste
knob of unsalted butter

Beat the eggs and seasoning with a fork. Melt the butter and tilt the pan to spread it over the bottom. Pour in the eggs and tilt the pan again so that they cover the base. Control the heat so that the egg just bubbles a little, but does not heave or burn. When the bottom is set and there is still some liquid egg in the centre of the top, fold each side of the omelette to the middle with a spatula, then slide it on to a plate and serve at once. Omelettes have to be made individually; they must be eaten at once as they cannot be kept warm.

Spanish omelette ⑩ P

Although the best Spanish omelettes are inevitably eaten in Spain, you can achieve very good results with this recipe. Be sure to cook the potato until slightly crisp, and only add the eggs when this is done. It makes a satisfying lunch with a crisp salad, and is also delicious eaten cold.

Variations
• *Add 1 sliced green pepper, 1 sliced red pepper and 1 sliced onion. Cook with the potatoes until soft, then proceed as before.*

• *Add some chopped fresh herbs in the last few minutes of cooking.*

3 tablespoons olive oil
225 g/½ lb potatoes, peeled and thinly sliced
6 eggs
150 ml/5 fl oz/⅔ cup single/light cream
3 tablespoons chopped parsley
seasoning to taste
25 g/1 oz/2 tablespoons butter

Heat the oil and fry the potatoes until brown and crisp. Pour off any excess oil. Mix together the eggs, cream, parsley and seasoning in a bowl. Melt the butter in the pan with the potatoes, then pour in the egg mixture. Cook until the eggs set. Do not try to fold the omelette. The more substantial these Spanish omelettes are, the more they have to be served like wedges of cake.

Basic cheese soufflé ⑩ P

It is important to follow a few basic rules in making soufflés. The egg whites should be chilled and whipped cold just before being folded in. Never leave them to sit out in the kitchen; if whipped they will go watery, and if not, they never will. Finally, do avoid opening the oven door during the cooking time. I prefer my soufflés to be uncooked in the centre so that everybody has a crisp brown risen part of soufflé as well as some sauce to go with it. This recipe serves six people.

Variations

Leek soufflé   *Use 25 g/1 oz/¼ cup grated Gruyère, but substitute the rest of the cheese with a purée made from 450 g/1 lb of leeks or spinach, or 100 g/4 oz mushrooms, cooked in 2 tablespoons of butter, then puréed.*

Piperade soufflé   *Use 25 g/1 oz/¼ cup grated Gruyère, but substitute the rest of the cheese with a piperade mixture (see page 144). Do this before the eggs are added.*

Summer pea soufflé   *Use 25 g/1 oz/¼ cup grated Gruyère, but substitute the rest of the cheese with 675 g/1½ lb fresh peas in their pods. Boil the peas and reduce to a purée with the cream, then add to the soufflé.*

6 large eggs, separated
25 g/1 oz/2 tablespoons butter
25 g/1 oz/2 tablespoons plain/all-purpose flour
300 ml/10 fl oz/1¼ cups milk
seasoning to taste
75 g/3 oz/¾ cup Gruyère cheese, grated
50 g/2 oz/½ cup mature Cheddar cheese, grated
25 g/1 oz/¼ cup Parmesan cheese, grated
150 ml/5 fl oz/⅔ cup single/light cream

Chill the egg whites in the refrigerator. Make a béchamel sauce from the butter, flour, milk and seasoning (see page 191). Add all the cheese and stir until it has melted. Remove from the heat and leave to cool a little. Stir in the cream and then the egg yolks. Generously butter a 2.75-litre/5-pint/3-quart soufflé dish and pre-heat the oven to 200°C/400°F/Gas mark 6. Beat the egg whites until they form stiff peaks. Fold in about a third of the egg whites to the soufflé mixture with a spatula. Do not worry if it is not all amalgamated. Fold in the remainder, then pour into the soufflé dish and bake on the top rack of the oven for 35-40 minutes.

Celeriac and sweet chestnut soufflé ⑳ P

Celeriac is a beautiful winter vegetable gradually finding favour worldwide. This soufflé is also excellent if made with pumpkin instead of celeriac; it then becomes a classic French dish.

100 g/¼ lb celeriac, peeled and chopped
4 tablespoons dry white wine
25 g/1 oz/2 tablespoons butter
seasoning
1 teaspoon celery salt
1 teaspoon kuzo flour or arrowroot dissolved in water
300 ml/10 fl oz/1¼ cups milk
50 g/2 oz/½ cup sweet chestnuts, chopped (see page 52)
50 g/2 oz/½ cup Gruyère, Cheddar or hard cheese, grated
4 eggs, separated

Simmer the celeriac in the wine, butter, seasoning and celery salt for 20 minutes. Mash coarsely. Heat the kuzo with the milk to make a sauce. Stir in the chestnuts, cheese and egg yolks. Pre-heat the oven to 220°C/425°F/Gas mark 7. Whip the whites stiffly and fold in gradually. Bake in a buttered 1.5-litre/2½-pint/1½-quart soufflé dish for 20 minutes.

Main Meals

In the old days of the vegetarian movement, perhaps twenty or forty years ago, a meal was still structured around the old cliché of 'meat and two veg' and a nut cutlet or rissole was substituted for the meat. This gave vegetarianism a bad name. All this has now changed. There is an infinite variety of meals and you can choose between one simple dish with several side dishes, or one intricate, substantial dish with perhaps just a side salad. There is no dish which is a meat substitute in itself. There is no need for one, nutritionally or aesthetically.

What dishes you eat depend on the occasion and the appetite. There can be simple meals of two courses beginning with, say, Danish apple soup, followed by dolmades and a tomato salad. Or you can have a more intricate meal, beginning with a terrine verte, followed by baked curry with whole spices, dry green curry, saffron rice, jajiki and pickles, then a pear and pistachio salad, a cheese, and to finish, Sussex pond pudding. These, as you might surmise, would be autumnal or winter meals, yet the latter is a great deal more substantial than the former, for no other reason than the vagaries of our appetite.

You can combine dishes from any part of this book to make a main meal. Any of the breads in the breakfast section will go with the soups, cheeses or pâtés. A main meal can also be made out of two or three vegetable side dishes - for example, mushrooms in red wine and mustard could be eaten with gingered pumpkin and a millet pilaf. A more simple meal could consist of Italian pasta balls served with broad/fava beans in garlic sauce. With any meal I would try to have a combination of raw vegetables with one hot, spicy vegetable, plus a grain and a fruit dish. Such a menu could be Caesar salad, followed by curried beans and buckwheat pilaf, then pears in red wine.

One of the most satisfactory discoveries is that, if you look at a meal which pleases aesthetically, it is nearly always nutritionally well balanced too.

The first recipes in this section are for stuffed dishes. There are two main components to a stuffing - the flavour, which is a vegetable or mixture of vegetables either puréed or chopped with herbs or spices, and the binding agent, which may be flour, eggs or cheese. A stuffing should taste very distinct and fairly strong. There is no point in stuffing a vegetable if the filling does not 'hold its own' in flavour and texture. At the same time, the flavours of the filling and vegetable should complement each other.

Try to keep a ratio of 3 to 1 between flavour and thickening agent. An excess of grains, rice or breadcrumbs will lead to stodge. Note that if you use beaten egg as your binding agent, the stuffing will seem rather wet until it is cooked.

Sometimes, against all judicious planning, a stuffing will turn out too dry to be palatable. It can generally be saved by making a sauce and, if the vegetable that it has stuffed is succulent enough, you will have a pleasant range of texture and flavour.

*Pumpkin, ginger and potato gratin served in a
hollowed pumpkin makes a spectacular
centrepiece (see page 161).*

147

Dolmades (Stuffed vine/grape leaves) ⑳ Ⓥ Ⓕ

Despite rumours to the contrary, this dish requires patience rather than skill. All Greek shops sell packets of vine/grape leaves soaked in brine. You need to place them in a bowl, scald them and allow the leaves to float and disentangle themselves from one another. Leave them to soak while you make the filling, but be careful to rinse the leaves in a colander beneath cold water before using them. As with all popular dishes, there is no definitive version of dolmades. Therefore, the following recipe can be the basis of your own experiments. It makes enough for 6 people as a first course.

225 g/8 oz/1¼ cups Patna/long grain rice
2 onions, finely chopped
4-5 garlic cloves, crushed
2 tablespoons celery leaves, finely chopped
1 teaspoon each crushed dill, thyme and oregano
seasoning to taste
225 g/8 oz vine/grape leaves, scalded and drained
150 ml/5 fl oz/⅔ cup olive oil
juice of 2 lemons

Scald the rice in boiling water and leave it for a few moments; then rinse it under a cold tap. Mix thoroughly with the onions, garlic, celery leaves, herbs and seasoning. Place a teaspoon of the mixture in the centre of each vine/grape leaf (larger leaves will need more, smaller ones less). Roll the leaf over the filling, tucking in the sides as you go. You should end up with a sausage shape. Put a layer of any vegetables, such as cabbage leaves, leek tops or onion skins, in a large saucepan to prevent the dolmades sticking or burning. Wedge the rolls in neatly together, adding a second layer if necessary. Fill any gaps with a slice of onion or garlic clove so that the dolmades do not unravel themselves. Pour over the olive oil and lemon juice and cover with 2-3 inches of water. Cover and cook slowly over a gentle heat, adding a *little* more water if they show any signs of drying out. They will need 1½ to 2 hours, depending on how gentle the heat is. When done, they have the appearance of plump little parcels.

Stuffed tomatoes ⑩ Ⓟ

This recipe is a simple classic; the Chanel suit of cooking. The following recipe is dedicated to those who dislike the traditional (sometimes wet) filling made from tomato pulp.

Variation
Stuffed courgettes/zucchini
Use medium-sized vegetables. Slice them in half lengthways and scoop out most of the flesh, leaving a 'shell' about 3 mm/⅛ inch thick. Simmer them in salted water for 3 minutes. Drain well. Make only half the quantity of stuffing, adding 2 tablespoons chopped walnuts and 2 or 3 crushed garlic cloves. Fill the vegetables and sprinkle with grated Parmesan rather than breadcrumbs. Bake as the tomatoes.

4-6 marmande/beefsteak tomatoes
2 tablespoons olive oil
2 large onions, finely sliced
seasoning to taste
50 g/2 oz/½ cup Gruyère cheese, grated
50 g/2 oz/½ cup Parmesan cheese, grated
generous handful of chopped parsley
2-3 tablespoons wholewheat breadcrumbs,
dried (see page 48)

Slice the tops off the tomatoes, gouge out the pulp and seeds, and discard everything but the tomato 'shells'. Heat the oil, add the onions, and cook covered over a gentle heat until soft and almost transparent. Add the seasoning, cheeses and parsley. Stir until the cheese melts. Pre-heat the oven to 200°C/400°F/Gas mark 6. Stuff the tomatoes, sprinkle with breadcrumbs and bake for 10-15 minutes.

Stuffed marrow/squash ⓔ

This is a traditional British dish and appears in every country kitchen as one of the autumn feasts. However, if marrows or squash get too large, they become tasteless and fibrous. Do not eat them after they have grown more than 30 cm/12 inches long; at this length, they can be satisfactorily stuffed. As marrows/squash contain a lot of water which they lose during cooking, it is important to stuff them with uncooked rice, which will absorb the water; breadcrumbs simply become soggy.

Variation
* *Use any variety of summer squash.*

1 vegetable marrow or squash, about 30 cm/12 inches long
3 tablespoons olive oil
1 onion, finely chopped
225 g/½ lb mushrooms, sliced
225 g/½ lb tomatoes, peeled and chopped (see page 52)
1 teaspoon each thyme and marjoram, ground
seasoning to taste
50 g/2 oz/½ cup mature/sharp Cheddar cheese, grated
75 g/3 oz/½ cup Patna/long grain rice

Pre-heat the oven to 200°C/400°F/Gas mark 6. Trim the ends of the marrow/squash, then cut a boat-shaped 'lid' out of its side. Dig the seeds out with a spoon, leaving the flesh inside. Grease a large piece of foil and sit the marrow/squash on it. Heat the oil in a pan and cook the onions, mushrooms, tomatoes and herbs for 5 minutes. When the onion and mushrooms are soft, add the seasoning, cheese and rice. Fill the marrow/squash with this mixture. Fit the lid back on and wrap the foil around the marrow/squash. Place on a baking sheet and bake for 50 minutes. Unwrap the marrow/squash carefully, as it retains its heat, and leave for a few minutes before slicing.

Stuffed onions ⓔ

Onions can sometimes taste powerfully sweet after cooking, so use a sharp-flavoured stuffing to offset this. Serve with a winter salad of chopped cabbage, carrots, apple and celery.

4 large onions
2 tablespoons olive oil
2 medium sized carrots, grated
50 g/2 oz/½ cup cooked chick peas,
broken up (see page 51)
1 teaspoon each caraway and coriander
seasoning to taste
3 tablespoons Gruyère cheese, grated

Trim and peel the onions and remove the centres, leaving a shell about 1 cm/¼ inch thick. Chop up the removed onion then gently simmer the onion shells in some salted water for 3 minutes. Drain carefully. Heat the oil in a pan and add the chopped onion, carrot, chick peas, herbs and seasoning. Cover and cook for 8 to 10 minutes over a low flame. Pre-heat the oven to 200°C/400°F/Gas mark 6. Fill the onion shells with the vegetable mixture and sprinkle some cheese over the top of each. Place in a greased oven dish and bake for 20 minutes.

Stuffed root vegetables ㉚ Ⓥ Ⓕ

These make an excellent snack or accompaniment to a main meal. Choose medium-sized potatoes, parsnips, turnips or sweet potatoes, cutting larger vegetables into several pieces, no smaller than 8 cm/3 inches thick. The preparation for all vegetables is the same: cut a lengthways indentation about 5 cm/2½ inches deep and scoop out the flesh, leaving a 'shell' about 1 cm/½ inch inside. (If you are not using the scooped-out flesh in the stuffing, it can be used in soups or stocks.) Boil the shells in a little salted water until just tender. Drain and stuff, cover with buttered paper and bake in a pre-heated oven at 200°C/400°F/Gas mark 6 for about 10 minutes. All the stuffings given here will fill 4-6 vegetables.

Stuffing 1
2 tablespoons corn oil
2-cm/1-inch piece root ginger, finely sliced
3 garlic cloves, chopped
2 red chillies, broken up
1 teaspoon each turmeric, mustard seed and fenugreek
2 red peppers
3 onions
inner vegetable flesh (see left)
sea salt

Heat the oil and fry the ginger, garlic, chillies and spices for a moment or two. Add the peppers, onions and vegetable flesh. Stir and cover. Cook over a low heat until it resembles a rough purée. Season and use.

Stuffing 2
450 g/1 lb spinach leaves, washed
inner vegetable flesh, chopped (see left)
50 g/2 oz/½ cup Parmesan cheese, grated
50 g/2 oz/½ cup Gruyère cheese, grated
75 g/3 oz/¾ cup flaked/slivered almonds,
toasted (see page 56)
seasoning to taste

Simmer the spinach and vegetable flesh over a low heat until soft. Drain well and chop coarsely. While still warm, add the cheeses, almonds and seasoning and use immediately.

Stuffing 3
2 tablespoons olive oil
1 teaspoon dried oregano
450 g/1 lb tomatoes, peeled and chopped (see page 52)
1 tablespoon tomato purée/paste
100 g/4 oz/1 cup mature/sharp Cheddar cheese, grated
seasoning to taste
100 g/4 oz/1 cup walnuts, half chopped, half ground
a few breadcrumbs

Heat the oil, simmer the oregano and tomatoes for 5 minutes, then add the purée/paste. Remove from the heat and mix in the cheese, seasoning and walnuts. Stuff your vegetables and scatter with the breadcrumbs before baking.

Stews

Most of the recipes in this section involve beans combined with various vegetables. Worldwide, the variety of dishes is immense. My selection ranges from fragrant spiced bean casserole, to rather more theatrical sweet potato and parsnip stew. There are also earthy lentil dahls from India and a Japanese influenced Hoppin' John.

All the beans in the ingredients lists are dried; most need cold water soaking overnight, or may be soaked in boiling water for one hour prior to cooking (see page 51). Some of the smaller members of the legume family, like lentils, can be cooked without pre-soaking. However, it will not do them any harm to be soaked and it cuts down on cooking time and the amount of water they absorb. Simmer all these dishes over a low flame so they soak up all the flavours slowly. Never add salt until the very last moment when checking the flavour; it hardens the beans and they will not cook.

Rainbow stew ⑮ Ⅴ Ｐ Ｆ

The orange juice and sliced apple added at the end of cooking give this pulse and vegetable stew a lift, making it a refreshing main course. Serve with a crisp green salad.

100 g/4 oz/½ cup black-eyed beans/peas,
pre-soaked (see page 51)
75 g/3 oz/½ cup yellow lentils, pre-soaked (see page 51)
1 vegetable stock/bouillon cube
3 tablespoons olive oil
1 tablespoon dried oregano
2 onions, sliced
5 garlic cloves, sliced
225 g/½ lb each potatoes, carrots and turnips, diced
1 head of celery
2 firm cooking apples
300 ml/10 fl oz/1¼ cups orange juice
seasoning to taste
chopped parsley for garnish

Drain the beans, then bring to the boil in plenty of fresh water, add the lentils and stock/bouillon cube, and simmer for 1 hour, or until the beans are tender. Meanwhile, heat the olive oil and add the oregano, onions, garlic and rest of the vegetables. Stir over a low heat and simmer for 10 minutes. Add the pulses in their stock, stir thoroughly and simmer for another 10 minutes. Slice and core the apples. Pour the orange juice into the stew and add the apples. Simmer for another 5 minutes. Season to taste. Sprinkle wih parsley and serve.

Basic spiced bean casserole ⑤ Ⓥ Ⓟ Ⓕ

The pleasure of this casserole is its infinite variability. It is amazing how all types of bean adapt to a huge range of different flavours. Serve with lettuce and egg mould (see page 162) for a satisfying main course.

Variations
● *Many other beans can be substituted in this casserole: try haricot/navy, butter, aduki, broad/fava and chick peas.*

Use all the ingredients, but replace the tomatoes, tomato purée/paste and paprika with the following:

● *Small chopped swede/rutabaga, 300 ml/10 fl oz/1¼ cups orange juice and some lightly fried caraway seeds.*

● *Delete the paprika and add 2 tablespoons peanut butter and 1 tablespoon tomato purée/ paste. These flavours go best with black-eyed beans/peas.*

● *Add 1 teaspoon each of crushed root ginger, turmeric, cloves, cumin and coriander, plus 1 cinnamon stick, 2 green cardamom pods and 2 black peppers.*

175 g/6 oz/1 cup red kidney beans,
pre-soaked (see page 51)
3 tablespoons olive oil
1 teaspoon each of cumin, coriander, fenugreek, turmeric
and asafoetida
2 garlic cloves, crushed
2 onions, sliced
2 red peppers, sliced
2 dried red chillies
450 g/1 lb tomatoes, peeled and chopped (see page 52)
1 tablespoon paprika
2 tablespoons tomato purée/paste
seasoning to taste

Drain the beans and then boil fiercely in fresh water for 10 minutes. Drain and put to one side. Heat the oil in a casserole, add the spices, garlic, onions, peppers and chillies. Cook for 3 to 4 minutes. Add the beans and cover with 5 cm/1½ inches of water. Simmer for 30 minutes or until the beans are just soft (see page 51), then add the tomatoes and cook for another 30 minutes. Finally, add the paprika, tomato purée/paste and seasoning.
Note: If you want a hotter casserole, break the chillies open to release the seeds.

Ful medames ⑤ Ⓟ Ⓕ

This is a famous dish which can be bought ready cooked as a snack from Egyptian street stalls. It is equivalent to the hamburger in its ubiquity. Traditionally it is eaten as a first course, but it goes well with Oeufs Florentines (see page 143), and cabbage or leek dishes.

225 g/8 oz/1 cup ful medames/brown beans,
pre-soaked (see page 51)
4 hard-boiled eggs
3 garlic cloves, crushed
8 tablespoons olive oil
generous handful parsley, finely chopped
juice of 2 lemons
seasoning to taste

Drain the beans well and cook in plenty of boiling water for 1½ hours, or until tender. Drain well. Peel and mash the eggs, and stir into the beans with the rest of the ingredients. Serve warm.

Hoppin' John ㉚ Ⓥ Ⓟ Ⓕ

This dish comes from the southern United States and is traditionally eaten on New Year's Eve. It is usually made with bacon, but I have substituted nori which adds a taste of its own, and is healthier than bacon.

150 g/5 oz/⅔ cup black-eyed beans/peas,
pre-soaked (see page 51)
3 tablespoons olive oil
5 garlic cloves, crushed
2 large onions, finely sliced
1 red pepper, finely sliced
1 green pepper, finely sliced
135 g/4 oz/⅔ cup brown rice
2 nori sheets, cut small (with scissors)
1.2 litres/2 pints/5 cups vegetable stock (see page 110)
seasoning to taste
generous handful of chopped parsley

Drain the beans. Heat the oil in a casserole and add the crushed garlic, onions and peppers. Cook over a low heat until they begin to soften, then add the beans, rice and nori. Stir thoroughly and cook for another minute or two. Pour in the stock and bring to the boil. Cover and simmer for 45 minutes, or until the beans and rice are tender. Cook uncovered for the last 5 minutes or so if the dish is too liquid. Season well and stir in the parsley.

Hot sweet potato and parsnip stew ⑮ Ⓥ Ⓕ

There are two kinds of sweet potato (sometimes called yams in the US) - one with yellow/white flesh, the other orange. The latter are a beautiful colour and look especially good in curry or spiced dishes. Do not overcook them; they cook more quickly than ordinary potatoes and should not be allowed to get mushy, which they will do very willingly. This recipe is more West Indian than Far Eastern. Eat it with brown rice or cous cous as one of several spiced dishes.

120 ml/4 fl oz/½ cup sunflower or corn oil
1 tablespoon mustard seed
1 teaspoon mace
2 green chillies, chopped
5 garlic cloves, crushed
25 g/1 oz root ginger, sliced (size of a golf ball)
1 tablespoon garam masala (see page 42)
2 onions, sliced
225 g/½ lb sweet potatoes, peeled and chopped
225 g/½ lb parsnips, peeled and chopped
450 g/1 lb tomatoes, peeled and chopped (see page 52)
4 tablespoons lemon juice or juice from 2 lemons
seasoning to taste

Heat the oil in a large pan and cook the mustard seeds and mace until the seeds pop. Lower the heat and add the chillies, garlic, ginger, garam masala and onion. Fry gently for a moment or two, taking care not to burn the spices. Add the sweet potatoes and parsnips and stir well. Bring to boiling point, then cover and simmer for a few moments. Add the tomatoes and lemon juice. Stir again thoroughly, then simmer for 15 minutes. Taste and season. If it needs pepper, add some, but it should be spicy and hot enough.

Curries

There are two main types of curry. In a dry curry the spices are ground and cooked in the ghee or oil. Their flavours are soaked up by the vegetables, and in the last stage of cooking the lid is taken off the dish, the heat turned up, and the vegetables cooked until crisp and the sauce largely evaporated. By adding yoghurt to this method of cooking, you will create a dry curd curry.

The other main type of curry has a good amount of sauce with it, which can be thickened with either gram flour or coconut milk, which will give a rich and delicious flavour. Remember, coconut milk is high in saturated fats, so use it judiciously.

Perhaps the most important ingredients in curries are the spices; they may be used whole, ground or made into a paste. These options are discussed on page 42. Do not be tempted to buy ready-made curry powder; it has little flavour or aroma.

This brings me to the question of how hot you want your curry. You can control the heat very easily by the amount of chillis or cayenne that you add. (See page 60 for notes on types of chilli and the amount of heat each generates.) It is the seeds of the chilli which are most fiery. If you want a very hot curry, chop the green chillis and add the seeds. Two or three green chillis added to a meal for six people would make it very hot. A slightly less hot curry could be made by using the same amount of dried red chillis broken up and crushed. A milder curry can be made using either of these without the seeds. Ginger is an important constituent of curry. It gives another kind of heat with a flavour of its own. Whatever heat you like your curries to generate, always add fresh spices carefully, as the hotness is never completely predictable and, once there, will be difficult to remove.

Baked spiced potatoes ⑳ Ⓟ Ⓕ

This is a classic dry curry that is a good accompaniment to other saucier curries, such as mattar paneer and curried mung beans.

4 large potatoes, peeled
2 tablespoons oil
5 bay leaves, crushed
1 teaspoon each turmeric powder, chilli powder and garam masala (see page 42)
½ teaspoon brown sugar
5 garlic cloves, crushed
seasoning to taste
300 ml/10 fl oz/1¼ cups plain yoghurt
handful of chopped coriander leaves

Pre-heat the oven to 200°C/400°F/Gas mark 6. Boil the potatoes whole for about 12 minutes. Meanwhile, heat the oil and fry the bay leaves and other spices for a few moments, then stir in the sugar and garlic. Add the seasoning and then mix in the yoghurt. Drain the potatoes well, prick them all over with a fork and then roll them in the yoghurt paste, making sure they are well covered. It is best to pour the paste into a large, shallow ovenproof dish to do this. Bake in the same dish for about 30 minutes, and sprinkle with the coriander leaves before serving.

Curried mung beans ⑤ Ⓥ Ⓕ

Recipes for spiced bean dishes are legion. You can use any sort of bean and any mix of spices. Finding one you like is a matter of trial and error. This is one of my favourites. Eat it with potato and mint tart and a fruit salad (see pages 125 and 177).

150 g/5 oz/⅔ cup mung beans
2 tablespoons olive oil
1 tablespoon curry powder (see page 42)
2 teaspoons garam masala (see page 42)
juice and zest from 1 lime
300 ml/10 fl oz/1¼ cups vegetable stock (see page 110)
seasoning to taste
2 tablespoons coriander leaves, finely chopped

Boil the mung beans for 20 to 30 minutes until tender. Drain well. Heat the oil in a casserole and cook the curry spices in it for a minute, until the flavours are released into the oil. Add the lime zest and juice and then the beans. Stir thoroughly for 2 minutes, then add the stock and seasoning. Cook for 5 minutes over a low heat, then stir in the coriander leaves just before serving.

Okra, potato and ginger curry ㉕ Ⓥ Ⓕ

This is a whole spice curry that is particularly flavoursome. Okra (or ladies' fingers) should be prepared with a wash and the merest trimming of the stalk. If you expose the inside, the juices run and they can be slimy, which come people find repellent. Serve with buckwheat, jajiki, spiced baked potatoes and a fruit salad (see pages 190, 154 and 120).

450 g/1 lb fresh okra
450 g/1 lb potatoes
150 ml/5 fl oz/⅔ cup olive oil
2 onions, sliced
5 garlic cloves, sliced
½ teaspoon each coriander, cumin and nutmeg, ground
1 teaspoon each mustard seed and fenugreek, ground
50 g/2 oz root ginger, grated
seasoning to taste
1 tablespoon sesame seeds, roasted (see page 56)

Wash and trim the okra. Peel the potatoes and cut into small dice. Heat the oil in a pan and add the vegetables with the onions, garlic, spices and ginger. Stir well and cook on a high flame for 2 or 3 minutes. Then lower the heat, cover and simmer for 20 minutes, or until the potato is cooked. Finally add the seasoning and sprinkle with sesame seeds.

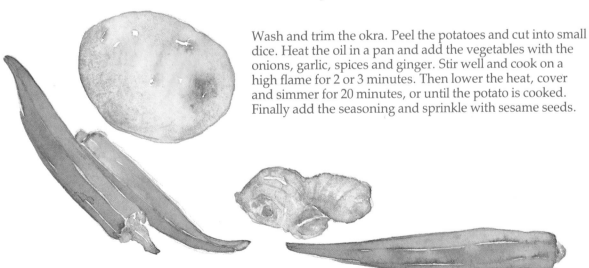

Dry curd curry ⑩ 𝐅

This is an excellent, medium hot dish which completely transforms a collection of root vegetables. Go for contrast in either colour or texture, as nothing is more dampening to the appetite than a dish where everything looks and tastes the same. Do not be nervous about the amount of root ginger included. When cooked, it has a beautiful flavour. Serve with basmati rice, jajiki and a selection of pickles (see pages 190 and 195).

Variation
● *Almost any vegetable can be used in this curry. Try baby turnips, parsnips, sweet potato, or any combination - even raw aubergine/eggplant, courgettes/zucchini or green beans.*

1½ tablespoons vegetable ghee or corn oil
3 cm/1½ inches root ginger, peeled and thinly sliced
1 teaspoon black mustard seeds
2 teaspoons poppy seeds
2 teaspoons turmeric, ground
250 g/½ lb each carrots, potatoes and celery
2 large onions, sliced
2 garlic cloves, finely chopped
a little sea salt
2 cloves
6 black peppercorns
2 teaspoons coriander seeds, ground
1 tablespoon lemon juice
150 ml/5 fl oz/⅔ cup plain yoghurt
handful of coriander leaves, chopped
pinch of garam masala (see page 42)

Heat the ghee or oil and fry the ginger, mustard and poppy seeds with the turmeric. Scrub the vegetables, cut into small chunks and fry in the spice mixture over a medium heat for about 10 minutes, stirring well. Add the onions, garlic and salt, and cook for 5 more minutes. Pre-heat the oven to 180°C/350°F/Gas mark 4. Add the remaining spices, sprinkle with the lemon juice and stir in the yoghurt. Cover and bake for 45 minutes. All the juices should be absorbed, the yoghurt forming a delicious crunchy coating. Sprinkle the curry with the coriander leaves and garam masala, and garnish with a slice of lemon or lime.

Mattar Paneer ⑮ 𝐏 𝐅

This is a favourite dish of the Punjab and a famous part of Indian vegetarian cuisine. Paneer is a fresh cheese made in the same way as Ricotta (see page 55), but you may substitute tofu if you like. Serve as one of several curries, or eat it as a light lunch with baked spiced potatoes (see page 154).

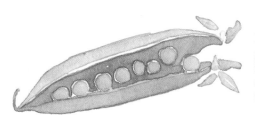

450 g/1 lb peas, shelled
corn or sunflower oil
1 large onion, finely chopped
5 garlic cloves, sliced
25 g/1 oz root ginger, peeled and sliced
1 teaspoon each coriander, cumin and turmeric
½ teaspoon each chilli powder and asafoetida
225 g/8 oz/2 cups Paneer or Ricotta cheese (see page 55)
sea salt

Boil the peas until tender; drain and reserve. Fry the onion, garlic, ginger and spices in the oil until the onion is soft. Stir in the Paneer and fry for a moment, then add the peas and salt. Stir and fry for 3 more minutes. Garnish with chopped tomatoes and spring onions/scallions.

Dry green curry ⑮ Ⅴ Ⓟ Ⓕ

We too easily ignore the green leaf family of vegetables in curry dishes. Vary your choice of greens and eat this as a side dish with another curry, plus plain rice and sweet chutney. This dish is medium hot.

450 g/1 lb spinach or broccoli
225 g/½ lb potatoes, diced small
Aromatic spices, ground together:
1 teaspoon cumin seeds
2 teaspoons coriander seeds
2 teaspoons turmeric
salt, cloves, nutmeg and cinnamon stick to taste
Second flavouring
1½ tablespoons ghee or oil
2 large onions, sliced
2 garlic cloves, crushed
2 small dried chillies (4 for really hot)
2 black cardamoms and 10 black peppercorns, crushed

Boil the vegetables in salted water until just tender - about 20 minutes. Drain, sprinkle with the aromatic spices, cover, and shake well. Leave for 10 to 15 minutes. Meanwhile, fry the onions in the ghee with the second spices until crisp. Add the spiced vegetables and fry for 1 minute over a high heat, stirring constantly.

Baked curry with whole spices ⑮ Ⅴ Ⓕ

Mushrooms and potatoes make a happy combination in a curry. In this recipe, baked in the oven, the mushrooms lose some of their liquid, which subtly flavours the spiced sauce. The potatoes soak up the spices and also take on a little of the mushroom flavour. Eat with brown rice or cous cous, jajiki, onion bhaji and lime chutney (see pages 123, 190 and 136).

Variation

● *If you want to ensure all the flavours are sealed in, make a sticky dough from flour and water and use it to seal round the edges of the casserole. It will bake hard, so you must chip it off at the end of the cooking time.*

3 tablespoons corn oil or ghee
450 g/1 lb large field mushrooms, washed and sliced
225 g/½ lb potatoes, peeled and cubed
2 teaspoons turmeric
2 cm/1 inch root ginger, crushed
3 garlic cloves (optional)
2 large onions and 1 large red pepper, finely sliced
2 teaspoons each cumin, coriander and mustard seeds, ground
cloves, cinnamon stick and black peppercorns to taste
3 green cardamoms, split
1-3 dried red chillis, split (depending on heat required)
salt and lemon juice to taste

Heat the oil in a large casserole. Add the mushrooms, potatoes, turmeric, ginger and garlic. Fry for 5 minutes, stirring constantly. Reduce the heat and simmer for 4 to 5 minutes. Remove from the heat and cover the vegetables with the onions and pepper. Pre-heat the oven to 180°C/ 350°F/Gas mark 4. Sprinkle with the cumin, coriander, mustard, cloves, cinnamon and peppercorns. Add the last four ingredients. Cover, shake firmly and bake for 1 hour.

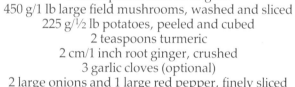

Baked Dishes

This section covers baked gratins, moulds and terrines. Gratins are vegetables mixed with cream or cheese and baked in the oven, or finished beneath a hot grill/broiler.

Moulds are vegetable mixtures encased in leaves, cooked in soufflé or mould dishes inside a bain marie and baked in the oven. They are allowed to rest for a few minutes before being unmoulded. Any leaves can be used to encase a mould - spinach, cabbage, lettuce, Chinese leaves/Nappa or celery cabbage, Swiss chard and vine/grape leaves. Moulds are much easier to cook than they might seem, and are among the prettiest main course dishes you can have. They can be made in individual ramekins and are a delicious way of starting a meal.

A terrine is defined as a mould, which has a chunkier texture than a purée or paste. But it can also be a mixture of both, and generally is. The exciting aspect of terrines is that they are highly decorative and single portions of them arranged on a plate can look as beautiful as an abstract painting. Any of the pâtés on pages 138-140 could be made into terrines by adding small cooked shapes of vegetables as the terrine is being filled.

Layered terrines take the aesthetics one step further because you can create colourful layers with additional decoration. It is wise not to go too far. A terrine with more than three colours will look vulgar.

Terrines are chilled, then sliced and served with a cold sauce or mayonnaise (see pages 192 and 129). They may also be served with cream or yoghurt-based purées, thinned to the right consistency with a little extra cream or yoghurt. Roux-based sauces are not suitable.

Since the advent of *nouvelle cuisine*, it has become fashionable to serve the sliced terrine on individual plates with the sauce beneath. This can look very beautiful but you may prefer to slice the terrine at table and let people help themselves to the sauce. The choice is yours.

Gratin Dauphinois ⑤ P F

If I were a condemned man, this dish would certainly be my last meal. It must be cooked in a slow oven to prevent the cream curdling, and to allow the potatoes to absorb all the flavour.

Variations

Gratin Lyonnais *Omit the nutmeg, and add 225 g/½ lb of thinly sliced onions softened in an extra 2 tablespoons of butter. Mix the onions with the potatoes and proceed as before.*

Gratin Savoyard *Mix 100 g/4 oz/1 cup finely grated Gruyère with the potatoes.*

Gratin Ardennais *Omit the nutmeg and add 1 tablespoon of roughly ground juniper berries and 4 tablespoons grated Parmesan cheese. Mix with the potato and layer as before.*

675 g/1½ lb potatoes, peeled
25 g/1 oz/2 tablespoons butter
1 teaspoon ground nutmeg
seasoning to taste
600 ml/1 pint/2½ cups single/light cream

Pre-heat the oven to 170°C/325°F/Gas mark 3. Slice the potatoes very thinly in a food processor or on a mandoline, then soak in cold water for 1 hour to remove the starch. Rinse under running cold water and dry carefully. Use a little of the butter for greasing a gratin dish. Layer the potatoes in it, sprinkling them with a little of the nutmeg, salt and pepper as you go. Pour in half the cream when the dish is half full, then continue to layer the rest of the potatoes, seasoning and cream until the dish is full. Dot with the remaining butter and bake for 2½ hours, or until the top has turned golden brown.

Creamy celeriac purée layered with
carrot and apricot purée makes Terrine
rose as pretty to look at as it is good
to eat. It is served with Sauce verte
(see pages 163 and 191).

Courgette/zucchini gratin ⑳ P F

*Another classic French dish from the
farmhouse kitchen. In gratins, the vegetables
are sometimes mixed with rice, eggs and
cheese, omitting the cream. The following
three recipes show the different methods.*

6 tablespoons olive oil
675 g/1½ lb courgettes/zucchini, thinly sliced
2 onions, thinly sliced
3 garlic cloves, crushed
50 g/2 oz/⅓ cup rice
3 eggs, beaten
50 g/2 oz/½ cup Parmesan cheese, grated
seasoning to taste

Pre-heat the oven to 200°C/400°F/Gas mark 6. Heat the oil in
a pan and cook the courgettes/zucchini and onions with the
garlic until just soft. Meanwhile, boil the rice until it is
tender, then drain and rinse under hot water. Mix the rice
with the vegetables and the rest of the ingredients and bake
for 10-12 minutes, or until it is brown and the eggs have set.

Chicory/Belgian endive gratin ⑩ P F

*Not enough people think of cooking chicory/
Belgian endive, but I love it cooked. It has a
completely different flavour than when raw.*

3 heads of chicory/Belgian endive
2 eggs, beaten
300 ml/10 fl oz/1¼ cups single/light cream
50 g/2 oz/½ cup Gruyère cheese, finely grated
seasoning to taste

Pre-heat the oven to 200°C/400°F/Gas mark 6. Slice each
chicory/endive head into four and blanch for 1 minute. Drain
and then lay them in a buttered gratin dish. Mix the eggs
with the cream, cheese and seasoning, and pour over the
chicory/endive. Bake for 20 minutes.

Spinach gratin ⑮ P F

*This dish originated in southern France near
the Italian border, hence the inclusion of
Parmesan cheese.*

50 g/2 oz/4 tablespoons butter
450 g/1 lb spinach leaves
300 ml/10 fl oz/1¼ cups single/light cream
2 eggs, beaten
50 g/2 oz/ cup Parmesan cheese, grated
seasoning to taste

Pre-heat the oven to 200°C/400°F/Gas mark 6. Melt the butter
in a pan and add the spinach leaves. Cover and cook over a
moderate heat until the spinach is one third of its bulk, then
chop roughly. Add the rest of the ingredients, pour into a
buttered gratin dish and cook for 10-12 minutes, or until it is
brown and the eggs have set.

Pumpkin, ginger and potato gratin

*The amber colour of the pumpkin flecked with
specks of ginger makes this lovely dish look
especially appetizing.*

Variation

• *Spoon the mixture into a hollowed-out
pumpkin, marrow or other squash which has
been parboiled for about 5 minutes and
drained well. Cover in foil and bake in a
pre-heated oven at 180°C/350°F/Gas mark 4
for about 45 minutes.*

6 tablespoons olive oil
1 medium size onion, chopped
1 garlic clove, crushed
25 g/1 oz root ginger, peeled and grated
1 teaspoon cumin, ground
6 green cardamoms, crushed
675 g/1½ lb/6 cups pumpkin flesh, cubed
675 g/1½ lb potatoes, cubed and boiled for 10-15 minutes
juice of ½ a lemon
300 ml/10 fl oz/1¼ cups Greek yoghurt (see page 45)
sea salt to taste
chopped fresh coriander to garnish

Heat the oil and cook the onion until soft and translucent
with the garlic, ginger and spices. Add the pumpkin and
potatoes and cook until slightly browned and crisp. Add the
lemon juice, yoghurt and seasoning, and heat through.
Transfer the mixture to a gratin dish and grill/broil until the
surface is nice and crisp. Sprinkle with the coriander.

Moussaka verde

*Unlike traditional moussaka, which tends to
be rather heavy because of its meat content,
this dish is light and much healthier. I also
find the aubergine/eggplant more palatable as
it does not become 'clogged' with meat juices.*

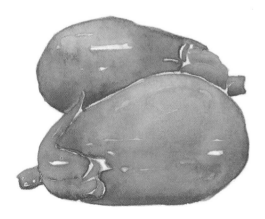

3 aubergines/eggplants, cut in 5-mm/¼-inch slices
450 g/1 lb spinach, washed and drained
450 g/1 lb courgettes/zucchini, sliced
2 eggs, beaten
flour for coating
corn oil for frying
225 g/8 oz tofu, chopped
300 ml/10 fl oz/1¼ cups parsley sauce (see page 191)
300 ml/10 fl oz/1¼ cups cheese sauce (see page 191)

Salt the aubergines/eggplants (see page 52). Meanwhile,
cook the spinach with the courgettes/zucchini over a low
flame for 8 to 10 minutes. Drain well. Dip the aubergine/
eggplant slices in beaten egg, then flour, and fry in the oil
until just crisp. Pre-heat the oven to 200°C/400°F/Gas mark 6.
Butter an oven dish. Lay half the aubergine/eggplant slices
on the bottom, spread the spinach and courgettes/zucchini
over them and sprinkle the tofu on top. Make the parsley
sauce and pour over the vegetables and tofu. Lay the
remaining aubergine/eggplant slices over the sauce. Make
the cheese sauce and pour it over the top. Bake for 25
minutes, or until the top is brown.

Lettuce and egg moulds ㉕ Ⓟ

Strong lettuce leaves are required for this recipe, but you may need to cut out the rigid spines after blanching in order to arrange the leaves in the mould. Serve warm or cold with a mayonnaise or sauce (see pages 129 and 191) as a first course or light lunch. This recipe makes enough for 6 people.

Variation
● *For a pretty effect when cut, fill the lined ramekins with a shallow layer of Ricotta. Put a ball of nut and mushroom pâté in the middle, surround it with carrot and apricot pâté, then finish with another layer of Ricotta. Bake as before.*

10 lettuce leaves (Webb's wonder/romaine or Iceberg)
225 g/8 oz/1 cup Ricotta cheese (see page 55)
seasoning to taste
1 egg per person
100 g/4 oz/1 cup Parmesan cheese, freshly grated
1 tablespoon single/light cream per person

Butter 6 ramekins. Blanch the lettuce leaves in boiling water for 1 minute, then drain carefully. Arrange the cooled leaves in each ramekin so that they cover the bottom and sides, and overlap the edges. Pre-heat the oven to 200°C/400°F/Gas mark 6. Place a tablespoon of Ricotta in each ramekin and season well. Break in an egg and cover with about 1 tablespoon of Parmesan. Pour the cream over each one. Fold over the lettuce leaves, place the ramekins in a bain marie (see page 53) and bake for 20 minutes. Allow to rest for 5 minutes before unmoulding.

Walnut and cabbage moulds ㉕ Ⓟ Ⓕ

A perfect marriage of flavours that looks mouthwatering when tucked inside a handsome savoy cabbage. Serve with aubergine/eggplant and pepper sauce (see page 193).

1 medium savoy cabbage
175 g/6 oz parsnips, peeled and sliced
175 g/6 oz/1½ cups walnuts, coarsely chopped
225 g/8 oz/1 cup cottage or curd cheese
100 g/4 oz/½ cup Quark, puréed cottage cheese or plain yoghurt
1 large egg, hard-boiled and chopped
25 g/1 oz/¼ cup Parmesan cheese, grated
seasoning to taste

Wash the cabbage and remove outer leaves as necessary. Plunge into a pan of boiling water and blanch for 2 minutes, then drain well. Boil the parsnips until soft then chop roughly. Mix well with the remaining ingredients. Pre-heat the oven to 200°C/400°F/Gas mark 6. Open out as many of the outer cabbage leaves as possible to provide pockets for the stuffing. Then, using a small sharp knife, very carefully remove the centre leaves of the cabbage, taking care not to damage the base. Fill the centre and the outer leaves with the parsnip mixture. Wrap the cabbage in foil or place in a roasting bag and bake for about 45 minutes or until the cabbage feels tender when pierced with a skewer and the filling is firm.

Terrine verte ㊺ P F

An attractively-striped and well-flavoured dish which needs a mild and creamy sauce to accompany it. Try any of those on page 193, and serve with a crisp salad.

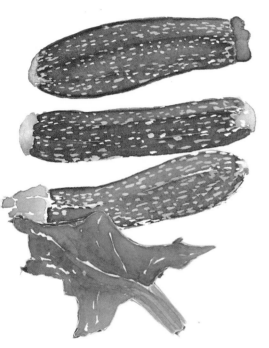

675 g/1½ lb spinach leaves, washed and drained
25 g/1 oz/2 tablespoons butter
1 courgette/zucchini
2 eggs
50 g/2 oz/½ cup Gruyère cheese, grated
50 g/2 oz/¼ cup Ricotta cheese (see page 55)
3 tablespoons Quark or puréed cottage cheese
seasoning to taste
300 ml/10 fl oz/1¼ cups cabbage and coriander
purée (see page 138)

Cook the spinach leaves in the butter over a low heat until soft. Chop coarsely and leave to cool. Cut out small 'U'-shaped channels along the length of the courgette/zucchini. Boil it for 3-4 minutes in a little salted water. Drain and cool. Slice into 5-mm/¼-inch pieces shaped like cog wheels. Purée the spinach with its liquid and add the eggs, cheeses and seasoning. Pre-heat the oven to 200°C/400°F/Gas mark 6. Generously butter a 1.2-litre/2-pint/5-cup terrine or loaf pan and pour in about 1 cm/½ inch of the cabbage and coriander purée. Into this stand some of the courgette/zucchini cog wheels, well spaced, in any pattern you choose. Cover with a layer of spinach purée, then another layer of the cabbage and coriander. Arrange a few more courgette/zucchini pieces in different places. You should be able to get in six layers altogether. Cover with buttered greaseproof/waxed paper and cook in a bain marie (see page 53) for 40-45 minutes. Let the terrine rest for 10 minutes before unmoulding. Then refrigerate for 2-3 hours or 1 day.

Terrine rose ㊺ P F

A prettily-coloured dish in shades of cream and peach. Serve as a first course with mayonnaise (see page 129), or eat with steamed vegetables as a main course.
Variation
● *Place a sheet of nori between each layer of the terrine. Apart from tasting good, it helps define the different colours.*

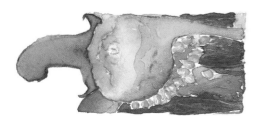

2 or 3 celeriac, peeled and chopped
1 red pepper, peeled (see page 52)
2 eggs
25 g/1 oz/2 tablespoons butter
75 g/3 oz/¾ cup Cheddar cheese, grated
300 g/10 oz/1¼ cups Quark or puréed cottage cheese
seasoning to taste
300 ml/10 fl oz/1¼ cups carrot and apricot
purée (see page 139)

Steam the celeriac until tender. Cut the pepper flesh into small diamond shapes. Purée the celeriac with the eggs, butter, cheeses and seasoning. Butter a 1.2-litre/2-pint/5-cup terrine or loaf pan and pour in 2 cm/1 inch of celeriac purée. Dot some pieces of pepper in it, and cover with carrot purée. Alternate the purées and the pattern of the pepper pieces until the terrine is full. Cover and cook as terrine verte.

 # Pasta

Italy consumes more pasta than any other country in the world and is the nation most strongly associated with it. However, the Chinese have eaten pasta for centuries and it is also made and eaten in Spain, Greece, the Middle East, North Africa and the United States. Nowadays, it is possible to buy pasta made from wholewheat and buckwheat, and traditional pasta is also available in several colours, depending on what ingredients were used to make it. All varieties come in a bewildering range of shapes and sizes.

There is a vast number of pasta dishes and those in this section are but a tiny number of my own favourites. Almost any vegetable sauce can be layered with pasta sheets, covered with a cheese sauce and baked in the oven. The plainest noodle is changed out of recognition by a sauce made with fresh herbs and, of them all, a basil sauce is perhaps supreme. But it is well worth experimenting with sauces based on seaweeds, as in spaghetti nori.

Pasta is one of the most versatile foodstuffs ever created, and lends itself to being successfully reheated, so nothing need go to waste. The mixtures we call croquettes, rissoles, cakes or balls are nearly always made from leftovers. If the food is not more than a day old, these can work well and are often more delicious than the original dishes. I must admit that anything called a rissole or a croquette usually depresses my appetite. I have therefore experimented with various combinations and I believe the ones I include in this section are light and well-flavoured.

Spaghetti nori ⑤ Ⓟ

Carbonara sauce is a popular one which some vegetarians miss, so here is a good alternative. You can use a sea vegetable like nori instead of the ham or bacon. The salt and mineral flavour of the nori imparts a bite to the pasta, and is the most adaptable and easy to cook of the sea vegetables. This dish is nutritionally high in protein, vitamins and minerals. It serves four as a light lunch or starter, or makes a substantial main course for two.

225 g/½ lb buckwheat spaghetti
4 nori sheets
3 tablespoons soy sauce
2 tablespoons water
3 eggs, beaten
50 g/2 oz/4 tablespoons butter
100 g/¼ lb mushrooms, thinly sliced
generous handful of chopped parsley
seasoning to taste

Cook the spaghetti in plenty of salted, boiling water (see page 49). Meanwhile, scissor two of the nori sheets into small strips and simmer in the soy sauce and water for 3 minutes. Add the nori and its liquid to the beaten eggs. Drain the spaghetti carefully. Melt the butter in a large saucepan and cook the mushrooms until just soft. Pour in some of the egg mixture followed immediately by the pasta. Stir well, then remove from the heat and pour in the rest of the egg mixture with most of the parsley and seasoning. Toss well so the egg cooks from the heat of the spaghetti. Transfer to a serving dish. Grill/broil the remaining nori until bubbly and partially green. Crumble over the spaghetti with the parsley and serve immediately.

Lasagne verde ㉚ P F

This is my favourite lasagne dish, which I sometimes make on my birthday, as it takes advantage of the summer pea crop. It serves 10-12 people, so is ideal for a big dinner party.

900 g/2 lb spinach leaves
900 g/2 lb fresh peas, shelled
450 g/1 lb courgettes/zucchini, sliced
300 ml/10 fl oz/1¼ cups single/light cream
12-14 lasagne sheets, boiled and drained (see page 49)
225 g/½ lb/2 cups Parmesan cheese, grated
225 g/½ lb/2 cups Gruyère cheese, grated
freshly ground black pepper
225 g/½ lb/2 cups mature/sharp Cheddar cheese, grated
300 ml/10 fl oz/1¼ cups béchamel sauce (see page 191)

Pre-heat the oven to 200°C/400°F/Gas mark 6. Chop and cook the spinach without water over a very low flame for about 5 minutes. Drain and reserve the liquid for the cheese sauce. Boil the peas and steam the courgettes/zucchini above them. Add the courgettes/zucchini to the spinach. Blend the peas to a thin purée with the cream. Butter a shallow dish and line the bottom and sides with lasagne. Add half the Parmesan and Gruyère to the spinach mixture, stir well then pour over the lasagne. Now pour the pea purée over the top and season with black pepper. You will not need salt because of the Parmesan. Place another layer of lasagne over the top. Make a béchamel sauce then add all the remaining cheese and spinach liquid. Leave to cool, then pour over the pasta. Bake for about 30 minutes, or until the top is brown.

Baked rigatoni ⑮ P F

Rigatoni are large ridged tubes used in baked dishes. This is a nice pasta because you can mix it up with a lot of sauce which will go inside the tubes as well as outside, hence you end up with a kind of pasta dish I like most of all where there is more sauce than pasta.

1 medium sized cauliflower
450 g/1 lb leeks
50 g/2 oz/4 tablespoons butter
25 g/1 oz/2 tablespoons plain/all-purpose flour
500 ml/10 fl oz/1¼ cups milk
seasoning to taste
150 g/6 oz rigatoni, boiled and drained (see page 49)
75 g/3 oz/¾ cup Gruyère cheese, grated
25 g/1 oz/¼ cup Parmesan cheese, grated
300 ml/10 fl oz/1¼ cups single/light cream

Pre-heat the oven to 200°C/400°F/Gas mark 6. Cut the cauliflower into florets, boil for 4 to 5 minutes and drain well. Trim the leeks and slice into 2-cm/1-inch chunks. Melt the butter in a pan and add the leeks; cover and cook for 10 minutes over a low heat. Sprinkle in the flour and add the milk and seasoning. Butter a large, shallow oven dish and spread the cauliflower and rigatoni over the bottom. Sprinkle with the cheeses, then stir in the leek sauce. Pour the cream over the top and bake for 20 minutes.

Cannelloni alla funghi trapanese ㉚ Ⓟ Ⓕ

It is preferable to use cannelloni sheets or small lasagne sheets for this recipe. Dried cannelloni tubes end up with very little 'bite' and need a lot of liquid to cook, which can dilute the stuffing.

8-10 cannelloni sheets, boiled and drained (see page 49)
For the stuffing
450 g/1 lb mushrooms
3 tablespoons olive oil
3 garlic cloves, crushed
450 g/1 lb tomatoes, skinned and chopped (see page 52)
1 tablespoon ground marjoram
1 tablespoon potato flour/starch
seasoning to taste
For the sauce
6 tablespoons dry red wine
1 tablespoon walnut oil
300 g/10 oz/1¼ cups Ricotta cheese (see page 55)
seasoning to taste

Pre-heat the oven to 200°C/400°F/Gas mark 6. Slice the mushrooms thinly. Heat the olive oil and cook the garlic and mushrooms in it. After a few minutes, add the tomatoes, marjoram, flour and seasoning. Continue to cook for 8-10 minutes until the liquid is reduced by a third. Taste and check the seasoning. Generously butter a large, shallow oven dish. Place some of the stuffing on each cannelloni sheet, roll them up tightly and lay them in the dish. Mix all the sauce ingredients together and pour over the cannelloni. Bake for 15 minutes.

Gnocchi di patate ⑳ Ⓟ Ⓕ

These are small balls of potato which are gently poached before eating. Italian cooks emphasize the necessity of floury/baking potatoes in this recipe to prevent the gnocchi breaking up when poached. It is also wise to purée the potatoes by hand or in a food mill; a food processor makes them too sticky. This recipe makes enough for six people as first course. Serve with a crisp salad and any pasta sauce (see page 192).

900 g/2 lb potatoes, such as King Edwards or russet
1 egg
1 teaspoon sea salt
200 g/7 oz/1¾ cups plain/all-purpose flour

Cook the potatoes and mash to a purée. Add the egg, salt and most of the flour. The mixture should be soft, smooth and slightly sticky. Knead for at least 5 minutes. Shape the mixture into sausage-like rolls about 2 cm/1 inch in diameter and cut into 1.5-cm/¾-inch pieces. To help hold the sauce, shape the gnocchi with a fork or butter pat so that they are ridged (see page 57). Place about two dozen gnocchi in a large pan of lightly-salted boiling water and cook for about 30 seconds, or until they rise to the surface. Drain well and transfer to a heated dish. Sprinkle with Parmesan and serve.

Walnut and buckwheat croquettes ㉟ Ⓟ Ⓕ

As buckwheat is such a lightweight cereal, these croquettes are particularly good. If, in the past, you have found nut mixtures stodgy, try these and surprise yourself. This recipe makes five handsome-size croquettes, enough to feed 4 people as a light lunch. Double the amounts if more are needed. Serve with tomato and malt whisky sauce, or salsa romesco (see pages 192 and 246).

225 g/8 oz/2 cups cooked buckwheat
100 g/4 oz/1 generous cup broken walnuts
4 garlic cloves, crushed
2 teaspoons oregano
1 egg, beaten
seasoning to taste
wholewheat breadcrumbs, toasted (see page 48)
corn or sunflower oil for frying

Mix the first six ingredients together thoroughly. Fashion into croquettes and roll in the breadcrumbs. Refrigerate for about 30 minutes, then fry in a little oil over a medium heat until crisp and golden.

Potato and rice croquettes ㉕ Ⓟ Ⓕ

This recipe is the simplest one of all and an excellent foil to a spicy stew or curry (see pages 151 and 154). You can flavour these croquettes with almost any spice or herb, but fresh herbs suit potato and rice the best.

450 g/1 lb potatoes, cooked and mashed
225 g/8 oz/1¼ cups rice, cooked
generous handful of parsley, finely chopped
seasoning to taste
1 egg, beaten
toasted sesame seeds for coating (see page 56)
corn oil for frying

Thoroughly mix the first 5 ingredients. Leave to stand for 1 hour. Shape into cakes, roll in the sesame seeds and shallow-fry in 1 cm/½ inch oil until brown and crisp.

Lentil, carrot and nut rissole ㉚ Ⓟ Ⓕ

This is a delicious creation, having a crunchy outside and a soft interior. The rissoles are easier to fry if refrigerated for 30 minutes after they have been shaped. Serve with a tomato sauce (see page 192).

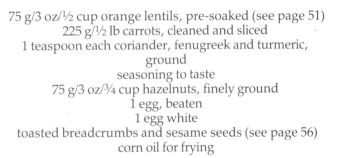

75 g/3 oz/½ cup orange lentils, pre-soaked (see page 51)
225 g/½ lb carrots, cleaned and sliced
1 teaspoon each coriander, fenugreek and turmeric, ground
seasoning to taste
75 g/3 oz/¾ cup hazelnuts, finely ground
1 egg, beaten
1 egg white
toasted breadcrumbs and sesame seeds (see page 56)
corn oil for frying

Boil the lentils with the carrots for 30 minutes, or until the lentils are tender. Drain carefully. Stir in the spices and seasoning. Purée the lentil mixture, pour into a mixing bowl and add the nuts and beaten egg. Stir well and refrigerate for 30 minutes. Roll the mixture into about 10 sausage shapes, dip them in the egg white, breadcrumbs and sesame seeds, then fry until crisp and brown.

Italian pasta balls ⑳ P

These are excellent and can be made from any leftover pasta. They are much lighter than they appear and should be served with a good sauce, such as aubergine/eggplant and pepper, tomato or green sauce (see pages 192-193).

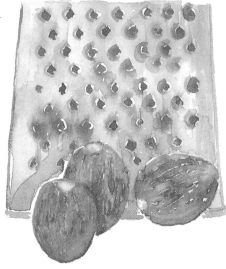

100 g/4 oz dried green tagliatelle
450/1 lb spinach leaves
100 g/4 oz/½ cup Ricotta cheese (see page 55)
50 g/2 oz/½ cup Gruyère cheese, grated
50 g/2 oz/½ cup Parmesan cheese, grated
2 tablespoons double/heavy cream
pinch of nutmeg
2 eggs
seasoning to taste
wholewheat breadcrumbs for coating (see page 48)
corn oil for frying

Cook the tagliatelle in plenty of boiling salted water until just soft. Drain well. Cook the spinach in a saucepan over a very low heat until it has reduced to one-third of its bulk. Drain well. Combine the pasta and spinach and blend to a rough purée. Add the rest of the ingredients, except one of the eggs and the breadcrumbs. Mix well. Place the mixture in a bowl and refrigerate for 1 hour. Beat the remaining egg. Fashion the chilled pasta mixture into balls, dip in the egg and coat with the breadcrumbs. Refrigerate again for 30 minutes, then shallow- or deep-fry until golden.

Falafel ⑩ P F

In Israel there are falafel bars which serve these delicious balls made from chick peas tucked inside pitta bread. They are eaten with various pickles made from aubergine/eggplant, courgettes/zucchini and onions. In Egypt they are called 'ta'amia' and are made from beans. They can be served hot with a sauce, or eaten cold with salad.

225 g/8 oz/1⅓ cups chick peas, pre-soaked (see page 51)
½ teaspoon micronized/active dry yeast (see page 41)
2 large onions, minced or grated
5 garlic cloves, crushed
2 teaspoons each coriander, fennel, cumin and caraway, ground
2 eggs, beaten
seasoning to taste
corn oil for frying

Drain the chick peas, fast boil in fresh water for 10 minutes, then simmer for 2 hours, or until tender. Drain well and blend. Transfer to a large bowl, add all the other ingredients and mix thoroughly. Cover and leave in a warm place for 1 hour. Roll into small balls, and shallow- or deep-fry until crisp and brown.

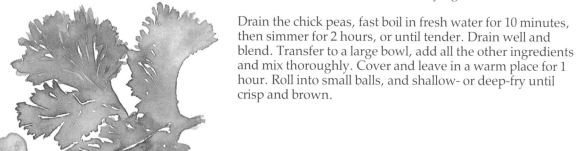

Mushroom and artichoke pudding ㉕ P F

The featherlight suet pastry in this pudding makes it a far cry from the institutional variety that you may remember from schooldays. Dried mushrooms have a greater intensity of flavour, which is closely sealed in this pudding, so that when you cut into the crust, the aromas are singularly enticing.

50 g/2 oz dried mushrooms
1 onion, finely chopped
225 g/8 oz canned artichoke hearts, drained and chopped
50 g/2 oz canned water chestnuts
3 courgettes/zucchini, sliced
bunch of parsley, chopped
For the dough
100 g/4 oz/⅔ cup shredded vegetable suet (see page 37)
175 g/6 oz/1½ cups strong white/all-purpose flour
1 teaspoon salt
1 tablespoon water
For the sauce
25 g/1 oz/2 tablespoons butter
1 tablespoon potato flour/starch
2 tablespoons soy sauce
150 ml/5 fl oz/⅔ cup dry white wine

Cover the mushrooms with cold water and soak for 5 hours. Drain and reserve the water. Mix all the dough ingredients together by hand. Roll out the dough thinly and use two-thirds to line a 1.7-litre/3-pint/2-quart pudding basin/ steaming mould. Lightly mix the vegetables and parsley together and place in the dough case. Make a roux from the butter and flour (see page 191), and then stir in the mushroom liquid, soy sauce and wine to make a smooth sauce. Pour over the vegetables. Roll out the remaining dough and fit on top of the pudding basin. Cover it with foil and tie securely with string. Steam in a covered pan for 2 hours (see page 200).

Scottish white pudding ⑩ P F

A traditional Scottish dish which is marvellous for cold winter days. It can be sliced and fried in oil for breakfast, or served with a sauce, such as tomato and black olive (see page 192), as part of a main meal.

225 g/8 oz/⅓ cups coarse/Scotch oatmeal
100 g/4 oz/⅔ cup shredded vegetable suet (see page 37)
2 large onions, thinly sliced
1 egg
2 teaspoons ground sage
1 teaspoon ground thyme
seasoning to taste

Roast the oatmeal by putting it in a dry pan and letting it brown slightly. Pour it into a large mixing bowl and add all the other ingredients. Place in a white cloth and tie tightly and securely. Bring a pan of water to the boil and place the pudding in it. Simmer for 1½ hours. Let the pudding cool, take from the cloth and slice it, then fry in olive oil and serve.

Rice and Grains

The dried seeds of various grasses are man's oldest food. The seed is a plant's storehouse of fuel, and for its size it is one of the richest sources of nutrition known to us. In the ancient world they rightly respected this treasure and named gods after grains.

Agricultural science and modern technology have improved and perfected the cultivation of many grains. We now have a 'green revolution', in which grain harvests can yield a third more, or even double than fifty years ago. Yet the tragedy is that we can still not feed the hungry world. We grow enough grain to be able to give two pounds to each person per day, but half of the grain cultivated in the world is taken by the West to feed livestock and factory-farmed animals, which are to be killed for meat. Another third of the half left is taken by the West for its own consumption.

All grains yield a flour, the most widely used being wheat flour. People suffering from an allergy to gluten and especially wheat gluten, have to experiment with other flours. These are as nutritious and often have more flavour than wheat flours (see page 84). Ideally we should all experiment and try foods that we are unfamiliar with.

We have learned from Chapter 1 that we should eat more whole grains in our diet, and there are many to choose from, buckwheat, bulgar, millet and cous cous being just a few. Use them instead of white rice for extra flavour and nutrition. Millet and cous cous have a slight nutty taste, which can be enhanced by the addition of a few chopped nuts. Any leftovers are useful for other dishes, like croquettes, so don't worry if you cook too much. They can also be added to thicken soups, stews and stuffings. I include two recipes for pilafs in this section, but almost any combination of vegetables and herbs can be chopped and added to grains. Rice and grains are both valuable sources of nutrition and flavour, so don't be afraid to experiment.

Risotto alla valtellinese ⑩ P F

The Italian dish, risotto, has many variations, but should always be made with a medium-grained rice. The risotto should be moist, with separate, al dente grains. The Italians traditionally use arborio rice and cook it to perfection very slowly on top of the stove with frequent stirring to avoid sticking. However, I make risotto in the oven and have always used long grain Patna rice, as I believe it is easier to keep this rice tender but al dente. This recipe is from Lombardy.

75 g/3 oz/6 tablespoons butter
2 tablespoons olive oil
150 g/6 oz/1½ cups broad/fava beans, shelled
1 medium savoy cabbage, finely sliced
275 g/10 oz/1½ cups Patna/long-grain rice
2 teaspoons sage, finely chopped
seasoning to taste
900 ml/1½ pints/3¾ cups vegetable stock (see page 110)
50 g/2 oz/½ cup Parmesan cheese, freshly grated

Pre-heat the oven to 200°C/400°F/Gas mark 6. Melt half the butter with the oil in a casserole and add the beans, cabbage and rice. Stir well and sprinkle in the sage and seasoning. Then add the stock and let it simmer for a minute before covering the dish and baking for 20 minutes. Remove from the oven and stir in the cheese. Check the seasoning before adding the remainder of the butter and serving.

Wild rice forestière is a mouthwatering combination of wild mushrooms sautéed in butter and served on a bed of al dente wild rice (see page 173).

 # Biryani ⑳ [F]

Created by chefs of the Moghul emperors, these dishes were originally highly complicated with many layers of rice, meat, fish and vegetables, all spiced in different ways. The rice is partly cooked before the dish is composed, and then baked in the oven. This recipe makes eight generous servings.

3 tablespoons corn oil
1 large onion and 5 garlic cloves, finely chopped
5-cm/2-inch piece root ginger, finely sliced
juice of 1 lemon
225 g/½ lb mushrooms, cleaned
225 g/½ lb each spinach, parsnips and swede/rutabaga, chopped small
1 head of celery, chopped small
sea salt
First spices
3 green cardamoms
1 teaspoon each cumin, coriander, fenugreek and asafoetida
½ teaspoon chilli powder

Rice
450 g/1 lb/2½ cups basmati rice
2 tablespoons milk
¼ teaspoon saffron
corn oil for frying
1 onion, chopped
150 ml/5 fl oz/⅔ cup vegetable stock (see page 110)
Second spices
3 green cardamoms and 3 whole cloves
2-cm/1-inch piece cassia bark
1 blade mace and 3 bay leaves
For garnish
2 tablespoons each raisins, currants and chopped almonds

Pre-heat the oven to 180°C/350°F/Gas mark 4. Heat the oil and fry the onion, garlic, ginger and first spices until the onion is soft. Add the lemon juice, vegetables and salt. Cover the pan and simmer over a low heat for 30 minutes. Meanwhile, boil the rice in salted water for 5 minutes. Drain and set to one side. Warm the milk and soak the saffron in it.

Heat a little oil and fry the onion. Add the milk, saffron and stock. Pour in the rice and heat, then strain again, reserving the liquid. Place half the rice in the bottom of an oven dish. Scatter the second lot of spices over it. Cover with the vegetables and then the remaining rice. Pour in the stock. Cover and bake for 45 minutes. Garnish before serving.

Persian millet pilaf ⑩ [V] [P] [F]

A classic Middle-Eastern dish. Millet has a pleasant nutty flavour, so it goes well with any other dish containing nuts. Alternatively, try serving it with a layered terrine as shown on page 159.

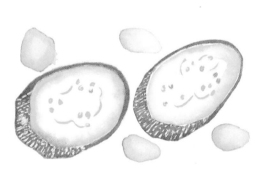

4 tablespoons olive oil
3 garlic cloves, crushed
150 g/6 oz/¾ cup millet
4 courgettes/zucchini, thinly sliced
2 onions, thinly sliced
2 green peppers, cored, seeded and sliced
50 g/2 oz/½ cup toasted almonds, chopped
3 tablespoons mint, chopped
juice and zest of 1 lemon
seasoning to taste

Heat half the oil in a large pan and add the garlic and millet. Cover with boiling water and simmer for 20 minutes, adding a little more water if it looks like drying out. Meanwhile, heat the rest of the oil in another pan and add the vegetables. Cover and simmer until just soft. When the millet is cooked, stir in the vegetables and the remaining ingredients. Stir well and heat for a second before serving.

Buckwheat pilaf ⑩ V F

Buckwheat makes a light dish and when stir-fried, as it is in this recipe, it is quite delicious. Eat it with a crisp salad, or any of the curry dishes (see pages 154-157).

100 g/6 oz/1 cup buckwheat groats
100 g/4 oz baby sweetcorn or ears of corn
2 tablespoons toasted sesame oil
3 garlic cloves, crushed
450 g/1 lb tomatoes, peeled and chopped (see page 52)
1 bunch spring onions/scallions, chopped
seasoning to taste

Place the buckwheat in a saucepan, cover with boiling water and simmer for 5 minutes. Keep the baby sweetcorn whole, but slice larger ears thinly. Heat the oil and fry the garlic. Add all the vegetables and stir-fry for 2 minutes. Drain the buckwheat and add to the pan. Stir-fry for another minute, season and then serve.

Saffron rice ⑤

Though saffron is absurdly expensive, one needs merely a pinch to colour and flavour a dish. No substitute will do for the particular colour of the rice is 24-carat gold. Serve with curries or bean stews (see pages 151-157).

Variation
● *To pep up plain boiled rice, gently fry 2 chopped onions, 3 crushed garlic cloves and 2 seeded, chopped green chillies, until soft. Add 1 teaspoon each ground cumin and coriander seeds, and 2 or 3 ground cardamoms. Fry for a minute, then stir into the rice.*

2 tablespoons milk
good pinch of saffron
600 ml/1 pint/2½ cups water
seasoning to taste
225 g/8 oz/1¼ cups Patna or basmati rice, washed
nuts and raisins for garnish

Warm the milk and soak the saffron for 20 minutes. Boil the water with the seasoning, then add the rice and saffron milk. Lower the heat and simmer for 7 to 10 minutes, until the rice is cooked through and the water absorbed. Turn on to a platter and garnish with nuts and raisins.

Wild rice forestière ⑮ P F

If you want to arouse the palate and please the eye, this is the perfect dish. Serve it at a special dinner party with a crisp green salad.

225 g/8 oz/1½ cups wild rice
450 g/1 lb mixed mushrooms: button, oyster, shiitake, pleurotes, dried morels, or boletus
25 g/1 oz/2 tablespoons butter
2 tablespoons sunflower oil
100 g/¼ lb shallots, peeled and chopped (see page 52)
2 tablespoons soy sauce
few fresh tarragon leaves
freshly ground black pepper to taste

Cook the rice (see page 50). Meanwhile, trim, clean and slice the mushrooms. Heat the butter and oil and fry the shallots until soft. Raise the heat and add the mushrooms, stirring constantly for a few minutes. Add the soy sauce. Remove from the heat, stir in the tarragon and season.

Savoury Pastries

I used to think it was impossible to make edible wholewheat pastry. I have been proved wrong, but I must add that it is very easy to make something brittle and bland.

The secret of making moist and crumbly wholewheat pastry is to work carefully and to add water cautiously. It is a good idea to add lemon juice instead of water because the ascorbic acid breaks down the gluten and helps to give the necessary crumbly texture.

The next golden rule to remember is that the flavour of your pastry will only be as good as your shortening. For the best texture, half butter and half vegetable fat is necessary. Use your shortening straight from the refrigerator, and grate it into the flour using a cheese grater. This is much easier than mixing it in with two knives, and makes the rubbing in by hand much quicker.

All pastry benefits hugely from a resting period in a cool atmosphere after being made. If you find it difficult to roll out, try sandwiching it between plastic wrap and rolling it out within that (see page 48).

In this section I give recipes for three types of pastry dish: tarts, quiches and pies. A tart is a pastry case in which vegetables are cooked with cream, or tofu. It appears not quite set and should run slightly when you cut it. A quiche is a pastry case in which vegetables are cooked with all or some of the tart ingredients, plus eggs. When cooked, the quiche is set and slightly firm.

Basically, there are two kinds of pie: one where the mixture is simply covered with a pastry lid, and one where the pastry also lines the pie dish and soaks up the flavours and juices from the filling. The main characteristic of a good pie is that it should have a delicious sauce. The pies I give are all extremely tasty, and can be made with either shortcrust/basic pie pastry or puff pastry.

Basic wholewheat pastry ⑤ P F

One of the secrets of successful pastry-making is to keep ingredients, utensils and your hands as cold as possible. This recipe makes enough pastry to line a dish 23 cm/9 inches in diameter and approximately 2 cm/1 inch deep.

Variations
Make the following substitutions for the wholewheat flour.
Oatmeal pastry   Use 100 g/4 oz/generous 1 cup oatmeal with 100 g/4 oz/1 cup wholewheat flour.

Cheese pastry   Mix 50 g/2 oz/½ cup finely grated hard cheese with the fats in the basic pastry recipe.

Sweet pastry   Use half wholewheat and half unbleached white flour. Mix with ¼ teaspoon salt, 150g/5oz/⅔ cup unsalted butter, 2 tablespoons mild honey, and 1 tablespoon ice-cold water if needed.

225 g/8 oz/2 cups wholewheat flour
½ teaspoon sea salt
50 g/2 oz/4 tablespoons unsalted butter
50 g/2 oz/4 tablespoons hard vegetable shortening
1 tablespoon lemon juice
1 tablespoon cold water

Sift the flour and then return the bran to the bowl. Add the salt and quickly grate both fats into the flour. Rub the mixture with your fingers until it resembles fine breadcrumbs. Now add the lemon juice and begin to make a dough. If it will not bind add the water. Divide into two balls and refrigerate for 1 hour before using.

*What could be more refreshing on a hot
summer's day than this cool, glazed tart?
The filling is a light mixture of soft
cheese, yoghurt, cucumber and
mint (see page 176).*

Cucumber and mint tart ㉑ P F

Refreshing to look at and delicious to eat, this tart never fails to please. It goes well with the avocado purée on page 189. Serve this tart and all its variations at room temperature, not chilled. Use a 23-cm/9-inch pastry case.

1 cheese pastry case, baked blind (see pages 174 and 48)
1 large cucumber
sea salt
150 g/5 oz/⅔ cup curd/small curd cottage cheese
75 ml/3 fl oz/6 tablespoons Greek yoghurt (see page 45)
or Quark or puréed cottage cheese
1 tablespoon lemon juice
2 teaspoons agar agar or arrowroot dissolved in 2 tablespoons boiling water (see page 40)
bunch of fresh mint
Glaze (optional)
3 tablespoons lime marmalade
1 tablespoon water
1 tablespoon fresh lime juice

Coarsely grate one-third of the cucumber and slice the remainder thinly. Place in separate colanders, sprinkle with salt and leave for about 1 hour to draw out excess liquid. Meanwhile, mix the remaining ingredients thoroughly. Rinse both lots of cucumber and pat dry. Add the grated cucumber to the curd/cottage cheese mixture, then spoon this filling into the pastry case. Smooth down the surface, then arrange the cucumber slices in an overlapping circular pattern on top. If you wish to glaze the tart, melt the marmalade in the water, add the lime juice and strain through a fine sieve. Brush the glaze over the cucumber, then leave to set. Garnish with a sprig of mint.

Variations

Watercress and spring onion/scallion tart
Substitute 1 bunch of watercress and 1 bunch of spring onions/scallions for the cucumber and mint.

Chop the cress and onions finely, mix with the rest of the ingredients and pile into the pastry case. Decorate with a few more leaves of cress.

Avocado and lemon tart *Substitute the cucumber and mint with 2 ripe avocados, 2-3 tablespoons aïoli mayonnaise (see page 129) and a little parsley.*

Purée the flesh of 1 avocado with the lemon juice and zest. Mix with the curd/cottage cheese and yoghurt and season well. Pile into the pastry case and decorate with slices of the other avocado. Cover with the mayonnaise and garnish with the parsley.

Celery and courgette/zucchini tart
Substitute the central stalks of 1 head of celery and 225 g/½ lb baby courgettes/zucchini for the cucumber and mint.

Grate the courgettes/zucchini into a bowl and slice the celery very finely. Mix well with the rest of the ingredients and pile into the pastry case. Garnish with parsley.

Potato and mint tart ⑳

Another classic marriage of flavours. The addition of raw kohlrabi gives texture to this lovely tart. It is better warm than hot, and is excellent cold.

1 wholewheat pastry case, baked blind
(see pages 174 and 48)
450 g/1 lb potatoes
1 large kohlrabi
75 g/3 oz/scant ½ cup tofu
150 ml/5 fl oz/⅔ cup single/light cream
150 ml/5 fl oz/⅔ cup plain yoghurt or Smetana/low-fat
sour cream
seasoning to taste
a generous handful of mint

Peel and boil the potatoes for 15 minutes. Drain well and slice into 2-mm/⅛-inch rounds. Peel and grate the kohlrabi into a bowl and mash in the tofu. Add the cream, yoghurt seasoning and mint and mix well. Pre-heat the oven to 200°C/400°F/Gas mark 6. Lay the potato in the pastry case and smooth the kohlrabi mixture between the potato pieces until the tart is full. Bake for 20 minutes, or until the top is just crisp and brown.

Variations
Root vegetable and onion tart
Substitute sweet potatoes, parsnips, swede/ rutubaga or turnips for the potatoes.

Boil for only 3 minutes. Grate 1 large onion instead of the kohlrabi, and use 2-3 tablespoons of fresh tarragon, finely chopped, instead of the mint.

Potato, marrow/squash and lemon tart
Substitute half a small marrow/winter squash, peeled, seeded and chopped, for the kohlrabi, and 2 lemons for the mint. Serve with sautéed mushrooms and steamed broccoli.

Melt 50 g/2 oz/4 tablespoons of butter in a pan and fry the marrow/squash with the zest of 1 lemon for 4 or 5 minutes. Squeeze in the juice from 1 lemon and cook for another minute. Mix thoroughly with the other ingredients. Spread over the potatoes in the pastry case. Bake as described earlier. Garnish with the second lemon, thinly sliced, and return to the oven for a minute so that the lemon is hot.

Leek and green peppercorn tart (25) [P] [F]

A deliciously light summer tart in shades of green. Serve with a crisp green salad and you have a perfect lunch.

1 wholewheat pastry case, baked blind
(see pages 174 and 48)
675 g/1½ lb leeks
50 g/2 oz/4 tablespoons butter
1 teaspoon green peppercorns
150 g/5 oz/⅔ cup Quark or puréed cottage cheese mixed
with 150 ml/5 fl oz/⅔ cup milk
seasoning to taste

Pre-heat the oven to 200°C/400°F/Gas mark 6. Slice the leeks lengthways and clean them, then cut them across into 5-mm/½-inch slices. Melt the butter in a pan and cook the leeks over a low flame for 5-7 minutes, or until soft. Pour into a bowl, add the rest of the ingredients and mix thoroughly. Pour into the pastry case and bake for 15 minutes.

Variations
Fresh pea and courgette/zucchini tart
Omit the butter, and use 450 g/1 lb fresh peas and 225 g/½ lb courgettes/zucchini instead of the leeks and peppercorns.

Boil the peas for 5-10 minutes, until cooked. Slice the courgettes/zucchini and steam briefly. Purée the peas, cream and seasoning, pour into the pastry case and decorate with the courgettes/zucchini.

Broccoli tart *Use 225 g/½ lb broccoli instead of the peas.*

Follow the instructions for the previous variation.

Watercress and asparagus tart *Use 1 bunch watercress and 225 g/½ lb fresh asparagus instead of the leeks and peppercorns.*

Trim and steam the asparagus, cut off the tips and reserve. Chop the watercress and fry in the butter for a few minutes. Blend the asparagus with the cream and seasoning. Mix with the watercress and bake as described earlier. Garnish with the asparagus tips in the last few minutes of baking.

Mushroom and red pepper tart
Substitute the leeks, peppercorns and butter with 225 g/½ lb mushrooms, 1 red pepper, cored, and 3 tablespoons olive oil.

Slice the mushrooms and pepper thinly and fry slowly in the oil for about 8 minutes. Leave to cool, then mix with the cream and seasoning, and bake as before.

Tomato and pumpkin quiche ㉛ Ⓟ Ⓕ

A delicious combination of flavours with crumbly oatmeal pastry.

1 oatmeal pastry case, baked blind (see pages 174 and 48)
50 g/2 oz/4 tablespoons butter
225 g/½ lb pumpkin flesh, cut into small cubes
450 g/1 lb tomatoes, peeled and seeded (see page 52)
1 bunch of basil leaves
3 eggs
300 ml/10 fl oz/1¼ cups single/light cream
50 g/2 oz/½ cup Gruyère cheese, finely grated
seasoning to taste

Pre-heat the oven to 200°C/400°F/Gas mark 6. Heat the butter in a pan and cook the pumpkin for 5 to 6 minutes until it is crisp on the outside and has just begun to soften in the centre. Chop the tomato flesh coarsely and add to the pumpkin. Chop the basil leaves finely and add these with the rest of the ingredients. Stir thoroughly and pour into the pastry case. Bake for 25 minutes.

Variations

Mushroom and walnut quiche   *Omit the pumpkin, tomatoes, basil and half the butter, and substitute 225 g/½ lb mushrooms, sliced and 100 g/4 oz/1 cup walnuts, freshly shelled and roughly chopped.*

Fry the mushrooms over a low flame for about 8 minutes. Mix the walnuts with the rest of the ingredients and add to the mushrooms. Bake as before.

Broad/fava bean and pistachio quiche   *Omit the pumpkin, tomatoes, basil and butter, and substitute 450 g/1 lb fresh broad/ fava beans, shelled, 75 g/3 oz/⅔ cup pistachio nuts, shelled and 1 tablespoon summer savory, finely chopped.*

Boil the beans until soft (see page 51). Cool, then blend with the cream, eggs and savory. Chop the nuts coarsely and stir into the purée with the cheeses and seasoning. Bake as before.

Celeriac quiche   *Omit the pumpkin and basil, and substitute 225 g/½ lb diced celeriac, and a generous handful of chopped celery leaves.*

Cook the celeriac in the butter for about 10 minutes. Add the celery leaves with the rest of the ingredients, stir well and bake as before.

Spinach quiche ⑳ Ⓟ Ⓕ

A classic dish that looks appetizing and is both delicious and sustaining. Eat with tomato and basil salad (see page 120).

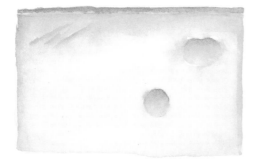

1 wholewheat pastry case, baked blind (see pages 174 and 48)
450 g/1 lb spinach leaves
50 g/2 oz/4 tablespoons butter
3 eggs, beaten
50 g/2 oz/¼ cup tofu
150 ml/5 fl oz/⅔ cup single/light cream
25 g/1 oz/¼ cup Parmesan cheese, grated
25 g/1 oz/¼ cup Gruyère cheese, grated
seasoning to taste

Pre-heat the oven to 200°C/400°F/Gas mark 6. Cook the spinach in the butter until it has reduced by one-third. Chop it coarsely with a wooden spoon, add the rest of the ingredients, mix thoroughly and pour into the pastry case. Bake for 25 minutes.

Variations

Cabbage and coriander quiche
Substitute half a medium-sized white/tight-head green cabbage for the spinach.

Slice the cabbage thinly and cook in the butter with 2 teaspoons of ground coriander until soft.

Swiss chard quiche   *Substitute 450 g/ 1 lb Swiss chard for the spinach.*

Cook the stalks in a little boiling water and chop them up finely when tender. Then add the butter and leaves, cook for about 5 minutes and proceed as before.

Kale quiche   *Substitute 250 g/1 lb kale for the Swiss chard.*

Boil the whole leaf for 2-3 minutes. Then chop it up and cook in the butter for a further 5 minutes.

Artichoke and mushroom quiche   ㉚ Ⓕ

Quick to make and good to eat, this quiche deserves a permanent place in your repertoire.

1 wholewheat pastry case, baked blind (see pages 174 and 48)
25 g/1 oz/2 tablespoons butter
225 g/½ lb mushrooms, cleaned and sliced
5 artichoke hearts
2 eggs, beaten
150 ml/5 fl oz/⅔ cup sour cream
50 g/2 oz/½ cup Gruyère cheese, grated
generous handful of chopped parsley
seasoning to taste

Pre-heat the oven to 200°C/400°F/Gas mark 6. Melt the butter, and cook the mushrooms until tender. Drive off the liquid by raising the heat. Add the rest of the ingredients, then pour into the pastry case and bake for 25 minutes.

Spiced potato and mushroom pie ㉚ P F

*The lightly curried filling in this traditional
English pie is particularly pleasant and
satisfying. It is rather like a large pakora.*

4 tablespoons olive oil
½ teaspoon each of mustard seeds, whole fenugreek,
cassia, cardomom, coriander and turmeric
25 g/1 oz root ginger, grated
1 onion, thinly sliced
450 g/1 lb potatoes, peeled and diced
225 g/½ lb mushrooms, stalks removed
seasoning to taste
For the sauce
1 teaspoon kuzu flour or arrowroot dissolved in 150 ml/
5 fl oz/⅔ cup stock or water
5 tablespoons soy sauce
1 tablespoon fresh coriander, chopped
juice of 1 lemon
75 g/6 oz shortcrust/basic pie pastry (see page 174)
1 egg, beaten, for glazing

Heat the olive oil in a pan and cook the spices and ginger for
a minute or two, before adding the onion, potatoes,
mushrooms and seasoning. Cover the pan and cook over a
gentle heat for 15 minutes. Pour into a pie dish. Pre-heat the
oven to 200°C/400°F/Gas mark 6. Make the sauce by bringing
the flour, stock and soy sauce to the boil. Once thickened,
add the coriander and lemon juice and pour over the
vegetables. Roll out the pastry to fit the top and glaze with
the egg. Bake for 25 to 30 minutes.

Variations
Sweet and sour pie *Substitute the
onions, potatoes and mushrooms with 450 g/
1 lb parsnips, 450 g/1 lb shallots, 75 g/3 oz/
scant ½ cup tofu and 2 hard-boiled eggs,
sliced. For the sauce use 25 g/1 oz/
2 tablespoons split pea flour, 25 g/1 oz/ 2
tablespoons butter, 6 tablespoons white wine
vinegar, 175 ml/6 fl oz/¾ cup vegetable
stock (see page 110) and 1 tablespoon honey.*

Scrub the parsnips and cut in small chunks. Peel the shallots
(see page 52) and boil with the parsnips in a little salted
water for 5 minutes. Drain and then fry for 5 minutes with
the spices. Place in a pie dish, cover with slices of egg and
crumble the tofu on top. Make the sauce and proceed as
before.

Two artichoke pie ㉕ P F

It is a pleasure to use two types of artichoke in this way, as they are similar in flavour, but totally different in texture. Serve with a steamed green vegetable, or raw grated carrots in lemon juice.

100 g/4 oz wholewheat pastry (see page 174)
4 large globe artichoke bottoms
225 g/½ lb Jerusalem artichokes
For the sauce
25 g/1 oz/2 tablespoons butter
25 g/1 oz/2 tablespoons potato flour/starch
300 ml/10 fl oz/1¼ cups dry white wine
75 g/3 oz/¾ cup Gruyère cheese, grated
chopped parsley (in sauce)
pinch of mace
2 bay leaves
seasoning to taste

Steam the globe artichokes for 30-40 minutes, discard the leaves and choke, but reserve the bottoms. Slice into quarters and place in a 1-litre/2-pint/1-quart pie dish. Clean but do not peel the Jerusalem artichokes and chop coarsely. Boil in a little salted water for 8 minutes. Drain and add to the globe artichokes. Pre-heat the oven to 200°C/400°F/Gas mark 6. Make a roux from the butter and flour (see page 191), then add the wine, cheese, parsley, mace, bay leaves and seasoning. Stir until you have a smooth sauce and pour in just enough to cover the vegetables. Roll out the pastry to fit the top of the pie and bake for 30 minutes.

Variation

Fennel and marrow/squash pie
Substitute 2 heads of fennel, 225 g/½ lb/1½ cups diced marrow/winter squash flesh, 25 g/ 1 oz/2 tablespoons butter, and 50 g/2 oz/¼ cup tofu for the previous filling. Omit the Gruyère in the sauce and substitute 25 g/1 oz grated root ginger and use half dry white wine, half vegetable stock to make 300 ml/10 fl oz/1¼ cups liquid.

Cook the marrow/squash in the butter until soft. Trim the fennel, slice into strips and boil in salted water for 5 minutes. Crumble the tofu into the drained fennel and marrow/ squash, and transfer to a pie dish. To make the sauce, sweat the ginger in the butter (see page 53), then make a roux in the usual way (see page 191). Proceed as above.

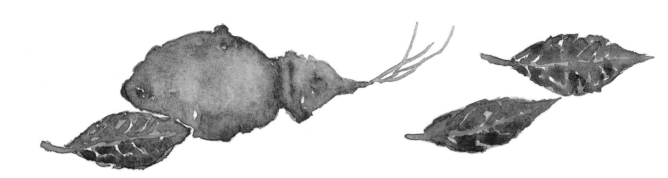

Pizza ⑳ P F

Pizzas are best made with a yeast dough. This is not difficult to make and will rise easily. It is a matter of taste whether to make the dough with unbleached strong white/all-purpose flour, wholewheat flour, or a mixture of both. I think pizzas taste good on any homemade base, but do remember that those made with wholewheat flour take longer to rise.

Variations

● *The fun of pizza lies in the almost infinite number of toppings you can devise. It is essential to start with a thick tomato sauce, but on this you can put anything that takes your fancy: olives, asparagus, pine nuts, raisins, fresh tomatoes, mushrooms, onions, Mozzarella, capers, herbs, garlic, tofu, spinach, eggs, or anything else that comes to mind. The final ingredient is a generous sprinkling of freshly-grated Parmesan; this gives the authentic taste of Italian pizza.*

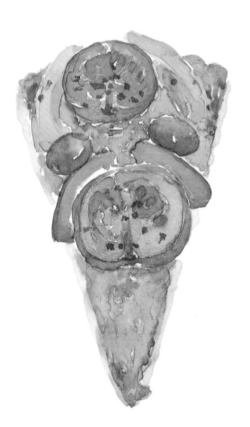

Dough
225 g/½ lb/2 cups strong white/all-purpose flour,
or 81% wholewheat flour, or 100% wholewheat flour
½ sachet micronized/active dry yeast (see page 41)
½ teaspoon sea salt
2 tablespoons olive oil
2 tablespoons warm milk
1 egg
2-3 tablespoons warm water

Mix all the ingredients together, knead thoroughly then cover and leave in a warm place to rise. Oil a baking sheet. Take the ball of dough and smooth it into a circular shape over the sheet with the sides of your hands, pressing and pulling it, and allowing a little more dough at the edges to hold in the filling. Cover with a cloth and leave for about 10 minutes before adding the filling.

Filling
1 medium-sized green pepper
2 medium-sized onions
2 tablespoons olive oil
1 teaspoon each of oregano and marjoram
5 garlic cloves, crushed
½ teaspoon sea salt
400-450 g/14-16 oz can of tomatoes
2 tablespoons tomato purée/paste
5 fresh tomatoes
2 tablespoons capers
12 black olives, stoned

Slice the pepper and onions. Heat the olive oil and fry the herbs for a few minutes, stir in the garlic, and then add the onions, pepper and salt. Cover and simmer over a low flame for 15 minutes, and then add the canned tomatoes. Bring to the boil then simmer again for 45 minutes. It should now be a thick sauce. Add the tomato purée/paste and cook uncovered for another 5 minutes so that the sauce thickens and reduces a little more. Smear this filling over the dough. Decorate with slices of fresh tomato, capers and olives. Let the pizza rest again for another 10 minutes. Heat the oven to 220°C/425°F/Gas mark 7 and bake the pizza for 15 minutes, then turn the oven down to 190°C/375°F/Gas mark 5 for a further 15 minutes. The filling should never dry out, so check at half time and if it looks too cooked, cover with foil. If you have any pizza left over, it can be gently warmed up in the oven, but it must be covered.

Basic pancakes ⑤ P F

This recipe makes 8 light, English-style pancakes (about 15 cm/6 inches in diameter) which are perfect for stuffing. If you want to use a sweet filling, add 1 teaspoonful of sugar or honey to the batter. For added richness and a thicker pancake you can use another egg, 1 teaspoonful of baking powder, and 1 tablespoonful of powdered skimmed milk.

100 g/4 oz/1 cup plain/all-purpose flour
100 g/4 oz/1 cup wholewheat flour
½ teaspoon salt
2 eggs
300 ml/10 fl oz/1¼ cups milk
300 ml/10 fl oz/1¼ cups water
corn or sunflower oil for frying

Sift the flours and salt into a bowl and return the bran from the sieve. Break in the eggs and mix to a thick paste. Combine the milk and water and whisk into the paste to make a thin batter. Leave for 1 hour, then whisk again just before using. Heat 1 teaspoonful of oil in a small frying pan and spread over the inside. Ladle in 2-3 tablespoons batter. Roll and tilt the pan until it covers the bottom. Cook rapidly until the surface begins to dry out. Turn over and cook the other side. Fill each pancake and fold (like an envelope) as soon as it is made. Arrange in a buttered shallow oven dish and dribble some sauce on top. Bake in a pre-heated oven at 190°C/375°F/Gas mark 5 for 10 minutes if the pancakes are cold, 5 minutes if warm.

Fillings

All the following fillings make enough to stuff 8 pancakes. They are also suitable as pie or tart fillings. Any that require cooking should be prepared beforehand, so the stuffed pancake will be in the oven no more than 10 minutes - any longer, and it will be leathery.

Ratatouille ⑮ V F

Although this is a vegetable stew, it makes a marvellous filling for pancakes and is part of a satisfying main meal if served with quiches or baked potatoes. It is excellent hot, warm or cold. If puréed, it also makes a good dip with crudités.

1 aubergine/eggplant, sliced and salted (see page 52)
6 tablespoons thick olive oil
2 onions, sliced
3 green peppers, cored and seeded
3 courgettes/zucchini, sliced
5 garlic cloves, sliced
675 g/1½ lb tomatoes, peeled and chopped (see page 52)
seasoning to taste

Heat the oil in a pan and fry the onions, peppers, courgettes/zucchini, garlic and aubergine/eggplant. Lower the heat and simmer gently for 20 minutes. Add the tomatoes and seasoning, and simmer for another 10 minutes until you have a rough purée.

Avocado and green pepper

*Do remember that avocado can be heated but
not cooked. If you want to make this filling in
advance, do not add the avocado until the last
few moments.*

50 g/2 oz/4 tablespoons butter
2 garlic cloves, crushed
1 green pepper, cored, seeded and sliced
1 small onion, sliced
1 ripe avocado, peeled, stoned and diced
150 ml/5 fl oz/²⁄₃ cup sour cream
3 tablespoons parsley, finely chopped
seasoning to taste

Melt the butter in a pan, add the garlic and then the pepper
and onion. Cook over a low heat for about 10 minutes, or
until just soft. Pour into a bowl and add the avocado with
the rest of the ingredients. Mix thoroughly.

Variations
Avocado, leek and Feta   *Substitute 2 or 3
leeks and 75 g/3 oz Feta cheese for the green
pepper, onion, garlic and parsley.*

Wash and trim the leeks, then slice into thin rings. Season
and cook in the melted butter until just soft. Crumble in the
Feta, stir well and cook for half a minute, until the cheese
just starts to become runny. Pour into a bowl, add the
avocado and sour cream, and mix thoroughly. (As Feta is
highly salted, you may not wish to add any extra salt.)

Avocado and turnip   *Substitute 75 g/3 oz
baby turnips, cooked and diced, and 1 bunch
spring onions/scallions, trimmed and chopped
for the green peppers, onion and butter.*

Mix all the ingredients together and use immediately.

Mushroom and celeriac

25 g/1 oz/2 tablespoons butter
225 g/½ lb mushrooms, thinly sliced
2 celeriac, peeled and sliced
100 g/4 oz/½ cup Quark or puréed cottage cheese or
Ricotta cheese (see page 55)
25 g/1 oz/¼ cup Gruyère cheese, grated
seasoning to taste

Melt the butter in a pan and cook the mushrooms until just
soft. Transfer to a mixing bowl. Steam the celeriac for about
15 minutes, then cut into small dice. Add to the mushrooms
with the rest of the ingredients. Mix thoroughly.

Purées, Sauces and Pickles

Purées are called 'dips' by some people. I think this is an unfortunate misuse of words, giving only an indication of what is done to the dish rather than what is in it. A purée which is stabbed by a stick of celery or sliced at with a cracker can quickly become an unsightly and unappetizing pottage.

Purées should be spooned out on to individual plates and then eaten with a fork or scooped up with bread. A plate of crudités with a selection of purées is a noble beginning to any meal, but people should be encouraged to stick the vegetables in their own serving, *not* in the communal pot.

Purées have many uses. They make an interesting stuffing for vegetables (see page 150), but remember to make the purées fairly firm - one does not want to be presented with a dry cleaning bill after a dinner party. They are also the basis of layered terrines.

When using a purée for another dish, it is important to remember one thing. If it is to be cooked, do not use a purée with an oil base. The oil tends to separate from the mixture, making the dish look and taste unpleasant. If the purée is made with a dairy product base, then it is perfect for baking; the butter becomes a binding agent.

Tapenade ③ Ⓥ ⑤

The classic tapenade includes anchovies, which add a resonance that I find quite unnecessary. The recipe below has all the flavour and resonance one could wish.

Variation
• *Follow the method for tapenade, but use half the oil to cook 225 g/½ lb of mushrooms. When they are soft, purée them in a blender with the rest of the ingredients, and taste before adding more salt.*

20 black olives, stoned
2 tablespoons capers
juice and zest of 1 lemon
5 garlic cloves, crushed
150 ml/5 fl oz/⅔ cup olive oil
seasoning to taste

Put all the ingredients in a blender or food processor and blend to a thick purée. Take care in adding salt, as both the olives and capers may well be salty enough.

Lentil purée ⑩ Ⓥ ⑤

All kinds of lentils make excellent purées, and when spiced are a staple part of Indian cuisine, known as dahls. Eat with curries, or serve with a mild-flavoured tart, such as avocado and lemon (see page 176).

Variation
• *If you want a thicker purée, place it in the oven for 20 minutes at 180°C/350°F/Gas mark 4, to evaporate the moisture.*

100 g/4 oz/½ cup yellow or orange lentils (see page 51)
2 bay leaves
1 tablespoon lemon juice
½ teaspoon coriander, ground
pinch of garam masala (see page 42)
3 garlic cloves, crushed
150 ml/5 fl oz/⅔ cup olive oil
seasoning to taste

Cover the lentils with boiling water and simmer for 20-30 minutes with the bay leaves. When soft, drain and remove the bay leaves. Transfer the lentils to a blender, add the rest of the ingredients and blend to a purée.

Spiced plums are an equally delectable variation of Spiced quinces. They are the perfect accompaniment to cheese (see page 197).

Skordalia ㉒ V

This is a purée for lovers of garlic and Greece. It is traditionally eaten with salt cod dishes, fried aubergine/eggplant and courgettes/ zucchini. It is also used as a first course.

2 slices homemade white bread
1 head of garlic, peeled and crushed (see page 52)
225 g/½ lb potatoes, peeled and steamed or boiled
juice and zest of 1 lemon
150 ml/5 fl oz/⅔ cup olive oil
seasoning to taste

Moisten the bread in water. Add the garlic to the potatoes and mix thoroughly. Squeeze all the water out of the bread and add to the potato mixture. Stir thoroughly and add the lemon juice and zest. Place everything in a food processor and liquidize at the slowest speed. (This may be done with a fork if you have no processor or blender.) Start adding the oil drop by drop, as you would when making mayonnaise. As the mixture absorbs the oil, pour in a steady stream and increase the speed of the machine. Add the seasoning.

Hummus ⑮ V P F

This is one of the most popular vegetable purées in the world. The earthy flavour of chick peas blended with the best olive oil, garlic and mint, is a most refreshing start to a meal. This is the classic recipe for hummus, but there are many variations.

Variations
• *For an even smoother paste add 150 g/ 5 oz/⅔ cup curd/small curd cottage cheese, fromage frais/cream cheese, Quark or puréed cottage cheese.*
• *For a lighter hummus, fold in a stiffly beaten egg white or some mayonnaise.*

175 g/6 oz/1 cup chick peas, pre-soaked (see page 51)
2 garlic cloves, crushed
juice and zest of 1 lemon
150 ml/5 fl oz/⅔ cup olive oil
generous handful mint, finely chopped
seasoning to taste

Boil the chick peas in 1.7 litres/3 pints/2 quarts water for 2 hours, or until tender. (Chick peas do not disintegrate if overcooked, but they will break up on the point of a knife.) Drain well, but keep back about 150 ml/5 fl oz/⅔ cup of the cooking liquid in case the purée is too thick. Blend everything until you have a smooth, creamy purée.

Purée of Swiss chard ⑤ F

The flavour of this vegetable is impossible to describe, the leaf and stalk having quite different flavours. When the whole vegetable is used, as in this purée, it is quite delicious. Eat it with gratin dauphinois (see page 158).

450g/1 lb Swiss chard
300 ml/10 fl oz/1¼ cups vegetable stock (see page 110)
50 g/2 oz/4 tablespoons butter
2 tablespoons double/heavy cream
seasoning to taste

Slice the stalks from the leaves and cook in the stock for about 10 minutes. Drain away the stock and add the butter and leaves to the stalks. Cook over a low heat for about 5 more minutes. Allow to cool, then place in a blender and reduce to a purée, adding the cream and seasoning. Pour into a warm oven dish and reheat gently.

Avocado purée ⑩

This is one of the best and simplest purées, which is why I kept it until last. I use it a lot and to accompany other dishes, such as pâtés and terrines (see pages 138 and 163).

2 ripe avocados
1 tablespoon juice and zest from 1 lime
1 garlic clove, crushed
225 g/8 oz/1 cup Greek yoghurt (see page 45)
seasoning to taste

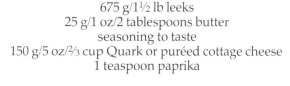

Scoop the flesh out of the avocados and place in a blender with the rest of the ingredients. Purée until smooth.

Leek purée ⑤ P F

Leeks have a delicate flavour which intensifies when puréed. Eat this as a hot side dish with the spiced potato pie or a cheese soufflé (see pages 181 and 145).

675 g/1½ lb leeks
25 g/1 oz/2 tablespoons butter
seasoning to taste
150 g/5 oz/⅔ cup Quark or puréed cottage cheese
1 teaspoon paprika

Trim and clean the leeks, by slicing them in half lengthways. Then slice them across in 1-cm/½-inch chunks. Melt the butter in a pan and add the leeks. Season, cover the pan and cook over a low heat for about 10 minutes. Stir and then blend to a purée. Add the Quark or cottage cheese and continue to blend until you have a smooth, thick sauce. Turn out on to a warm serving dish and sprinkle with the paprika.

Cauliflower and coriander purée ⑩ F

The Arabs introduced coriander to Spain, and this dish stems from that marriage of cultures. Eat this purée with crudités.
Variation
● *Omit the cauliflower and parsley, and substitute 225 g/8 oz/1 cup of cooked orange lentils, a pinch of garam masala and a squeeze of lemon.*

1 large cauliflower, boiled or steamed
1 large potato, cooked
1 teaspoon coriander, ground
seasoning to taste
150 ml/5 fl oz/⅔ cup double/heavy cream
chopped parsley for garnish

Purée the cauliflower in a blender, then drain it again as it will have absorbed water during cooking. When it is as dry as you can manage, return it to the blender with the potato, coriander and seasoning. Blend and add the cream. Garnish with the parsley.

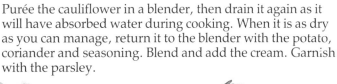

Sauces

For health reasons, the current trend is to make sauces by reduction and without flour. This is done by reducing 300 ml/10 fl oz/1¼ cups of wine, stock and flavourings to only a few tablespoons of liquid. The sauce may then be thickened with 1 tablespoon of double/heavy cream.

In my view, you might just as well use some butter in the first place; quite often it is used anyway, to sweat the vegetables in. As trends go, making sauces by reduction has its pros and cons. The value is that it generally makes a lighter and better-flavoured sauce than a flour-based one.

The disadvantage is that the method of reduction takes time and skill, which only experience gives you. Do try this method by all means, but if the sauce includes either cream or butter, it is no healthier than the sauces made from a roux (see page 191). My feeling is that it is quicker and easier to make sauces out of a light roux base, ensuring that whatever liquid used is well flavoured, so that the sauce is never floury or watery. Light, flour-based sauces can satisfy on both flavour and health counts, and most of us will continue with them while the fad of fashion passes us by.

Beurre blanc (White butter) ⑩

This is a classic French sauce with the distinctive flavour of shallots. Pour over steamed root vegetables, or eat with baked potatoes. I think this sauce is so good, I would have it with almost anything.

Variation
- *Steep a few saffron strands in 2 tablespoons of hot water for 30 minutes. Strain and add to the sauce.*

3 shallots, peeled and finely chopped (see page 52)
250 ml/8 fl oz/1 cup dry white wine
100 g/4 oz/½ cup butter
1 tablespoon double/heavy cream
seasoning to taste
1 teaspoon lemon juice

Place the shallots and white wine in a saucepan and simmer until reduced by about a third. Cut the butter in flakes and add one by one with the cream, whisking as you go. Season with salt, pepper and lemon juice. The sauce can be further seasoned by adding a tablespoon of fresh herbs.

Jajiki ⑤

This is a Greek dish which is renowned all over the Middle East. It is a lovely combination of yoghurt, mint and cucumber. Serve it as an appetizer with pitta bread, or eat with curry (see pages 154-157).

1 large cucumber
sea salt
2 or 3 garlic cloves, crushed
150 ml/5 fl oz/⅔ cup plain yoghurt
freshly ground black pepper
3 tablespoons fresh mint, finely chopped

Dice and salt the cucumber as described on page 52. Mix all the other ingredients together in a large bowl and stir in the cucumber. Chill thoroughly before serving.

Basic béchamel sauce ④ P F

*Much of cooking relies on the sauce. As many
sauces are variations of the white sauce called
béchamel, it is vital to understand a few
simple rules in making the roux - the flour
and fat base for the sauce. If you follow the
technique here you will create smooth and
lump-free sauces every time.*

Variations
*Different flours may be used in a béchamel to
give subtly different flavours. Try yellow split
pea flour, gram/chick pea flour, or potato
flour/starch (see page 86).*

Cheese sauce (Mornay)
*Follow the béchamel method and add 2
tablespoons each of freshly grated Parmesan
and Gruyère cheese when the sauce has
thickened. Season to taste.*

Parsley sauce
*Follow the béchamel method and add a
generous handful of finely chopped parsley
and a tablespoon of double/heavy cream.
Season carefully.*

Mustard sauce
*Follow the basic béchamel method and add
1 tablespoon each of Meaux mustard, Dijon
mustard and double/heavy cream.*

Green sauce (Sauce verte)
*Add two tablespoons each of finely chopped
spinach and sorrel to the parsley sauce above.*

Onion sauce
*Soften 225 g/½ lb onions in 2 tablespoons
butter. Add the flour and seasoning with a
dash of nutmeg. Then add the milk to make a
thick sauce.*

Soy and ginger sauce
*Coarsely chop 25 g/1 oz root ginger and infuse
it in 150 ml/5 fl oz/⅔ cup of water, leaving it
for 10 minutes. Make the basic roux and
strain the ginger water into it. Add 150 ml/
5 fl oz/⅔ cup of soy sauce and mix thoroughly.
If you find soy sauce too strong, use 300 ml/
10 fl oz/1¼ cups of water to infuse the
ginger and then add as much soy sauce as
your palate will take.*

25 g/1 oz/2 tablespoons butter
25 g/1 oz/2 tablespoons plain/all-purpose flour
300 ml/10 fl oz/1¼ cups milk or vegetable
stock (see page 110)

Melt the butter in a pan and then sprinkle in the flour. Stir
with a wooden spoon over a low heat to make a paste and
just cook the flour a little. Pour in the liquid slowly, stirring
all the time to make sure there are no lumps.

Basic tomato sauce ⑤ Ⅴ Ｆ

An excellent basic tomato sauce can be made from fresh tomatoes throughout the year, but the price of fresh tomatoes in the winter may make it a bit of a luxury. If you make a sauce out of canned tomatoes you will achieve a very predictable flavour whatever you add to it. The same applies to tomato paste or purée. They all have their uses, but can be over-used in the kitchen. The recipe for basic tomato sauce has many variations.

Variations
Red wine and tomato sauce   *Instead of sherry add 300 ml/10 fl oz/1¼ cups of dry red wine and a tablespoon of paprika.*

Tomato and chilli sauce   *Add two dried red chillies to the basic tomato sauce. Their flavour is pungent enough to make the sauce a fiery one. The chillies should be discarded with the rest of the vegetable debris.*

Tomato and malt whisky sauce
Substitute malt whisky for the sherry. This gives the sauce a piquant and unusual flavour that is particularly good with a rather subtle pâté or terrine, such as cabbage and coriander (see page 138).

Sauces for pasta

All the sauces given here are enough for 225 g/8 oz dried pasta or 175 g/6 oz fresh pasta – enough to feed 4 people as a starter.

Tomato and black olive sauce ⑤

A strongly-flavoured sauce from southern Italy which has a lovely colour and texture.

900 g/2 lb tomatoes
6 tablespoons dry sherry
3 garlic cloves, crushed
seasoning to taste

Cut the tomatoes in half and place in a saucepan with the rest of the ingredients over a low heat. Put a lid on the pan and leave to simmer for 10 minutes. Allow to cool, then put through a sieve. Discard the vegetable debris and reheat the liquid. If the resulting sauce, after sieving, is too thin, reduce a little by raising the heat and removing the lid. This also applies to all the variations.

3 tablespoons olive oil
3 garlic cloves, crushed
900 g/2 lb tomatoes, peeled and chopped (see page 52)
12 black olives, stoned and thinly sliced
1 teaspoon ground marjoram
150 ml/5 fl oz/⅔ cup dry red wine
seasoning to taste

Heat the oil in a pan and add the garlic and tomatoes. Stir well and cook for a minute or two, then add the rest of the ingredients and simmer for 20 minutes.

Creamy herb sauce ⑩

A smashing sauce to have with baked potatoes or steamed vegetables.

Variation
● *Cream sauces can be made with a thinned purée of such vegetables as leek, fennel, spinach and watercress, following this principle.*

200 ml/7 fl oz/1 scant cup dry white wine
3 shallots, peeled and chopped (see page 52)
bouquet garni (see page 56)
200 ml/7 fl oz/1 scant cup vegetable stock (see page 110)
150 ml/5 fl oz/⅔ cup single/light or sour cream
50 g/2 oz/4 tablespoons butter
1 tablespoon each of freshly chopped chervil, tarragon, parsley and chives
seasoning to taste

Simmer the white wine, shallots, bouquet garni and stock until reduced by half. Remove the bouquet garni and whisk in the cream, butter, herbs and seasoning.

Green sauce ⑮ Ⓟ

This is a subtle sauce from southern Italy which is excellent with pasta.

50 g/2 oz/4 tablespoons butter
675 g/1½ lb courgettes/zucchini, coarsely grated
2 garlic cloves, crushed
150 ml/5 fl oz/⅔ cup single/light cream
1 tablespoon green peppercorns, crushed
1 tablespoon walnut pieces
75 g/3 oz soft blue cheese
seasoning to taste

Melt the butter in a pan and cook the courgettes/zucchini with the garlic for 2 minutes, or until the vegetable liquid has evaporated. Add the cream, peppercorns and walnuts, then add the cheese and allow to melt. Season and serve.

Aubergine/Eggplant and pepper sauce ⑤ Ⓥ Ⓕ

A hearty, peasant sauce from Sicily, which has a chunky texture and superb flavour.

1 small aubergine/eggplant, thinly sliced and salted (see page 52)
2 green peppers
4 tablespoons olive oil
3 garlic cloves, crushed
1 tablespoon green peppercorns
150 ml/5 fl oz/⅔ cup dry red wine
6 tablespoons vegetable stock (see page 110)

Chop the aubergine/eggplant into small chunks. Core and slice the peppers. Heat the oil in a pan and cook the vegetables with the garlic. Stir well and cook for a moment before adding the rest of the ingredients. Simmer for 15 minutes until you have a thick, rough purée.

Curry sauce ⑤

An excellent sauce to have with plain steamed vegetables or pakora (see page 136).

Variation

● *For a hot curry sauce, add ¼ teaspoon cayenne pepper or chilli powder to the curry powder.*

3 tablespoons olive oil
1 tablespoon curry powder (see page 42)
3 tablespoons lemon juice
300 ml/10 fl oz/1¼ cups water
seasoning to taste
150 ml/5 fl oz/½ cup plain yoghurt or sour cream

Heat the oil in a pan and cook the curry powder for 1 minute. Add the lemon juice and water and simmer for 5 minutes. Season the sauce and then stir in the yoghurt or sour cream.

Sweet and sour sauce ⑤

There are many variations of this popular sauce, which may be completely liquid, or contain a mixture of julienne vegetables. Serve with any of the rice dishes, or as a dipping sauce with tempura (see page 136).

150 ml/5 fl oz/⅔ cup water
150 ml/5 fl oz/⅔ cup red wine vinegar
3 tablespoons lemon juice
3 tablespoons honey
2 tablespoons soy sauce
1 teaspoon kuzu flour or arrowroot dissolved in a little cold water

Mix the first five ingredients together and heat until simmering. Then add the kuzu to thicken the sauce. Stir briskly to avoid lumps. The Chinese add food colouring as they like their sauce to be red.

Peanut sauce ⑩ P

This is a classic Indonesian sauce which we associate with small kebabs called satay. It's also good with crudités.

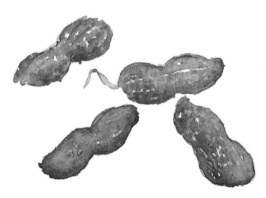

4 tablespoons groundnut/peanut oil
1 onion, finely chopped
3 garlic cloves, crushed
1 dried red chilli
100 g/4 oz/½ cup smooth peanut butter
4 tablespoons soy sauce
juice of 1 lemon
1 teaspoon brown sugar
sea salt to taste
150 ml/5 fl oz/⅔ cup milk

Heat the oil in a pan and cook the onion and garlic with the chilli until soft. Add the peanut butter, soy sauce, lemon juice, sugar and salt. Stir well and continue to cook until you have a smooth sauce. Take out the chilli and add the milk.

Chutneys and Pickles

Homemade pickles are particularly good with curries and two or three served in small dishes will enliven any meal. They are useful too for packed lunches or picnics, as a relish in sandwiches, or mixed with some of the spreads. Some of the pickles can be chopped small and added to mayonnaise to create a texture similar to sauce tartare.

When bottling chutneys or pickles, it is unnecessary to use Kilner or special preserving jars. Any wide-necked, screw top jar will do, as long as it has been properly sterilized. To do this, immerse the jars and their caps in a large pan of cold water. Bring to the boil and keep them at boiling point for 2 minutes. Remove the jars with tongs and leave to dry. Fill the jars to the brim with the pickles. (It is important not to leave any space.) When cool, screw the cap on tightly and store in a cool, shady place. I have always used this method, and find that pickles I made three years ago are still in perfect condition.

However, the USDA recommends that special preserving jars are used and filled to within 1 cm/½ inch of the top. They should then be sealed, placed in a pan of hot water and boiled for 10 minutes. (Do not attempt this with ordinary jars; they will not withstand the temperature.) This is an additional precaution against spoilage during storage. Leave to cool, then store.

Sweet pumpkin pickle ⑳

Delicately flavoured with celery, this amber-coloured pickle is delicious with Brie and Camembert. Store for three months before eating.

Variation
● *Any variety of squash can be used instead of the pumpkin.*

1 medium size pumpkin
225 g/½ lb honey
600 ml/1 pint/2½ cups cider vinegar
2 tablespoons celery seed
1 tablespoon each celery salt and sea salt

Extract the flesh from the pumpkin and discard the seeds. Chop up coarsely and place in a pan with the rest of the ingredients. Bring to the boil and simmer for 20 minutes. Cool, bottle and seal.

Hot green tomato chutney ⑮ Ⅴ

This is a beautiful chutney and an excellent way of using up green tomatoes. The recipe includes many whole garlic cloves, but don't worry - they become soft and subtle after cooking. This is a fairly hot and sharp chutney - a perfect foil for mature Cheddar. It can be eaten after five months and is perfect for brightening those February blues.
Note: Tomatoes sometimes make a lot of liquid, so you may not need to add all the vinegar suggested.

1 kg/2¼ lb green tomatoes, coarsely chopped
20-25 large garlic cloves, peeled (see page 52)
3 green chillies, chopped
100 g/4 oz root ginger, peeled and thinly sliced
1 tablespoon brown sugar
1 teaspoon sea salt
600 ml/1 pint/2½ cups apple cider vinegar

Place all the ingredients in a preserving pan with half the vinegar. Bring to the boil and simmer, stirring often, for about 20 minutes. Then add the rest of the vinegar, bring to the boil again and simmer until the chutney thickens a little. Leave to cool and then bottle.

Marrow/winter squash and ginger chutney ⑮ Ⓥ

Do not use marrows or squash more than 45 cm/18 inches long; they have no flavour. When fused with ginger, they make an excellent chutney which goes well with blue cheese, such as Roquefort or Fourme d'Ambert. Store this chutney for six months before using.

Variation
- *Pumpkin may be substituted for the marrow/squash.*

1 vegetable marrow/squash
75 g/3 oz root ginger, peeled and thinly sliced
1 teaspoon each of cloves, mace, juniper berries, pimento berries and crushed coriander seeds
600 ml/1 pint/2½ cups cider vinegar
1 tablespoon brown sugar
1 teaspoon sea salt

Peel and seed the marrow/squash and chop the flesh coarsely. Put everything in a large saucepan and simmer for 20 minutes. Leave to cool and then bottle.

Parsnip, cucumber and garlic chutney ⑮ Ⓥ

There is a pleasant variety of textures among the vegetables in this chutney, which also uses whole garlic cloves. Store for six months, then eat with a smooth pâté, such as cabbage and coriander (see page 138).

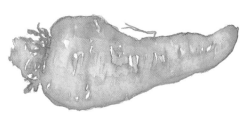

900 g/2 lb parsnips
2 cucumbers
4 heads of garlic, peeled (see page 52)
600 ml/1 pint/2½ cups cider vinegar
1 teaspoon each cloves, mace, juniper berries, cumin and crushed coriander
2 dried red chillies
1 tablespoon tamarind
2 tablespoons brown sugar
2 teaspoons sea salt

Peel the parsnips and cut into chunks. Coarsely cut the cucumbers without peeling them. Add the garlic to the parsnips and cucumbers. Cook the vegetables in a large saucepan with all the other ingredients for 30 minutes. Leave to cool before bottling.

Mustard pickled cauliflower ⑳ Ⓥ

How good this is! It is made with cider vinegar, which is milder than malt and is a lovely speckled yellow. Despite the spicy name, it is not at all hot. Store for six months before eating.

2 large cauliflowers
900 g/2 lb shallots, peeled (see page 52)
2 tablespoons Meaux/wholegrain mustard
2 tablespoons Dijon mustard
2 teaspoons sea salt
600 ml/1 pint/2½ cups cider vinegar

Divide the cauliflowers into florets and blanch in boiling water (see page 52). Pack the cauliflower and shallots into a large sterilized jar. Put the mustards into a pan with the salt and slowly add the vinegar. Bring to the boil and pour over the vegetables in the jar. Cool and seal.

Gingered pickled onions ⓴ Ⓥ

I believe this recipe is a triumph. Try it and find out. Eaten with homemade bread and mature Cheddar, you have a meal fit for an Emperor.

100 g/4 oz/⅓ cup sea salt
1 litre/1¾ pints/1 quart water
1.5 kg/3 lb pickling onions, peeled (see page 52)
1 tablespoon pickling spices
50 g/2 oz root ginger
600 ml/1 pint/2½ cups cider vinegar

Make a brine from the salt and water and soak the onions in it for 24 hours. Drain and place the onions in a large sterilized jar with the pickling spices. Slice the unpeeled ginger thinly and stick the pieces down among the onions. Heat the vinegar until it just begins to simmer and pour over the onions. Screw the top on the jar and keep for 6 months before trying one.

Pickled beetroot/beets and garlic ㉕

This must surely be the perfect marriage. The garlic beautifully flavours the beetroot and the beetroot beautifully colours the garlic. Store this pickle for a minimum of three months before using.

2.25 kg/5 lb beetroot/beets
5 heads of garlic, peeled (see page 52)
600 ml/1 pint/2½ cups cider vinegar
3 dried red chillies
1 teaspoon each of cloves, mace, juniper berries and pimento berries
1 teaspoon sea salt

Boil the beetroots/beets in lots of water until tender - about 1 hour - and leave to cool. Peel and quarter the beetroots/beets. Place in a large sterilized jar with the garlic. Bring the cider to the boil with the remaining ingredients. Pour over the beetroot/beet and garlic, and seal.

Spiced quinces ⑩

You may find quinces hard to get hold of, but it is worth the effort as they look stunningly beautiful when they turn a dark reddish amber in their juice. They also taste as good as they look and are edible after one month. The flavour of quince defies definition, being part pear, apple and lemon, yet very much itself.
Variation
● *Plums may be used instead of quinces.*

1.5 kg/3 lb quinces
175 g/6 oz/1 cup brown sugar
600 ml/1 pint/2½ cups cider vinegar
juice and rind of 2 lemons
50 g/2 oz root ginger
2 cinnamon sticks
2 vanilla pods/beans
1 teaspoon cloves
1 teaspoon sea salt

Slice the quinces in half and core them. Melt the sugar in the vinegar and add the rest of the ingredients. Add the quinces and simmer for 30 minutes. Cool and bottle.

Desserts

For ease of reference, this section is divided into hot and cold desserts. The hot dishes are mainly steamed puddings, which seem curiously English, but in fact, are found throughout northern Europe. They may be either savoury or sweet, and all are high in carbohydrate. Steamed puddings are traditionally made with beef suet. Fortunately, one can now buy vegetable suet from healthfood stores, which has been processed to work like beef suet. In my opinion, this fat works better than beef suet, giving a much lighter, more sponge-like crust (see page 37).

Fresh fruit or fresh fruit salads, with or without added fruit juices, are perhaps the most delicious way of ending a meal. This kind of dish can be broadened to include dried fruits and nuts. Instead of cream, one can use plain yoghurt, or yoghurt with beaten egg white whipped into it. You can also scatter various chopped nuts into this mixture.

Of all dried fruits, apricots are the most nutritious and have excellent flavour. When buying any dried fruit, however, do make sure it is unprocessed and untreated with preservative. The good thing about dried fruits is that their intensified sugars are so sweet, no other sugar need be added.

Apart from tarts and fruit salads, the cold desserts in this section also include syllabubs and fools. The name 'syllabub' derives from Sille, which was part of the Champagne country from which came sparkling Sill wine, and 'bub' which was Elizabethan slang for a bubbling drink. The first syllabubs were made by milking a cow directly into a pot of cider or wine, the object being to produce a clear drink with froth on top.

Fruit fools are a distant cousin of the syllabub; they date from the same time and were based on a pulp of cooked fruits beaten together with sugar and cream. Sometimes eggs were added, the raw yolks beaten in with the cream and sugar, and the egg whites whipped separately and folded in afterwards. Many of the most delicious desserts are still to be found among the syllabubs and fools.

Indian pudding ⑩

Similar in texture to corn bread, this pudding is best served with Greek yoghurt (see page 45) or whipped cream.

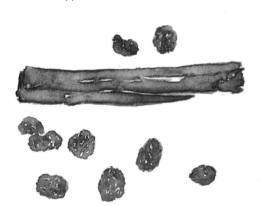

175 g/6 oz/1½ cups corn meal
600 ml/1 pint/2½ cups milk
50 g/2 oz/4 tablespoons butter
6 tablespoons molasses
6 tablespoons honey
½ teaspoon each salt, ginger and cinnamon
2 eggs, beaten
100 g/4 oz/1 cup raisins

Pre-heat the oven to 200°C/400°F/Gas mark 6. Mix the corn meal with the milk and heat in a saucepan, stirring all the time. When the mixture has begun to thicken, remove from the heat and stir in the butter, molasses, honey, salt and spices. When it has cooled a little, beat in the eggs and stir in the raisins. Pour into a well-buttered, shallow oven dish and bake for 45 minutes.

*Sussex pond pudding is a traditional
English dessert. It has a light suet
crust encasing a whole lemon, which sits
in a syrupy pool of brown sugar (see page 200).*

Steamed ginger pudding with marmalade sauce ⑮

*A deliciously satisfying winter pudding
served with a rich, orange and wine sauce -
perfect for keeping the cold out.*

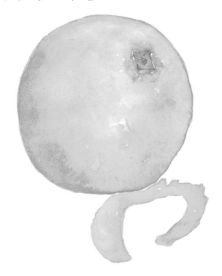

75 g/3 oz/6 tablespoons butter
50 g/2 oz/¼ cup caster/superfine sugar
2 eggs
100 g/4 oz/1 cup wholewheat flour
1 teaspoon baking powder
100 g/4 oz preserved stem ginger, chopped
2 tablespoons ginger syrup
½ teaspoon ground ginger
scant 150 ml/5 fl oz/½ cup milk
120 ml/4 fl oz/½ cup dry white wine
3 tablespoons strong marmalade
1 teaspoon arrowroot mixed with a little cold water

Cream the butter and sugar. Mix in the eggs, then the flour,
baking powder and ginger ingredients. Mix thoroughly and
add the milk slowly. Butter a 1.5-litre/2½-pint/1½-quart
pudding basin/steaming mould and put the dough inside.
Cover with greaseproof/waxed paper and foil, tie firmly with
string and steam (like the Sussex pond pudding) for 2½
hours. Just before serving, heat the marmalade with the
wine. Thicken the sauce with the arrowroot and serve hot.

Sussex pond pudding ⑮

*This pudding has the most wonderful
appearance when cut open. The lemon sits in a
golden brown, silky pool of sugar, lemon juice
and butter. Absolute bliss!*

225 g/8 oz/2 cups self-raising flour
100 g/4 oz/1 cup shredded vegetable suet (see page 37)
150 ml/5 floz/⅔ cup equal parts milk and water
100 g/4 oz/½ cup butter
100 g/4 oz/⅔ cup soft brown sugar
1 large lemon

Thoroughly mix the flour and suet. Slowly add the milk and
water and mix into a dough. Set aside a quarter of it and roll
out the rest in a circle. Line a 1.5-litre/2½-pint/1½-quart
pudding basin/steaming mould with the pastry and trim the
edges. Chop the butter into small pieces and mix it with the
sugar. Prick the lemon all over with a sharp needle, going
through the skin and into the flesh. Place the lemon in the
basin and cover with the butter and sugar mixture. Roll out
the remaining pastry, place it on top of the basin, trim and
seal the edge. Cover with greaseproof/waxed paper and foil,
and tie firmly with string. Half fill a large saucepan with
water, place the pudding in it so that the water comes almost
to the top. Cover and leave to boil for 3 hours. As the water
evaporates, top it up with boiling water. To serve, remove
the foil and paper, cover with a large plate and invert to turn
it out. Cut into the pudding at table and give everyone a
portion of the lemon with the juices and suet crust.

Baked apple with apricot purée ⑩ Ⓥ Ⓕ

A traditional English dessert with the added goodness and sharpness of apricots. It can also be made with almost any other fruit purée.

Variation

● *Fruit purées can be made from almost any fruit. Cook the fruit gently in butter until it becomes thick and mushy, then sieve the mixture. Generally these purées need no additions - not even sugar.*

4-6 large cooking apples
300 ml/10 fl oz/1¼ cups apricot purée (see page 201)
1 tablespoon flaked/slivered almonds

Pre-heat the oven to 200°C/400°F/Gas mark 6. Core the apples without peeling them and place on a buttered baking sheet. Fill the cavities with the apricot purée and cover the top with the almonds. Bake for 20 minutes.

Hot apricot soufflé ⑦ Ⓟ

This is identical in preparation to the cheese soufflé (see page 145), and like it, should be slightly runny in the middle after baking. Almost any fruit purée can be used instead of apricot, but avoid citrus fruits because they will curdle the eggs. This soufflé is delicious with whipped cream.

100 g/4 oz/⅔ cup dried apricots
300 ml/10 fl oz/1¼ cups apple juice
50 g/2 oz/½ cup raisins
150ml/5 fl oz/⅔ cup brandy
4 eggs
300 ml/10 fl oz/1¼ cups single/light cream

Soak the apricots overnight in the apple juice and soak the raisins overnight in the brandy. Simmer the apricots for 5 minutes. Leave to cool, then blend to a purée. Separate the eggs and add the yolks and cream to the apricot purée. Pre-heat the oven to 200°C/400°F/Gas mark 6. Butter a 1.5-litre/2½-pint/1½-quart soufflé dish. Whip the egg whites until stiff and fold into the apricot purée. Pour into the soufflé dish and bake for 20 minutes, or until well risen and lightly brown. Before serving, pour the raisins and brandy on top.

Apricot syllabub ⑩

The idea of a flavoured cream goes back to the sixteenth century. This one is particularly good, having the sharpness of the apricots set against the smoothness of the cream. Serve it in individual glasses with a sprig of mint.

Variations

● *Combine 175 ml/6 fl oz/¾ cup of dry sherry with the zest and juice of 1 lemon. Add 2 tablespoons of caster/superfine sugar and a pinch of nutmeg. Slowly add 300 ml/10 fl oz/ 1¼ cups of double/heavy cream, then whisk until it just holds its shape.*

● *Substitute half brandy, half white wine for the sherry.*

100 g/4 oz/⅔ cup dried apricots
300 ml/10 fl oz/1¼ cups apple juice
2 eggs
150 ml/5 fl oz/⅔ cup double/heavy cream

Soak the apricots overnight in the apple juice. Then bring them to the boil and simmer for 5 minutes. Leave to cool and purée in a blender. Separate the eggs and add the yolks to the purée. Whip the whites until stiff and fold in carefully. Lightly whip the cream and fold into the purée as well. Chill for 1 hour before serving.

Layered fig and cream cheese mould ⑩ P F

*This is a sensational-looking dessert which is
very rich, so you need only a little. Note: If
you do not have a spring-release pan, line a
straight-sided dish with foil in order to turn
out the mould.*
Variation
- *Apricots can be substituted for the figs.*

175 g/6 oz dried figs
300ml/10 fl oz/1¼ cups apple juice
6 tablespoons brandy
175 g/6 oz/⅔ cup cream cheese
75 g/3 oz/⅔ cup chopped walnuts
3 tablespoons apple and pear fructose syrup (see page 43)

Soak the figs in the apple juice overnight. Then bring them
to the boil and simmer for 5 minutes. Leave to cool and then
blend to a purée with the brandy. Mix the rest of the
ingredients together in a bowl. Lightly butter a deep
17-cm/7-inch spring-release cake pan and place a 2-cm/l-inch
layer of fig purée at the bottom. Cover with a layer of the
cream cheese mixture. Continue alternating the layers until
the pan is full. Freeze for 1 day. Unmould 2 hours before
serving. When it reaches room temperature, slice like a cake.

Pomegranate coupe ⑩

*The combination of pomegranate and kiwi
fruit is a pleasing one in both appearance and
taste. This elegant dessert is easy to make and
the addition of rum gives it a surprising
flavour.*

4 kiwi fruits, peeled and chopped
2 pomegranates, seeded
1 tablespoon white rum mixed with 1 tablespoon clear
honey
150 ml/5 fl oz/⅔ cup double/heavy cream, whipped until
it holds its shape
1 egg white, stiffly beaten
2 tablespoons caster/superfine sugar
few sprigs of mint (optional)

Place the chopped kiwi fruit and all but 2 tablespoons of the
pomegranate seeds in separate bowls. Divide the rum and
honey mixture between the fruits. Fold the whipped cream
into the stiffly beaten egg white, then fold in the sugar.
Layer the fruits and cream mixture into tall glasses, finishing
with a layer of the cream mixture. Chill for about 30 minutes.
Decorate the tops with a few of the reserved pomegranate
seeds, and a small sprig of mint if you wish.

 *Pomegranate coupe is an elegant dessert
combining deep red pomegranate seeds with
pale green kiwi fruit. They are flavoured
with rum and layered with whipped cream
(see page 202).*

Blackcurrant tart ⑤ F

*I think blackcurrants are sublime summer
fruit and particularly good when tasting cold
and sharp against crumbly pastry.*

Variation

● *Blueberries or bilberries may be substituted
for the blackcurrants.*

1 sweet pastry case, baked blind (see page 204)
450 g/1 lb blackcurrants
2 tablespoons blackcurrant fructose syrup (see page 43)
6 tablespoons cassis

Cook the blackcurrants with the fructose syrup. Simmer for
a few minutes until just soft. Pour in the cassis and leave to
marinate for several hours. Drain off any excess liquid and
either drink it or mix it with whipped cream to make a
syllabub (see page 201). Fill the pastry case with the
blackcurrants. Chill for 1 hour before serving.

Glazed apple tart ⑮

*This recipe is based on a great French classic
dessert, but I have changed the filling from the
usual confectioner's cream to an apple purée.
It tastes nicer and is far healthier.*

Variations

● *Substitute the apple purée with one made
from dried apricots (see page 201). Sliced
pears may be used instead of sliced apples.*

● *Omit the apples and substitute 450 g/1 lb
quinces to make a purée. Arrange 3 fresh
sliced peaches on top, then bake and glaze as
before.*

450 g/1 lb eating apples
2 large cooking apples
3 tablespoons apple and pear fructose syrup (see page 43)
3 tablespoons apple or apricot jelly
6 tablespoons calvados
For the pastry
225 g/8 oz/2 cups plain/all-purpose flour
½ teaspoon salt
90 g/3½ oz/½ cup castor/superfine sugar
100 g/4 oz/½ cup butter
4 egg yolks
½ teaspoon vanilla essence/extract

Make the pastry by mixing the dry ingredients with the
butter. Then add the egg yolks and vanilla to make a dough.
Cover with plastic wrap and refrigerate for 1 hour. Roll out
the pastry to fill a 20-cm/8-inch tart pan and bake blind (see
page 48). Peel and core the cooking apples. Cook over a low
flame with the fructose syrup until they become a soft purée.
Now peel and core the eating apples and slice thinly.
Pre-heat the oven to 200°C/400°F/Gas mark 6. Arrange the
pieces in the purée in a circular pattern slightly overlapping
one another. Bake for 15 minutes. Melt the apple or apricot
jelly in a pan with the calvados and use to glaze the tart.
Leave to cool and serve with whipped cream.

Rosewater fruit salad ⑤

You will find this refreshing and fragrant dessert ideal for cleansing the palate after a spicy meal.

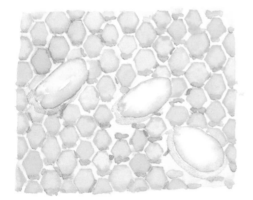

a piece of watermelon weighing about 450 g/1 lb
50 g/2 oz/½ cup flaked/slivered almonds, toasted (see page 56)
4 peaches, stoned and quartered
Syrup
300 ml/10 fl oz/1¼ cups water
3 tablespoons honey
2 tablespoons distilled rose water
1 cinnamon stick
juice of 1 lemon

Cut the watermelon flesh into bite size pieces. Combine the syrup ingredients in a shallow pan, bring to simmering point and briefly poach the peach slices. Remove them with a slotted spoon and reserve the syrup. Arrange the fruit and almonds in a serving dish. Heat the syrup to boiling point, then simmer until reduced by half. Cool a little then pour over the fruit mixture. Chill well before serving.

Brown bread ice cream ⑮ F

This ice cream is not only one of the most delicious ices ever devised, having a crunch and flavour like praline, but also, in its use of wholewheat breadcrumbs, a healthy part of the diet - that is, if we close our eyes for a moment to the cream and sugar content. The ice cream should be transferred from the freezer to the refrigerator about 30 minutes before serving so it is not too hard.

225g/8 oz/4 cups wholewheat breadcrumbs (see page 48)
225 g/8 oz/1⅓ cup Demerara/light brown sugar
1.2 litres/2 pints/5 cups whipping cream
2 tablespoons brandy

Pre-heat the oven to 200°C/400°F/Gas mark 6. Mix the breadcrumbs and sugar together, lay them out on a baking sheet and bake until brown and crisp, *not* burnt. When cool, crush them fairly small. You do not want a powder, so don't use a food processor. Lightly whip the cream and add the brandy. Stir in the crumbs and place in an ice cream machine or a freezer. If using a freezer take the ice cream out after 1 hour and stir it. Freeze again, repeating the stirring process after another hour. Refreeze, then decorate with mint leaves and/or crystallized violets.

Gooseberry fool ⑩ P

This was a favourite in Elizabethan times, as it is now. Chill it for 1 hour before serving with langues de chat.
Variation
• *Fools can be made out of the same weight of pears, apples, quinces, plums, damsons and rhubarb.*

450 g/1 lb gooseberries, washed and trimmed
50 g/2 oz/¼ cup castor/superfine sugar
6 tablespoons Beaumes de Venise
2 eggs, separated
300 ml/10 fl oz/1¼ cups double/heavy cream, whipped

Gently cook the gooseberries with the sugar until they become a pulp. Stir in the wine. When cool, stir in the egg yolks. Whip the whites stiffly and fold into the gooseberry purée, followed by the cream.

CHAPTER 5

Festive Occasions

Claudia Roden's Midsummer Picnic

Food is specially important on an outing. It has to be good because you have so much time on your hands and because nature has its way of unleashing the senses and the appetite. But it is part of the leisurely atmosphere and in the spirit of the occasion to make things easy for yourself when you are out among the trees.

My favourite picnics have always been spontaneous ones and those where the work was shared and resources pooled - when friends came to cook with me before we set off, or when we each brought a dish made in advance. Together we have prepared all kinds of things, from sandwiches and salads to hot pastas and soups, which we rushed out steaming in their pans, as well as pies, tarts, stuffed vegetables, omelettes and fruit salads. When you have a car it is easy to bring out almost anything.

A wonderful instant feast can simply be an assortment of vegetables bought on the way. You can have carrots, cauliflower, celery, little turnips, courgettes/zucchini, mushrooms, endive, fennel, tomatoes, peppers, cucumbers, spring onions/scallions and radishes, as well as cress and fresh herbs. Bring water to wash them and knives to peel them. Cut them up or leave them whole, and dress them simply with a mixture of olive oil, salt and pepper, adding lemon juice or vinegar if you like, and sprinkling with the chopped herbs.

Lay everything out in a beautiful, even spectacular, array. It is easy enough if there are many hands and if you have something like a tray to do it on. All you need to complete the feast is fresh bread, olives and pickles, a couple of cheeses, fruit and a hearty wine to wash it all down. Here are a few dishes which can be prepared in advance and are good cold.

Claudia Roden

Carrot and sweet potato dip

Although the main ingredients of this dip are both sweet, the spices and other flavourings give it a lovely piquancy. Serve this spicy appetizer with bread.

450 g/1 lb carrots, peeled
450 g/1 lb sweet potatoes, peeled
3 garlic cloves, crushed
2 teaspoons cumin

1 teaspoon cinnamon
4 tablespoons olive oil
3 tablespoons wine vinegar
good pinch of cayenne pepper

Boil the carrots and sweet potatoes in salted water until soft. Drain, then purée with the rest of the ingredients. Garnish with a few olives and serve.

A delicious and unusual selection of dishes to take on an open-air jaunt. From top right, the dishes are Bananas and dates with yoghurt, Orange pudding, Spinach omelette, Carrot and sweet potato dip, and a salad platter containing Okra with chick peas and tomatoes, Exotic fruit salad, and Lentils and rice with onions.

Spinach omelette

Served warm or cold, this omelette is really delicious. As it is quite substantial, cut it in wedges like cake and eat it with some of the following salads.

1 medium onion, finely chopped
3 tablespoons oil
675 g/1½ lb spinach, washed, drained and shredded

seasoning to taste
pinch of nutmeg
3 tomatoes, peeled and chopped (see page 52)
6 eggs, lightly beaten

Fry the onion in the oil until golden. Add the spinach, seasoning, nutmeg and tomatoes and stir until the spinach crumples. Mix the eggs in gently and cook covered over a very low heat for about 10-15 minutes until they set. Put under a grill or broiler to dry the top, then turn out.

Okra with chickpeas and tomatoes

A colourful and substantial salad which is perfect to eat in the open air. The subtle flavour of okra combines deliciously with the earthy taste of chick peas, and both are given a lift by the sharp lemon and garlic dressing.

225 g/½ lb button onions, peeled (see page 52)
4 tablespoons olive oil
2-3 garlic cloves, crushed
675 g/1½ lb okra, washed and trimmed
450 g/1 lb tomatoes, peeled and quartered

175 g/6 oz/1½ cups chick peas, cooked (see page 51)
seasoning to taste
juice of 1 lemon
bunch of coriander, chopped

Fry the onions whole in the oil until golden, then add the garlic, okra, tomatoes and chick peas with some of their water. Add the seasoning and lemon juice, and cook until the okra is tender and the liquid is reduced. Add the coriander and cook for a minute longer.

Exotic fruit salad

Despite the quantity of fruit in this recipe, this is a savoury salad. It is beautifully cool and particularly refreshing on a hot summer's day.

flesh of 1 avocado, cubed
1 pawpaw/papaya, peeled, seeded and cubed
flesh of ½ a melon, cubed
2 kiwi fruits, peeled and sliced
juice of 1 lemon

4 tablespoons olive oil
seasoning to taste
small bunch of chives, finely chopped
few sprigs of mint, finely chopped

Dress the fruits with a mixture of lemon juice, olive oil, seasoning and chopped herbs.

Lentils and rice with onions

Use green or brown lentils in this recipe; they have a lovely, nutty flavour, and go particularly well with the slightly sweet taste of caramelized onions.

450 g/l lb/2 cups lentils, soaked for 1 hour and rinsed
225 g/8 oz/1¼ cups long grain rice

seasoning to taste
675 g/1½ lb onions, halved and thinly sliced
150 ml/5 fl oz/⅔ cup olive oil

Bring the lentils to the boil in about 900 ml/ 1½ pints/3¾ cups water. Simmer until nearly tender. Add the rice and seasoning, and cook covered for about 15 minutes until the rice is done, adding more water if necessary. Fry the onion in a little of the oil until practically caramelized. Stir this into the rice and add the rest of the oil.

Bananas and dates with yoghurt

Surprise yourself with the wonderful combination of flavours in this simple dessert. It may be made in advance or just before eating.

5 bananas, thinly sliced
350 g/¾ lb fresh dates, peeled and halved

600ml/1 pint/2½ cups Greek yoghurt (see page 45)
2 tablespoons rose water

Put alternate layers of bananas and dates in a bowl. Mix the yoghurt and rose water and pour on top.

Orange dessert

If you like the taste of marmalade, you'll love this dessert. Every part of the oranges, except the pips, are puréed to a bitter pulp, combined with eggs and brandy, and baked. The result is a golden creation similar in texture and appearance to a soufflé. Eat it hot or cold.

2 large oranges
6 eggs
juice of 2 more oranges

juice of ½ lemon
3 tablespoons brandy or orange liqueur
10 tablespoons sugar to taste

Boil the oranges whole for about 1 hour until very tender. Cut open and remove the pips. Blend with the eggs, orange and lemon juice, the brandy and sugar. Bake in an ovenproof dish at 150°C/300°F/ Gas mark 2 for about 1 hour, or until firm.

Yoghurt drink

In the Middle East and India, the combination of whisked yoghurt and water is a classic. It makes a deliciously refreshing summer drink.

600 ml/1 pint/2½ cups plain yoghurt
450 ml/12 fl oz/1½ cups water
salt (optional)

few sprigs of fresh mint
several lumps of ice

Beat the yoghurt in a jug, then whisk in the water and a little salt if you like. Pour it into a thermos flask, add mint and several lumps of ice.

Alice Waters' Spring Fever Brunch

I really don't like eating breakfast at all, but this menu, based on current seasonal ingredients is an ideal late morning meal. It happens to be early spring in California right now; asparagus is coming up, the blood oranges are ripe, wild mushrooms abound, and strawberries are just coming on the market from San Diego.

There could be many variations with these ingredients. One way I think about menus is to imagine all the chosen food on the table at the same time. Then I mentally combine flavours, textures and colours that will subtly complement each other. You could make blood orange ice cream in buckwheat crêpes, mix wild mushrooms and asparagus, have bitter lettuce salad with blood oranges, buckwheat crêpes with wild mushrooms, or asparagus with blood orange vinaigrette. The combinations are endless.

Bandol Rosé or champagne are perfect for drinking during the meal, but I suggest you start with creamy café au lait. Make one espresso per person and top up with steamed milk to taste. Follow this with buckwheat crêpes and a sweet preserve such as plum jelly. The crêpes will not be too sweet because buckwheat has a naturally sour flavour.

The blood orange and strawberry compote that follows should be simple, cold and very refreshing before the buttery, warm asparagus. I think the rich taste of wild mushrooms would be delicious at this point, served with very thin slices of crusty peasant bread, grilled over charcoal, rubbed with raw garlic while still hot, and drizzled with olive oil. The salad of bitter greens and garlic offsets the richness of these flavours.

I love to end the meal with something not too big or too sweet. In this menu the biscotti seem right - full of nuts and raisins. Dip them into Italian Vin Santo and the dipping and sipping can go on into the afternoon!

Buckwheat crêpes

Buckwheat makes a very light crêpe, and the inclusion of beer in this recipe adds to its naturally sour flavour. The batter will keep refrigerated for 5 days to a week. If you like, the crêpes can be made several hours in advance, but keep them covered. (You may rub the pan with butter and wipe it out with absorbent paper to keep the first crêpe from sticking; you won't have to do it again.) This recipe makes enough for 32 crêpes, approximately 15 cm/6 inches in diameter. Serve with the preserve of your choice.

475 ml/16 fl oz/2 cups milk
¼ teaspoon salt
½ teaspoon sugar
50 g/2 oz/¼ cup unsalted butter
100 g/4 oz/1 cup plain/all-purpose flour

40 g/1½ oz/generous ¼ cup buckwheat flour
1 tablespoon vegetable oil
3 eggs
120 ml/4 fl oz/½ cup lager/light beer

Heat the milk, salt, sugar and butter until the butter melts. Mix the flour with the oil and eggs. Gradually add the milk until you have a smooth batter. Mix in the beer and strain into a clean bowl. Cover and chill for 2 hours. Let the batter warm slightly. Heat your crêpe pan until a drop of water sizzles when thrown into it. Lift the pan off the heat and add 2 tablespoons of batter. Tilt the pan to spread the batter, then cook for 1 minute on each side until brown and lacy. Fold the crêpes in half and warm through in a hot oven for 3 or 4 minutes. Drizzle with butter and fold into quarters.

*Clockwise from middle left: Café au lait,
Buckwheat crêpes, Biscotti, Asparagus with
shallot butter, Blood orange and strawberry
compote, Salad of bitter greens with Wild
mushrooms on toast*

Blood orange and strawberry compote

In the spring blood oranges aren't as sweet as they are later in the season, when they can be served alone. For this reason I have mixed them with early strawberries to make a delicious maroon compote. It is important to add the strawberries at the very last minute to preserve their texture.

4 blood oranges, washed
250 ml/8 fl oz/1 cup each water and champagne
90 g/3½ oz/½ cup sugar

2 tablespoons brandy or Cognac, to taste
350 g/12 oz/2 cups strawberries, hulled and sliced lengthways

Cut the zest in very thin slivers from 2 of the oranges. Place in a saucepan, cover with the water and champagne and bring to the boil. Remove from the heat, and steep for 15 minutes. Add the sugar then bring the mixture to the boil. Simmer for 20-30 minutes, or until a thin syrup forms. Cool and add brandy to taste. Chill the strawberries. Remove all the skin and pith from the oranges and cut the fruit into 5-mm/¼-inch slices. Layer them in a bowl, sprinkling with the syrup and peel. Chill for 1 hour, add the strawberries and serve.

Wild mushrooms on toast

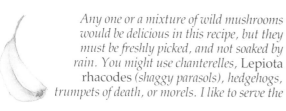

Any one or a mixture of wild mushrooms would be delicious in this recipe, but they must be freshly picked, and not soaked by rain. You might use chanterelles, Lepiota rhacodes *(shaggy parasols), hedgehogs, trumpets of death, or morels. I like to serve the mushrooms on grilled slices of peasant bread that has been drizzled with olive oil and rubbed with the cut edge of a garlic clove while still warm. Arrange the heaped slices of toast round the edges of a large platter, and pile the salad of bitter greens in the centre.*

225 g/½ lb wild mushrooms, brushed clean
1 tablespoon butter
1 tablespoon virgin olive oil

2 garlic cloves, crushed
seasoning to taste

Sauté the mushrooms in the hot butter and oil, seasoning to taste. As they brown, add the garlic. Stir for a few minutes more, but do not allow the garlic to burn. Serve on toast.

Salad of bitter greens

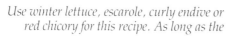

Use winter lettuce, escarole, curly endive or red chicory for this recipe. As long as the mixture is bitter, it is the perfect foil to the rich flavours of the wild mushrooms on toast.

4 large handfuls mixed bitter salad greens
2 tablespoons red·wine vinegar
1 teaspoon balsamic vinegar

1 garlic clove, crushed
seasoning to taste
4 tablespoons virgin olive oil

Wash and dry the greens well. Mix the vinegars with the garlic and a little salt. Let the mixture sit for a moment or two, then add the oil. Add pepper to taste. Toss the greens in the dressing and serve.

Asparagus with shallot butter

If the shallots you use are old they will be particularly strong and need a lot of cooking, which they get in the butter sauce. Pour over individual servings of the asparagus and, if you like, add a dollop of lightly whipped cream seasoned with salt and pepper.

2 large shallots, peeled and finely chopped (see page 52)
250 ml/8 fl oz/1 cup white wine
100 g/4 oz/½ cup unsalted butter, cut into flakes
seasoning to taste
dash of champagne vinegar
fresh asparagus to serve 4 (amount depends on size)

Heat the shallots with the wine and reduce the liquid to 1 tablespoon. Whisk in the butter bit by bit, keeping the heat low. Remove from the heat, season to taste and add the vinegar. Strain the mixture through a fine sieve and keep warm in a bain marie. Trim and peel the asparagus. Drop into a large pan of boiling salted water and cook until just tender - about 3 or 4 minutes. Drain and serve with the butter sauce.

Biscotti

I think these Italian biscuits are the perfect ending to this meal, being neither too heavy nor too sweet. They are densely packed with nuts and dried fruit and are easy to make.

6 eggs, separated
450 g/1 lb/2½ cups sugar
225 g/8 oz/1 cup unsalted butter, melted and cooled almost to room temperature
1½ teaspoons anise seed
175 g/6 oz/1½ cups chopped walnuts and almonds
75 g/3 oz/¾ cup sultanas/golden raisins
½ teaspoon vanilla essence/extract
1 kg/2¼ lb/9 cups plain/all-purpose flour
1½ teaspoons baking powder
pinch of salt

Beat the egg yolks with the sugar until pale yellow and the sugar has dissolved. Beat the egg whites stiffly and fold in the remaining sugar a bit at a time. Fold the white into the yolks and then add the butter. Add the anise seed, nuts, dried fruit and vanilla. Mix the flour with the baking powder and salt. Fold the flour into the egg mixture a quarter at a time. It will be stiff at the end and require a wooden spoon. Pre-heat the oven to 180°C/350°F/ Gas mark 4. Roll the dough into cylinders about 20-25 cm/8-10 inches long and 4 cm/1½ inches in diameter. Place on lightly buttered baking sheets and bake for 15-20 minutes until golden. Cut them into pieces about 2 cm/¾ inch wide at a 45° angle. Return them to the baking sheets, cut surface down, and bake for 5-10 minutes, until crisp.

Arabella Boxer's Dinner Party

Although I think of myself as 'almost a vegetarian', happy to exist on dishes of grain, pasta and vegetables most days of the week, I still rely on meat or fish for a special occasion. Many of my friends, even one of my children, call themselves vegetarian, but they still eat fish, and this makes dinner parties no problem whatsoever. Trying to create a festive meal without meat or fish, or quantities of butter and cream, which I prefer to do without anyway, is both demanding and challenging, but fun.

I decided to make mine an autumnal meal for 6-8 people, using to advantage the warm, earthy flavours of root vegetables, mushrooms, chestnuts, ginger and sesame seeds. As a bonus, I hoped to be able to find a few late autumn raspberries as a garnish for the dessert.

The meal starts with a pretty array of stuffed vegetables, or vegetable slices, with three different stuffings divided between them. It is served at room temperature, glowing with all the colours of autumn: yellow, brown, green and red. This is followed by a dish of mixed root vegetables - pickling onions, small leeks and carrots, fennel, parsnips and Jerusalem artichokes - lightly glazed in a sticky sauce with chestnuts and toasted sesame seeds. This is

served with, or around, a mound of basmati, wild and brown rice edged with feathery sprigs of dill.

After two dishes of mixed vegetables, I chose a simple salad: sprigs of watercress, with chopped shallots, in a light fruity dressing. With the salad, I would serve just one cheese - probably a vacherin or chèvre - with water biscuits and unsalted butter.

As the first two courses are quite a lot of work, a homemade ice cream seemed a sensible choice for dessert, since it can be made two or three days beforehand. A ginger ice cream is good in cool weather, since the warm ginger flavour offsets the chill of the ice and makes a perfect foil for a few raspberries. I'd serve it with some ginger biscuits, crisp and lacey, like tuiles d'amandes.

Having just returned from a trip to Turin, I decided on Piedmontese wines. As an aperitif, and with the first course, I would have a dry and delicate Gavi dei Gavi, or a flinty Arneis. Then, with the main course, one of the lighter Piedmontese reds, probably a Barbaresco, preferably Gaja 1978 or '79. With the ginger ice cream what could be better than a Moscato d'Asti (preferably Fontanafredda), with the sweet fragrance of the muscat grape, and a slight sparkle.

Arabella Boxer.

Clockwise from bottom right: Mixed stuffed vegetables, Wild rice timbale with glazed root vegetables, Watercress salad with Vacherin cheese, Ginger ice cream with thin ginger biscuits

 # Mixed stuffed vegetables

The dinner party will have a colourful start with this glowing array of vegetables. They should be stuffed just before eating. Serve at room temperature.

Stuffing A
1 large pepper, peeled and seeded (see page 52)
4 tomatoes, peeled and seeded (see page 52)
1 large garlic clove, roasted and peeled
¼ mild Spanish onion
1 celery heart, including leaves
2 tablespoons olive oil
1 tablespoon lemon juice
½ teaspoon coriander, ground
seasoning to taste
Stuffing B
3 tomatoes, peeled and seeded (see page 52)
1 small green pepper, finely chopped
½ bunch spring onions/scallions, chopped
1 chilli pepper, seeded and chopped (optional)

2 tablespoons lemon juice
1 tablespoon olive oil
1 large avocado
Stuffing C
225 g/8 oz/2 cups Ricotta or fromage frais
2 tablespoons horseradish, grated
½ bunch spring onions/scallions, chopped
2 tablespoons dill, finely chopped
seasoning to taste
Vegetables
12 large, flat mushrooms
1 large beetroot/beet, cooked and peeled
1 large aubergine/eggplant, salted (see page 52)
3-4 tablespoons olive oil
10 small, ripe tomatoes, peeled (see page 52)

Stuffing A   Chop the pepper, tomatoes and celery, and place in a bowl. Add the garlic and onion, finely chopped. Mix the oil, lemon juice and coriander, stir into the vegetables and season.
Stuffing B   Chop the tomatoes, place in a bowl and add the pepper and spring onions/scallions. Add the chilli then the olive oil and lemon juice and set aside. *Just before using the stuffing*, peel the avocado, chop the flesh finely and add to the mixture.
Stuffing C   Beat the Ricotta until smooth, then mix in the remaining ingredients
Vegetables   Pre-heat the oven to 175°C/350°F/ Gas mark 4. Wipe the mushrooms, cut off the stalks, and lay the caps gills uppermost

on oiled baking trays. Brush with a little oil and bake for 15 minutes. Cut the beetroot/beet into 6 or 8 slices about 5 mm/¼ inch thick. Brush the aubergine/eggplant slices on each side with olive oil and grill until golden. Drain on a cloth. Cut the tops off the tomatoes and scoop out the insides. Leave upside down to drain for 15 minutes. Discard the seeds and juice, but chop any firm parts, including the lids. Add to the stuffing. Put mounds of stuffing A on each mushroom cap, pile stuffing B on to slices of beetroot/beet and aubergine/eggplant, and arrange on a large platter. Finally, fill the tomatoes with stuffing C and dot them in between the other vegetables.

 # Watercress salad

Freshen the palate between the main course and dessert with this simple salad. I would serve it with a whole cheese (or part of one), such as Vacherin, chèvre, unpasteurized Camembert or Brie - whatever happens to be in really perfect condition on the day. Accompany it with water biscuits and unsalted butter.

4 bunches watercress
3 shallots, peeled and finely chopped (see page 52)
black pepper

6 tablespoons olive oil
2 tablespoons orange juice
2 tablespoons lemon juice

Wash and dry the watercress, selecting only the tender tips for the salad. Pile loosely in a bowl and scatter with the shallots. Add a little coarsely ground black pepper. Mix the olive oil with the fruit juices, and set aside. Pour over the salad just before serving and toss well.

Glazed root vegetables with wild rice timbale

Here is a dramatic main course. Turn out the timbale into the centre of a really big, round dish and surround with the vegetables, sprinkling them with sesame seeds and chopped parsley, and using dill or flat parsley as a garnish.

For the wild rice timbale
150 g/5 oz/¾ cup wild rice, washed
150 g/5 oz/¾ cup short grain brown rice, washed
150 g/5 oz/¾ cup basmati rice, washed
50 g/2 oz/¼ cup melted butter
seasoning to taste
For the vegetables
450 g/1 lb pickling onions, peeled (see page 52)
450 g/1 lb small leeks, weighed after trimming
450 g/1 lb small carrots, scraped
450 g/1 lb fennel, weighed after trimming
225 g/½ lb parsnips, peeled

225 g/½ lb Jerusalem artichokes, weighed after peeling
225 g/½ lb chestnuts, weighed after shelling
1.2 litres/2 pints/5 cups vegetable stock
For the glaze
75 g/3 oz/⅓ cup butter
3 tablespoons dry vermouth
1½ tablespoons white wine vinegar
seasoning to taste
1½ tablespoons sugar
1 tablespoon cornflour/cornstarch
5 tablespoons sesame seeds, toasted (see page 56)
5 tablespoons parsley, chopped

Cook the 3 types of rice (see page 50). Drain and mix with the butter and seasoning. Turn into an oiled 1.5-litre/2½-pint/6-cup pudding basin/steaming mould, cover and keep hot. Chop all the vegetables, except the onions, into 2-cm/1-inch pieces. (If the carrots are tiny, leave whole.) Shell and quarter the chestnuts (see page 52). Boil the carrots for 5 minutes, then drain. Melt 4 tablespoons of the butter in a deep frying pan or casserole. Add the onions, leeks and fennel. Cook until brown. Heat the stock and add just enough to cover the vegetables. Cover and simmer until just tender. Drain, adding the liquid to the reserved stock. Put these vegetables, plus the chestnuts, with the others. Reduce the reserved stock to 450 ml/15 fl oz/2 scant cups. Add the vermouth, vinegar, seasoning and sugar. Mix the cornflour/cornstarch with 2 tablespoons of the hot liquid. Add to the pan, stirring continuously until it boils. Simmer for 2 minutes. Pour over the vegetables, add the sesame and parsley, then mix gently.

Ginger ice cream

Ice cream is best when freshly made and eaten within 2-3 days of making. Rest it at room temperature for 30 minutes before serving it scattered with fresh raspberries or chopped preserved stem ginger. Eat with thin ginger biscuits.

600 ml/1 pint/2½ cups milk
4 eggs and 4 egg yolks, beaten
50 g/2 oz/4 tablespoons castor/superfine sugar

6 tablespoons preserved stem ginger syrup
600 ml/1 pint/2½ cups double/heavy cream, lightly whipped

Heat the milk until almost boiling. Gradually add the sugar to the eggs. When smooth, place the bowl over a pan of simmering water. Pour on the hot milk, beating steadily with a wire whisk as it cooks. When it thickens very slightly (in about 10 minutes), and just coats the back of a wooden spoon, remove the bowl and stand it in cold water, stirring often. When merely warm, remove the bowl, stir in the syrup, then fold in the cream. Transfer the mixture to an ice cream machine or a 1.5 litre/2½-pint/6-cup plastic container in the freezer. If using a freezer, beat the mixture thoroughly after 1½ hours. Freeze again and repeat the process twice more after 30-45 minutes.

Martha Rose Shulman's Thanksgiving

The reason I chose to be a cook in the first place has as much to do with my sense of conviviality as it does with my passion for cooking good, healthy food. Give me an excuse for a celebration and the table will be set. Sharing food and wine with friends and family is what Thanksgiving is all about, and for this reason it's my favourite holiday.

Every year my menu changes. I don't miss the turkey, but I couldn't do without the trimmings - the pumpkin, sweet potatoes, cranberries, and the other foods that are at the height of their season in late November - pears, mushrooms, dark leafy vegetables. Choosing one of those foods as the basis for a main dish is a challenge I enjoy.

For this menu (designed for 6 people) I've taken all the fruit and vegetables that mean Thanksgiving to me, and fitted them in where you might not expect them. Champagne kicks off the festivities. Serve it before the meal with light hors d'oeuvres - crudités with a dip of herbed goat cheese mixed with yoghurt, apple slices tossed in lime juice. and mixed nuts and raisins - just enough to whet the appetite.

The first course, a puréed mushroom soup, accompanied by a tawny-coloured, grainy bread, is heady with garlic and the savoury, 'meaty' flavour of wild mushrooms. Serve salade mesclun aux clementines between this earthy soup and the main dish. Make a mixture of salad greens such as dandelion, chicory, curly endive (frisée) and arugula, tossed with tangerine sections and a simple vinaigrette. The bitter greens and sweet tangerines complement each other, and the salad has a clean, refreshing taste which readies the palate for the next course.

Pumpkin ravioli might sound rather strange, but it's a traditional Northern Italian dish, and it's unforgettable - not at all like pumpkin pie wrapped in pasta, as one friend imagined it would be. Serve with plain steamed broccoli.

November is the month for drinking the first wines of the season, the 'primeurs'. Both Beaujolais Nouveau and Gamay Touraine have light, festive, fruity flavours which go beautifully with the dishes in this meal. If the primeurs aren't good this season, choose another reputable year.

The final dish, a cranberry-pear tarte is especially striking: as it bakes, the cranberry juices run between the slices of pear and the tarte looks like a colourful pinwheel.

At most Thanksgiving dinners, sounds of ecstasy gradually give way to groans of surfeit, but this meal is essentially a light one: you don't leave the table feeling stuffed. That's another reason to add it to your holiday repertoire.

Clockwise from top: Salade mesclun aux clementines, Steamed broccoli, wholewheat bread with oatmeal, bulgar and corn meal, Mixed mushroom soup, Pumpkin ravioli, Cranberry-pear tarte

 # Mixed mushroom soup

This is a warming and delicious start to the meal. Any wild mushrooms can be used - chanterelles, pleurotes, cèpes - but if you can't find them, use more dried cèpes or 'porcini' instead; the soup will still be delicious. The broth is an infusion obtained by soaking the dried mushrooms in boiling water; the mushrooms are cooked in a small amount of butter, olive oil and red wine with shallots and garlic before simmering in the broth. Finely chopped, sautéed cèpes, stirred into the soup after it has been puréed, add texture and a savoury touch. This is easy to make and can be kept for a day in the refrigerator.

50 g/2 oz dried cèpes or 'porcini'
550 g/1¼ lb fresh cultivated mushrooms, or a mixture of wild mushrooms
juice of 1 lemon
2 tablespoons butter
3 medium shallots, peeled and finely chopped (see page 52)
3-4 large garlic cloves, crushed
2 tablespoons olive oil

scant 1.2 litres/2 pints/5 cups vegetable stock or water (see page 110)
1 medium size potato, peeled and diced
150 ml/5 fl oz/⅔ cup dry red wine
2 tablespoons soy sauce
½ teaspoon each thyme and rosemary, chopped
seasoning to taste
4 tablespoons crème fraîche
chopped fresh parsley for garnish

Soak the dried cèpes in boiling water for 20-30 minutes. Thinly slice 6 attractive mushrooms, toss in lemon juice and set aside for the final garnish. Quarter the remaining mushrooms. Melt the butter over a medium heat and sauté the shallots with 1 garlic clove until brown. Drain the cèpes, reserving the liquid. Rinse thoroughly and squeeze dry. Set aside 6 heaped tablespoons, and add the remaining cèpes to the shallots with 1 tablespoon olive oil, the fresh mushrooms and the remaining garlic. Cook over a medium heat for 5-10 minutes; add the rest of the wine, then the soy sauce, thyme and rosemary, and sauté for another 10 minutes. Strain the reserved mushroom liquid and add stock to make up to 1.2 litres/2 pints/5 cups. Pour into the mushrooms, add the potato, bring to the boil, then cover and simmer for 30 minutes.

Meanwhile, finely chop the reserved cèpes, heat the remaining oil and sauté them for 5 minutes. Season to taste. Purée the soup and return to the heat. Season, then add the remaining wine. Whisk in the crème fraîche and stir in the sautéed cèpes. Heat through and serve, garnished with parsley and the reserved lemon mushrooms.

Wholewheat bread with oatmeal, bulgar and corn meal

There are two stages to making the loaves in this recipe. First of all you make a 'sponge' batter, richly flavoured with honey and molasses. When this has 'worked' and become bubbly, the rest of the ingredients are added to make a dough. The mixed grains give it a delicious texture and appearance. If you are new to bread-making, read the notes on page 102 before embarking on this recipe.

10 g/½ oz/1 tablespoon micronized/active dry yeast
750 ml/1¼ pints/3 cups lukewarm water
2 tablespoons mild-flavoured honey
2 tablespoons molasses
225 g/8 oz/2 cups unbleached white flour
225 g/8 oz/2 cups wholewheat flour
4 tablespoons melted butter or safflower oil

1 tablespoon salt
100 g/4 oz/scant 1 cup flaked oats
175 g/6 oz/1 cup bulgar or cracked wheat
75 g/3 oz/¾ cup corn meal
350 g/12 oz/3 cups wholewheat flour
1 egg, beaten for glaze
2 tablespoons sesame seeds for topping

Mix the yeast with the water, honey and molasses. Gradually whisk in the first two lots of flour until you have a smooth batter. Cover and leave in a warm spot for 1 hour, until bubbling. Add the butter and salt, then fold in the oats, bulgar and corn meal. Gradually add the remaining flour and make a dough. Knead for 10 minutes. If sticky, flour your hands and the work surface. Form the dough into a ball, place in an oiled bowl, cover and leave to rise for 1½ hours. Punch down the dough, divide into two loaves and place in oiled loaf pans. Cover lightly and leave to rise for 1 hour. Pre-heat the oven to 180°C/350°F/Gas mark 4. Brush the loaves with beaten egg and sprinkle with sesame seeds. Make 3 slashes across each loaf with a sharp knife and bake for 50-60 minutes.

 ## Pumpkin ravioli

It is not difficult to make pasta, and the end result from this recipe is well worth the time involved. The filling consists of baked, puréed pumpkin combined with Parmesan, breadcrumbs and ground almonds simmered in red wine and sage. It's the sage that makes this dish come alive. Serve the ravioli simply, heated through in melted butter and sprinkled with Parmesan.

450 g/1 lb homemade pasta (see page 49)
1.25 kg/2½ lb fresh pumpkin, seeded
50 g/2 oz/½ cup almonds, toasted and ground
25 g/1 oz/½ cup fresh breadcrumbs (see page 48)
1 teaspoon dried sage, or 7 fresh sage leaves, chopped
120 ml/4 fl oz/½ cup red wine, such as Gamay or Beaujolais
¼ teaspoon each nutmeg and cinnamon
175 g/6 oz/1½ cups Parmesan, freshly grated
seasoning to taste
6-8 tablespoons melted butter

Pre-heat the oven to 200°C/400°F/Gas mark 6. Bake the pumpkin until tender. Peel, and then purée the flesh. Simmer the almonds, breadcrumbs, sage and wine in a large saucepan, evaporating most of the liquid. Stir in the pumpkin and spices and heat through. Remove from the heat, stir in two-thirds of the Parmesan, and season. If the mixture seems watery, add breadcrumbs or Parmesan. Make the ravioli (see page 49). Cook gently in a large pot of boiling, salted water for about 3 minutes, until they float to the surface. Drain, then toss in melted butter and sprinkle with the remaining Parmesan.

  ## Cranberry-pear tarte

Thanksgiving wouldn't be Thanksgiving without cranberries, and in this menu I've worked them into the dessert. This tarte is as beautiful to look at as it is to eat. Use a shallow 30-cm/12-inch tarte pan.

1 sweet pastry case, baked blind (see page 174)
175 ml/6 fl oz/¾ cup fresh orange juice
3 tablespoons cornflour/cornstarch
150 g/5 oz/scant ½ cup mild-flavoured honey
450 g/1 lb cranberries, picked over
2 tablespoons orange zest, grated
3 large Comice pears, peeled, cored and thinly sliced
2 tablespoons lemon juice
2 tablespoons apricot jam

Whisk the orange juice, cornflour/cornstarch and all but 2 tablespoons of honey in a large saucepan. Add half the cranberries and bring to the boil, stirring. Remove from the heat and stir in the remaining cranberries and orange zest. The mixture should be quite thick. Set aside. Pre-heat the oven to 200°C/400°F/Gas mark 6. Toss the pears in the lemon juice and remaining honey. Arrange them in an overlapping ring around the outside edge of the pastry case. Pour the cranberry mixture into the middle. Bake for 25-30 minutes. Meanwhile, melt the jam in a saucepan with any honey and lemon left over from the pears. Use to glaze the cooked tarte. Cool before serving.

Caroline Conran's Christmas Celebration

I like a feeling of abundance at Christmas, with generosity and overflowing glasses, dressing-up, jokes and crackers, and a table covered with fruit, flowers, chocolates, candles and silver sugared-almonds; the extravagance makes everything seem heightened and exciting when Christmas day finally arrives.

Drink lots of champagne, starting well before the meal and continue through the first course, which is an exquisite salad topped with poached eggs and fried green coriander. If you don't like the idea of eggs, you could have small grilled goats' cheeses instead with a few lightly grilled walnuts.

The main course is a glorious tamale pie made of filo pastry. It has a delicious light filling of tomatoes, onions and peppers in a corn meal batter, and can be a spectacular centrepiece if you make it very large.

According to Anne Lindsay Greer in her book, *Cuisine of the American Southwest* (from which I got the idea for this pie), tamales were called 'food of the gods' by the Aztec Indians, and they do indeed taste heavenly. Accompany the pie with dishes of brightly coloured vegetables and bowls of salsa and guacamole. The ideal wine with this is a rich, full Burgundy - a 1976 Moulin à Vent or Nuits St-Georges, or a well-aged Rioja.

Finish the meal with my light version of Christmas pudding, accompanied by syllabub sorbet. If you prefer something even lighter, you could serve an exotic fruit salad, perhaps a combination of pink grapefruit, blood oranges, mangoes, passion fruit and pomegranate. Sprinkle with lemon juice and leave for a few hours before serving. Accompany the dessert with Beaumes de Venise or Monbazillac.

Caroline Conran

Herb salad with oyster mushrooms and poached eggs

This is the ideal beginning to an elaborate meal because the separate parts can be made in advance and then assembled just before you are ready to eat.

3 teaspoons sherry vinegar
1 teaspoon lemon juice
1 garlic clove, crushed
6 tablespoons each olive oil and sunflower oil
salt to taste
350 g/¾ lb oyster or button mushrooms
½ lemon

mixed salad greens, washed and dried (choose from lamb's lettuce, young spinach leaves, watercress, curly endive, chervil, continental parsley, chives, or sorrel)
6 poached eggs (see page 54)
1 bunch fresh coriander, chopped
1 teaspoon sweet paprika

Mix the first 3 ingredients with 2 tablespoons of each oil to make a dressing and set it aside. Trim the mushrooms and rub clean with half a lemon. Keep oyster mushrooms whole or halved, but slice button mushrooms finely. Heat 2 tablespoons of each oil until smoking, and fry the mushrooms until brown. Set aside in the pan. Just before serving, toss the greens with the dressing and put a generous handful on six plates. Reheat the mushrooms briskly. Heat the remaining oil, fry the coriander until it sizzles, then add the paprika. Scatter the mushrooms over each salad and place a poached egg in the middle. Pour some of the coriander mixture over each egg and serve at once.

Clockwise from top: Herb salad with oyster mushrooms and poached eggs, Steamed mange-tout/snow peas, Tamale pie, Christmas pudding, Syllabub sorbet

Tamale pie

This beautiful pie is made from filo pastry which can be bought from delicatessens and good supermarkets. Be sure to buy from somewhere with a reasonably fast turnover, as filo becomes brittle and difficult to work with when old. Keep it in the freezer if you are *storing it for more than a day or two. The pie is served with two Mexican accompaniments: spicy salsa, a red sauce that keeps for up to three days in the refrigerator, and a purée of avocados called guacamole. The pie requires a 32-cm/12½-inch loose-bottomed tart pan.*

For the salsa
1.5 kg/3 lb very red tomatoes
3 Spanish onions, finely chopped
30 sprigs coriander, chopped
4-5 green chillies, grilled, skinned, seeded and chopped
4-5 red chillies, seeded and chopped
2-3 small teaspoons salt
For the pie
3 large peppers, 1 yellow and 2 red, grilled and skinned
2 large Spanish onions, finely chopped
corn oil
2 fresh cobs of corn, boiled and cooled
175 ml/6 fl oz/¾ cup sour cream
3 eggs
2 tablespoons melted butter

225 g/8 oz/2 cups corn meal
65 g/2½ oz/generous ½ cup plain/all-purpose flour
1 teaspoon each bicarbonate of soda and baking powder
½ teaspoon sugar
1 small teaspoon salt
175 ml/6 fl oz/¾ cup milk
6-9 large rectangles filo or strudel pastry
225 g/8 oz/2 cups sharp Cheddar cheese, grated
For the guacamole
flesh of 3 ripe avocados, mashed with a fork
juice of 1-2 lemons
2-3 garlic cloves, finely chopped
cayenne pepper and seasoning to taste
1 tablespoon olive oil (optional)
toasted cumin seeds for garnish

Grill/broil the tomatoes about 12-15 cm/5-6 inches away from a very hot grill until tender and black all over. Leave to cool. Place the onions in a sieve and wash thoroughly, squeezing to remove all the acrid juices. Mix the onion, coriander and chillies. Skin and chop the tomatoes, but include a few bits of blackened skin cut into small pieces. Add to the onion mixture and season with salt.

Core the peppers and cut them into uneven strips or pieces. Soften the onion in 2-3 tablespoons corn oil for 30 minutes, stirring occasionally until tender and transparent, but not brown. Shuck the corn (see page 137). Mix it in a bowl with the cream, eggs and butter, then liquidize for a few seconds to blend the mixture. Sieve the dry ingredients into a large mixing bowl and beat in the egg mixture followed by the milk.

Pre-heat the oven to 175°C/350°F/Gas mark 4. Working quickly to prevent it drying out, lay a sheet of filo on a dampened cloth and brush all over with oil. Place it in the oiled tart pan, covering the bottom and overlapping the sides. Repeat this process with the remaining sheets, pushing them carefully into the sides of the pan and leaving an increasing amount overlapping the edges. Eventually the pastry must cover the top of the pie, so leave enough overlap to meet in the middle. Pour half the corn mixture into the pan and cover with a layer of cooked onions. Arrange the peppers on top - red in the middle, yellow round the outside. Cover with cheese and top with one-third of the salsa. Spread the remaining corn mixture over the top, then fold in the pastry, leaving the corners pointing upwards, so they look like petals. You can cut some more filo triangles to make more petals, but remember to brush them with oil. When the top is to your liking, bake the pie for 40-45 minutes in the middle of the oven until just set. Rest for 10 minutes before serving. Mix the guacamole ingredients together, season to taste and serve.

Christmas pudding

Unlike the traditional heavily fruited pudding, often made several months before the holiday, my pudding is light and made at the last minute. Before it is served, turn it on to a plate, douse it in brandy and set it on fire. The flaming pudding always evokes cries of delight. Make sure you use only the best organic ingredients (untreated and sun-dried) from a good health store.

50 g/2 oz/⅓ cup glacé cherries
225 g/8 oz/2 cups sultanas/golden raisins
225 g/8 oz/2 cups large, seedless raisins
50 g/2 oz/½ cup dried apricots, pre-soaked and chopped
50 g/2 oz/⅓ cup candied peel, chopped
50 g/2 oz/½ cup whole almonds, cut into large pieces
75 g/3 oz/⅔ cup ground almonds
100 g/4 oz/⅔ cup demerara sugar

75 g/3 oz/1½ cups fresh brown breadcrumbs (see page 48)
200 g/7 oz/1 scant cup softened butter
nutmeg, cinnamon and mixed spice to make 1 teaspoonful
juice and zest of ½ an orange and ½ a lemon
2 eggs
3 tablespoons brandy
1-2 tablespoons milk
pinch of salt

Mix the fruit, peel, whole and ground nuts, sugar and breadcrumbs together. Rub in the butter with your fingers, then stir in the spices. Beat the remaining ingredients in a bowl, then mix into the fruit. Let everyone stir the pudding and make a wish, then transfer it to a well-buttered 1-litre/1¾-pint/1-quart pudding basin/steaming mould. Cover loosely with buttered greaseproof/waxed paper, then cover with foil and tie tightly with string. (You must leave room for the pudding to expand.) Place the pudding in a saucepan and add boiling water to about 2 cm/1 inch below the string. Boil for 4 hours, making sure it doesn't boil dry. On Christmas Day, replace the foil cover with a fresh one and boil the pudding for a further 1-2 hours. Serve with the syllabub sorbet.

Syllabub sorbet

The traditional accompaniment to Christmas pudding is brandy butter, a rich and rather cloying taste. I think it's a good idea to eat the pudding with this sorbet. Serve it on separate little plates, and have a mouthful of deliciously hot pudding followed by a cooling mouthful of icy sorbet. It will make you very merry, so if you don't want it to be quite so alcoholic, heat the wine and sherry to boiling point and then allow to cool before you make the sorbet.

450 ml/15 fl oz/scant 2 cups Beaumes de Venise or other muscatel
300 ml/10 fl oz/1¼ cups very pale, dry sherry

juice and zest of 3-4 lemons
225-300 g/8-10 oz/1-1½ cups brown or white sugar
4 egg whites, beaten

Mix the wine with the sherry, lemon juice and zest, then chill in the refrigerator. Dissolve the sugar in 150 ml/5 fl oz/generous ⅔ cup water in a saucepan, then bring to the boil and boil for 5 minutes. Cool in a basin of cold water, then add to the chilled wine mixture, tasting to see how much is needed. Chill well, then add the egg whites and transfer to the freezer or sorbetière. If using a freezer, beat the mixture at least twice while it is freezing; this gives a much better texture.

Barbara Kafka's Wedding Salutation

I am a sentimentalist. I see a happy wedding, not a shotgun. I see a mild spring or summer day with fluffy clouds, no rain, and a garden flourished with bloom. Of course, all that may not be true, but the flavours and style of the wedding feast can at least evoke that happy image. Moistened by champagne or prosecco, spirits can soar.

This meal (designed for 12 people) is as beautiful to see as it is good to eat, and may be easily divided or multiplied. It starts with elegant individual portions of quails' eggs in 'aspic' and is followed by a sumptuous mound of steamed cous cous and 'baby' vegetables. (If you have difficulty in finding baby vegetables, cut large ones into attractive shapes. They will require less cooking than whole vegetables.)

The cous cous is served with a pungent, red sauce called 'harissa'. It can be made as spicy as you like, or think your guests might enjoy, by upping the quantities of sambal and harissa. Increase the other seasonings proportionately to maintain the balance.

No wedding would be complete without a cake. I have chosen to make a layered genoise - three tiers sandwiched together and iced with delicious camomile buttercream. Crushed caramel is scattered all over the cake and sparkles like jewels. All the work on this menu can be done ahead up until the final steaming of the cous cous and vegetables, which can be done without surveillance while the first course is being eaten. I hope it brings added joy and good memories to this day.

Barbara Kafka

Oeufs en gelée

This is a first course in festive miniature. The tender green gel tastes lightly of tarragon and looks like all springtime if nestled into lightly dressed greens set off by a peppery yellow or orange nasturtium blossom. If it is too early for nasturtiums, use a sprinkling of violets or old-fashioned rose petals, or the petals from chive flowers. Green glass or majolica plates would be ideal. If you have never worked with agar agar to make a gel, I think you will be pleasantly surprised. It sets at room temperature; which makes it easy to use.

18 quail's eggs, hard-boiled and peeled
(see page 54)
450 g/1 lb spinach, stemmed and washed
juice of 1 lemon
475 ml/16 fl oz/2 cups water

12 fresh tarragon leaves
25 g/1 oz prepared agar agar (see page 40)
2 teaspoons kosher salt
⅛ teaspoon white pepper, freshly ground

Cut the eggs in half lengthways, then cover and reserve. Purée the spinach with the lemon juice, pour into a large piece of double-thickness cheesecloth and squeeze all the liquid into a saucepan. (There should be 250 ml/8 fl oz/1 cup of brilliant green juice.) Add the water and bring to the boil. Drop in the tarragon, cover and infuse for 10 minutes. Stir in the agar agar, add the salt and pepper, then strain through a fine mesh. Put a tablespoon of spinach liquid in each of 12 ramekins. Allow to set, then arrange 3 egg halves on top - 2 with yolks down. Carefully fill the ramekins with the remaining spinach liquid and allow to set. Refrigerate covered until ready to use. Unmould and serve individually on a bed of tender salad greens dressed with vinaigrette.

Clockwise from top left: Harissa sauce,
Vegetable cous cous, Oeufs en gelée,
Wedding cake

 # Vegetable cous cous

In contrast to the first course which is served in elegant individual portions, this main course is startling and ample - a contemporary variant on a classic Bedouin marriage dish that would be made with lamb and other meats. Here it is made with the most beautiful of tiny, early vegetables in a brilliantly garish plethora of vivid colours. Serve this splendidly festive dish with small bowls of spicy harissa sauce. Note: The best harissa paste is French, available in tubes. Sambal olek is a spicy Oriental chutney available from delicatessens. Kosher salt is blessed.

Traditionally the Bedouin bride would have divided the grains with her own silver comb. I am indebted to Paula Wolfert's classic, Cous Cous and Other Good Food from Morocco, *for the Bedouin information, as well as for hints on the basic method of preparing cous cous.*

For the cous cous
1.5 kg/3 lb/6 cups cous cous, not instant
1.5 litres/2½ pints/6 cups tomato juice
1.5 litres/2½ pints/6 cups water
12 garlic cloves, peeled and crushed (see page 52)
1 teaspoon anise seed
2 teaspoons each cumin, coriander and ginger, ground
¼ teaspoon each allspice and fresh nutmeg, ground
4 teaspoons kosher salt
1 teaspoon each crushed red pepper and cardomom, ground
½ teaspoon cinnamon, ground
4 tablespoons olive oil
1 small bunch fresh coriander sprigs
For the vegetables
10 baby artichokes
juice of 1 lemon
24 baby carrots, scraped with 1 cm/½ inch stem left

24 baby turnips, scraped with 1 cm/½ inch stem left
24 small, fresh okra pods, trimmed (see page 155)
24 ears fresh baby corn, shucked (see page 137)
8 fresh tomatoes, seeded and quartered
12 tiny purple finger aubergines/eggplant
50 pearl onions, peeled (see page 52)
24 spears fresh asparagus, snapped and peeled
For the harissa
250 ml/8 fl oz/1 cup tomato stock or juice
225 g/½ lb tomatoes, peeled, chopped and seeded (see page 52)
1 garlic clove, crushed
1 teaspoon each sambal olek and harissa paste
½ teaspoon anise seed
¼ teaspoon coriander seed, ground
⅛ teaspoon cinnamon, ground
½ teaspoon cumin, ground
2 tablespoons each fresh lemon and lime juice
1 tablespoon olive oil

Prepare the cous cous as described on page 123, but for this quantity use 2.75 litres/5¼ pints/3 quarts. A large roasting pan is the ideal receptacle. Place the rest of the ingredients in a 4.5-litre/4-quart casserole and bring to a rolling boil. Meanwhile, line a steamer with a double thickness of cheesecloth large enough to extend over the sides. Fill with the prepared cous cous and place over the now simmering tomato sauce for 20 minutes. Dump the cous cous back in the roasting pan, break up any lumps and leave to swell and dry. Cut 4-5 cm/1½-2 inches off the top of the artichokes. Remove the small, discoloured basal leaves. Cut the stems even with the bases, then cut each artichoke in half lengthways and rub all over with lemon juice. Pour the remaining lemon juice into a bowl and add 475 ml/16 fl oz/2 cups of water. Immerse the artichokes in this until ready to use.

When the cous cous is dry and lump-free, replace it in the cheesecloth-lined steamer. Return the tomato sauce to a simmer, drain the artichokes and put them cut side down in the sauce. Place the cous cous steamer on top and steam for 10 minutes. Add all the vegetables, except the asparagus, to the sauce, replace the steamer and cook for 5 minutes. Finally, add the asparagus and cook for 5 minutes. Remove from the heat and toss the cous cous in the oil. Pile on to a large, flat platter. Make a deep, wide well in the mound and heap in the drained vegetables. Wreath with the coriander sprigs. Drizzle the cous cous with a *little* of the tomato sauce, adding tomato juice and more seasoning if necessary. Bring all the harissa ingredients, except the oil, to the boil, then simmer for 5 minutes. Turn off the heat, stir in the oil and serve.

 # Wedding cake

One could, of course, have a traditional wedding cake with white layers studded with candied fruit and coated with virtually inedible hard, white royal icing. Instead I think a gentler cake, although gala in form and decoration, would be this layered cake made with wholewheat, honey and an infusion of camomile. The icing is pale ivory and irresistible. Once again, the fresh flower decoration is edible. If the cake seems heavy on butter, sugar and eggs, don't worry; a small portion won't damage your health!
Note: This recipe requires 3 round cake pans: 30 x 6 cm/12 x 2½ inches (large), 23 x 6 cm/9 x 2½ inches (medium), and 15 x 6 cm/6 x 2½ inches (small). As most home mixers are not very big, prepare the mix in two batches and divide it proportionally between the layers.

For the cake
225 g/8 oz/2 cups wholewheat flour
100 g/4 oz/1 cup white flour
18 large eggs
300 g/10 oz/1½ cups sugar
1 tablespoon orange zest, finely grated
1 tablespoon vanilla essence/extract
175 g/6 oz/⅔ cup melted butter
For the imbibing syrup
350 ml/12 fl oz/1½ cups Marsala
3 tablespoons mild honey (preferably camomile)

For the camomile buttercream
900 ml/1½ pints/4 cups milk
175 ml/6 fl oz/¾ cup camomile tea
21 egg yolks
800 g/1¾ lb/4 cups granulated sugar
1.25 kg/2½ lb unsalted butter, softened and cut into 2-cm/1-inch pieces
For the honey caramel garnish
120 ml/4 fl oz/½ cup water
2 teaspoons camomile
175 g/6 oz/½ cup mild honey

Pre-heat the oven to 180°C/350°F/Gas mark 4. Butter the cake pans and line the bottom of each with greaseproof/waxed paper. Butter each paper and lightly dust each pan with flour. Sift the flours together twice and reserve. Whisk the eggs, sugar and zest in a large heat-proof bowl. Place over a pan of simmering water and whisk again until warm and frothy. Remove from the heat and beat at high speed for 10 minutes, until tripled in volume and cooled. Using a rubber spatula, gently fold in the flours, followed by the vanilla and butter. Pour into the pans and bake for 20-30 minutes, or until just firm to the touch. Rest for 5 minutes, then turn on to wire racks to cool completely. Mix the syrup ingredients together in a saucepan and cook over a low heat until just combined. Cool and reserve. Scald the milk, remove from the heat and add the camomile tea. Cover the pan and allow to infuse for 10 minutes. Strain. Beat the egg yolks with the sugar, then gradually beat in the infused milk. Transfer to a saucepan and cook over a medium heat, stirring constantly with a wooden spoon until the mixture thickens enough to coat the back of the spoon. Pour into a large bowl and beat with an electric mixer until completely cooled. Beating at medium speed, gradually incorporate the butter bit by bit.

Refrigerate until ready to use. Butter a sheet of greaseproof/waxed paper on both sides. Place on a buttered baking sheet and chill. Bring the water to the boil in a small, heavy saucepan, add the camomile, then cover and infuse for 10 minutes. Strain, and clean the pan. Return the infusion to the pan and stir in the honey. Cook over a medium heat to hard crack (150-155°C/300-310°F on a sugar thermometer). Pour on to the buttered paper, tilting the sheet to get a thin layer. When set, grind the caramel into small pieces (not a powder).
Final presentation
Cut each cake layer in half horizontally. Beginning with the large layer, lightly soak the cut sides in the syrup. Sandwich the layers together with 5 mm/¼ inch of buttercream. Keep in the freezer while preparing the other layers in the same way. Generously frost the large layer, smoothing the sides and top, then return to the freezer. Repeat with the other layers. Freeze all the layers for 15 minutes, then smooth with an icing spatula dipped in warm water. Place the ground caramel in a bowl. Hold each layer at an angle and press caramel on to the sides. Centre the layers on top of each other, finishing with the smallest. If you like sprinkle caramel over the rest of the cake or garnish with wreaths of fresh camomile flowers.

CHAPTER 6

The Vegetarian Family

Though most people are aware that a vegetarian diet is a healthy one, there are underlying anxieties about some nutritional aspects of daily meals, especially if you have a large family with babies, young children and perhaps elderly members all living under one roof. Of course, these worries exist if you are living alone, but they can seem excessive in a large family. So how does one achieve a balanced vegetarian diet without a great deal of hassle and chore?

One of the most constant worries is whether the vegetarian gets enough protein without animal foods. The answer is yes. Even the most spartan of vegetarians can get sufficient protein from grains, legumes and nuts, while more sybaritic vegetarians like myself will have it in eggs and dairy products, tofu, sesame and a hundred other delicacies and combinations.

Another basic worry is that going vegetarian will cause the cook a lot more trouble, and that it needs special skills and expertise. I believe vegetarian cooking is far *less* trouble than a carnivorous diet - once you're organized. (Follow the suggestions in Chapter 2 to help you.) The only skills involved are the basic cooking ones that you would need anyway, which are easily acquired. You probably do need to have at least some imagination, and it also helps to be willing to experiment with new foods and flavours. If everyone in the family is vegetarian, there's no problem. It is when individuals have different dietary preferences and requirements that meals can be a little more awkward. Planning and preparation is the answer - a well-stocked store cupboard and refrigerator.

Remember, the greater the range of foods in your diet and the more varied the dishes, the more likely you are to get all the nutrients you need. Basically, this message is true for every member of the family at every stage throughout life, though at each stage there will be different requirements.

Fig fudge ㉚ Ⓥ

A treat for all the family. Although the sugar content is high, an occasional indulgence won't do any harm. This recipe makes about 450 g/1 lb of fudge.

225 g/½ lb dried figs
zest and juice from 1 lemon
225 g/½ lb/1 generous cup castor/superfine sugar
75 ml/3 fl oz/⅓ cup water
25 g/½ lb ground almonds
50 g/2 oz/scant ½ cup carob powder
1 teaspoon cinnamon

Purée the figs. Mix the sugar, lemon and water and bring slowly to the boil, until the sugar has dissolved. Mix all the ingredients thoroughly. Cook until the mixture comes away from the sides of the pan. Transfer to a shallow dish, cool, and then cut into small squares and dust with icing sugar.

*Tempura - slices of vegetables dipped in
light batter and deep-fried - can be made at
table with all members of the family
participating. Here it is served with Rice
and almond salad, and two dipping sauces.
Fresh lychees and pawpaw/papaya are the
perfect dessert (see page 136, 123 and 194).*

Babies and toddlers

It should go without saying that all babies have the same nutritional requirements whether they are vegetarian or not. Babies under a year old will need three times as much protein per pound of body weight as do adults. Children over a year and up to the age of twelve will need twice as much.

For babies up to six months old, breast milk will provide enough nutrients, though an iron supplement may be advised at three months. Consult your doctor on this. There will, nevertheless, be some other foods you can introduce at this stage, such as puréed avocado or sweet potato, and up to the time when your baby is weaned. By the age of one, he/she should be on solid foods.

The diet of a vegetarian child at this stage should contain grains, legumes, vegetables, fruit and dairy products and at least one meal in the day should involve complementary protein, although, since adult foods fall naturally into a complementary pattern, children's probably will as well. Remember that seeds have high nutritional content, particularly sesame seeds. Because it is extremely bland, tofu is one of those foods which can be flavoured with anything your baby is fond of. It can, for example, be added to milk shakes flavoured with carob or fruit.

One of the great standbys after weaning is bean and vegetable soup with milk. Remember, avoid all foods with added sugars, such as fruits in heavy syrups, jams and jellies, for the baby will quickly acquire a taste for sweet foods.

There are two main concerns for babies and toddlers - calcium and iron. Lacto-vegetarian children will be getting enough calcium from dairy products but vegan children must get it from such things as broccoli and raisins and should also have sufficient vitamin D intake, as this enables calcium to be absorbed (a good source of vitamin D is fortified soya milk).

The other worry is whether baby and mother are getting enough iron. Sometimes iron supplements may be needed with premature babies. Certainly, when the baby is six months old, foods rich in iron, such as legumes and seeds, should be an habitual part of the diet and consuming vitamin C at the same time to aid the iron absorption is sensible. A third area of concern for vegan children is adequate vitamin B_{12} consumption (in, say, fortified soya milk). Take advice from your doctor or paediatrician. The recipe ideas following make one serving unless stated otherwise.

Split pea soup ⑩ Ⓥ Ⓟ Ⓕ

The flavour of split peas is always popular. This soup is best eaten hot or warm, as it tends to thicken when cold. This recipe makes enough for 4 servings.

75 g/3 oz/¾ cup split peas, soaked for 1 hour
1 carrot, grated
1 onion, grated
900 ml/1½ pints/3¾ cups water
1 tablespoon wheatgerm

Mix the split peas with the carrot, onion and water, and simmer for 40 minutes. Add the wheatgerm, cool and then blend to a purée.

Apple cheese ③ Ⓟ

This is a traditional English dish that makes an ideal breakfast or lunch and will slip down easily.

1 eating apple, peeled and grated
3 tablespoons cottage cheese
1 tablespoon wheatgerm

Mix everything together thoroughly.

Rice and lentils ⑮ Ⓟ Ⓕ

This dish, which may be eaten hot or cold, is an ideal source of complementary protein.

2 tablespoons cooked brown rice (see page 50)
1 tablespoon lentils, cooked (see page 51)
1 baby courgette/zucchini, grated
1 tablespoon plain yoghurt

Mix everything together.

Bean and buckwheat pilaf ⑩ Ⓥ Ⓟ Ⓕ

It is important to peel the cooked beans in this recipe, as the skin is indigestible - get your toddler to help. The inner bean is deliciously moist and tender.

3 tablespoons buckwheat, cooked (see page 50)
1 tablespoon French/snap beans, cooked and finely chopped
1 tablespoon broad/fava beans, cooked and finely chopped

Mix everything together thoroughly.

Rice and asparagus pilaf ⑮ Ⓥ Ⓕ

This is a rather special meal for a toddler. It can be made with the cheaper, thin pieces of asparagus, sometimes called 'sprue'.

3 tablespoons brown rice, cooked (see page 00)
3 asparagus spears, steamed and chopped
1 tablespoon wheatgerm

Mix everything together thoroughly.

Soya beans and tomato ⑮ Ⓥ Ⓟ Ⓕ

You won't have any problems in getting your child to eat this mixture, as babies love the sweet taste of ripe tomatoes.

1 tablespoon soya beans, cooked and finely mashed (see page 51)
2 tablespoon brown rice, cooked (see page 50)
1 tomato, peeled and blended to a purée

Mix everything together thoroughly.

Sandwich spread ② P F

Children adore this mixture. The sweetness of the banana offsets the powerful taste of peanut butter.

3 tablespoons cottage cheese
1 tablespoon peanut butter
1 banana, thinly sliced

Mix everything together.

Lentil burgers ② V P F

Seduce your child with this lentil burger - a delicious mixture of flavours and a good alternative to hamburgers. Pop them into a bun, or serve with homemade baked beans. Enough for 4 burgers.

75 g/3 oz/¾ cup lentils, cooked until soft (see page 51)
1 egg
pinch each of garlic salt, parsley, sage and thyme
1 tablespoon crushed walnuts
1 tablespoon brown breadcrumbs (see page 48)
2 tablespoons chopped onion
slices of hard cheese

Pre-heat the oven to 180°C/350°F/Gas mark 4. Mix everything together, except the onion and cheese. Mould into cake shapes and roll in the onion. Place on a baking tray, put a slice of cheese over each burger and bake for 12-15 minutes.

Tofu and raisins ② V P

Tofu is perfect for babies, as it is soft and bland. The broccoli is high in iron and the raisins add a pleasant sweetness to this dish.

25 g/1 oz tofu
10 raisins (soaked for 2 hours, then chopped)
small sprig broccoli, finely grated

Mix everything together thoroughly.

Orange and apricot drink ③ V F

Although your children won't appreciate the fact that this drink is high in vitamins and minerals, they will love the taste.

50 g/2 oz/½ cup dried apricots, soaked overnight in
200 ml/7 fl oz/1 scant cup fresh orange juice
3 teaspoons clear honey

Blend the apricots with the orange juice to a smooth purée. Add the honey and mix thoroughly.

 *Everyone likes 'finger food' - particularly
children. This selection of crudités and
crackers is served with three dips: Yoghurt
and sesame, Lentil purée and Avocado purée
(see pages 186 and 189)*

Young children

Many children automatically want to eat the same meals as their parents, because they like to feel 'grown up' so there is generally no problem in introducing new foods and flavours to them. But it is wise never to make anyone eat what they do not want to. Some children, for example, do not take easily to strongly spiced food. Very young children will still be wanting some of their foods mashed or puréed.

Growing children need more protein than fully grown adults (with the exception of pregnant women who also need more). So provide meals with complete or complementary protein. Examples of complete protein foods are milk, eggs and cheese, and an easy way of ensuring it is to add skimmed milk to recipes when baking. Examples of complementary protein are combinations of cereal with milk, rice with legumes, or legumes and sesame seeds. Another example is any form of wheat with cooked dried beans, or soya beans and peanuts. Toast with baked beans is an excellent meal, but a sandwich of miso and sesame spread (see page 138) with added salad vegetables would be ideal.

Looked at this way, one can clearly see that good nutritional food can be very simple and everyday; it need not be a banquet which has taken hours to prepare.

Remember that all dried beans and peas are an excellent substitute for protein from animal flesh, provided they are combined correctly (see chart on 25). Do not ignore the nutritional riches of nuts and seeds; few of them need to be eaten to enrich a meal in dietary terms, and when they are combined with rice and grains or legumes, you achieve complete protein.

Though we tend to forget it, there is also protein in vegetables. A large potato has as much protein as half a glass of milk, but it is not the complete protein found in milk.

It is not difficult to find good but popular children's foods and make them at home, thus ensuring that they are additive-free and wholesome. Pizzas are eternal favourites and there are dozens of excellent toppings with cheese. Near cousins to the pizza - tarts and quiches - work out almost as popular when made with vegetables, eggs and cheese.

There are many other delicious possibilities: bean dishes, as in baked beans, or chilli beans or bean moussaka; pasta dishes made with wholewheat spaghetti; outdoor barbecue food like vegetable kebabs and all the variety of burgers made from soy beans and tofu; baked potatoes with various fillings, barbecued corn, stuffed turnovers and pitta bread, cheese and nut spreads and raw vegetables with pâtés and dips.

Tofu comes into its own in desserts, for it can be puréed with fruit, sprinkled with nuts and made into ice cream. It can also be added to eggs and cream to enrich desserts.

Winter salad ⑩

As children frequently dislike greens, this salad is a good way to ensure that they eat them nonetheless. It is a kind of coleslaw made with yoghurt rather than mayonnaise. This recipe makes enough for 4.

¼ white/tight-head green cabbage, finely grated
2 red eating apples, finely grated
2 tablespoons raisins
4 tablespoons beansprouts
3 tablespoons plain yoghurt

Mix everything together thoroughly.

Sandwich fillings

Sandwich fillings are most delicious when there is a combination of crunch and softness which is why sliced cucumber and tomato are so successful. A sandwich composed of salad leaves needs a little mayonnaise (or low-fat soft cheese) to moisten it.

Cottage or curd cheese makes a good filling if mixed with chopped fresh herbs, especially parsley or finely chopped onion and celery.

Peanut butter is a favourite with most children, but try to buy one without sugar or chemical additives. All peanut butter needs a little salt.

Fillings for baked potatoes

Split baked potatoes in half and mix the insides with finely chopped onion and two tablespoons of Smetana/low-fat sour cream, or 1 tablespoon grated Cheddar cheese. Alternatively, mix them with finely sliced mushrooms, peppers, sweetcorn, cream cheese or blue cheese and chopped herbs.

Filling for pitta bread ⑤ P F

Almost as lavish as a club sandwich, but more delicious. Use wholewheat pitta bread, cut them in half and fill the pockets. Children will enjoy making these themselves. Serves 2.

10 g/½ oz/1 tablespoon butter
2 eggs
2 tomatoes, peeled and chopped (see page 52)
2 sticks of celery, chopped
2 tablespoons haricot/navy beans, cooked (see page 51)

Melt the butter in a pan and scramble the eggs with the tomatoes. When cooked, mix in the chopped celery and beans and stir well.

Egg custard ⑩ P̄

*It's worth making real egg custard as it tastes
so much better than the packet variety, and it
provides lots of nutrition for growing
children. This recipe serves 4.*

Variation
● *A richer custard can be made by
substituting single/light cream for milk; this is
a famous dish called crème brûlée.*

4 eggs
25 g/1 oz/2 tablespoons castor/superfine sugar
½ teaspoon vanilla essence/extract
600 ml/1 pint/2½ cups milk

Pre-heat the oven to 160°C/325°F/Gas mark 3. Lightly butter
a baking dish. Beat the eggs, sugar and vanilla together in a
bowl. Heat the milk to just below boiling point, add to the
eggs and mix thoroughly. Place the baking dish in a bain
marie (see page 53), pour the custard into it and bake for 45
minutes or until set.

Tofu and almond dessert ⑤ V̄ P̄

*Your child won't need much encouragement
to eat this delicious dessert, and you'll have
the added satisfaction of knowing that it's high
in protein. Makes 4 servings.*

125 g/5 oz tofu
1 tablespoon honey
25 g/1 oz/2 tablespoons ground almonds
1 teaspoon vanilla essence/extract
25 g/1 oz/¼ cup almonds, flaked/slivered

Purée the tofu with the honey, vanilla and ground almonds.
Place in a dish and decorate with the flaked/slivered
almonds.

Baked Alaska ⑮ P̄

*This is a particularly startling combination of
hot and cold that is exciting to look at and to
eat. Use the ice cream recipe on page 217,
adding 1 teaspoon of vanilla essence/extract
instead of the ginger syrup.*

1 sponge flan case
1 pint vanilla ice cream (see page 217)
4 eggs, separated
225 g/8 oz/1 generous cup castor/superfine sugar

Pre-heat the oven to 220°C/425°F/Gas mark 7. Whisk the egg
whites until stiff (using the yolks in the ice cream). Fold in
the sugar a tablespoon at a time. Generously fill the flan case
with ice cream and heap the meringue on top. Bake for only
a few minutes - until the meringue is golden brown. Serve
immediately.

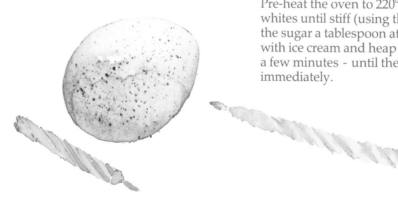

It's a good idea to relax the rules about
children eating sugar, particularly on
birthdays. This Baked Alaska - a sponge
base filled with ice cream and topped with
meringue - is a special treat that will
satisfy any child's longing for sweet things.

Adolescents

Adolescence is a time when the young are searching for their identity, and much experimentation occurs. Limitations and restrictions will be tested, tried and probably broken; parental feelings often trampled on and disregarded. Food is often a major area of conflict between parent and teenager and it is important that as a parent you do not use food as a weapon in any conflict or become over-anxious about it. This can so easily create eating problems in the teenager.

As a parent you will have little control over what a teenager eats or when they eat it. But there are a few basic things you can do, such as making sure the whole family eats a good, healthy breakfast together. That way you can at least know that your child has had one good meal a day. If you are *really* worried about what they're eating, keep plenty of healthy and enticing snacks in the larder or refrigerator so that these places are tempting for them to raid.

However, in life, there are as many problems as there are human beings. What happens, for example, if the younger members of your already-established vegetarian family suddenly feel they want to be like other kids who eat hamburgers and sausages? There's not much a parent can do in situations like this, for rebellion is natural to the growing teenager, and in one sense, should be encouraged. The quicker and fiercer the rebellion, the quicker it will burn itself out. Vegetarian children quite often try out meat and poultry as they grow up and very often later return to the diet of their childhood.

Alternatively, you may recently have taken the decision to be vegetarian and your children resist. Again, there's not much you can do; teenagers, in their attempt to find their adult identity will almost certainly do the opposite to their parents. I, personally,

would always encourage this as I am concerned that the individual should have freedom to find his/herself. The important thing is for the parent always to offer a range of choices to teenagers so that they can choose for themselves.

Perhaps a more common situation today is one where the parents are not vegetarian, but one or more of their children is. A dedicated vegetarian teenager in a meat-eating household will tend to strike the hard-working mother as a daunting problem. The best ploy is to slowly introduce delicious new vegetable dishes to the family diet which will tempt everyone else. Thus, you can slowly widen the repertoire and give everybody more choice.

Another problem parents often have to face is the teenager with a sudden obsession about not eating meat which comes out of a commitment to some movement or political ideal, such as one of the Animal Rights groups that have recently gained in popularity. The danger with vegetarianism arrived at in this way is that it is usually extreme, with little or no thought given to nutritional balance. Parents in this position should never fight any of this but just be quietly watchful that, however extreme the ideas are when expressed in food, some kind of rough balance is kept. If teenagers try fasting, make sure they drink plenty of fluids and do not fast for longer than thirty-six hours.

All parents should be particularly watchful and concerned for two extremes: anorexia and exaggerated overweight.

Anorexia nervosa is a refusal to eat. Sufferers believe that however thin they are, they are still overweight. It happens among girls more than boys (90% of sufferers are female, though the incidence is growing now with boys) and is a psychological problem rooted in rebellion against the system, the family structure, or even society itself. Food is the weapon that is used. Sufferers will go to extremes to hide the obsession, eating or pretending to eat a little, then making themselves vomit afterwards. (Chronic eating and purging is actually called bulimia nervosa, and as the sufferer may not look especially thin, it is a difficult condition to spot.) As a parent you should be concerned at the sight of flagrant thinness and immediately get professional advice from your doctor or a self-help group for eating disorders. This condition is serious; sufferers have been known to starve to death.

The other problem is the exact opposite, over-eating. Plumpness sometimes occurs around puberty and it will go away in time. But most adolescent fat is caused by the consumption of too much food (often of the wrong sort) and too little exercise. Unfortunately, however sensibly a child has been brought up eating a healthy diet, once out in the world, at school and college, the temptation of convenience foods is huge. Try not to worry. A child who has a good nutritional grounding will often need to experiment with all kinds of food but will probably, in time, return to the sensible diet of the home.

Today, everyone thinks they are fat. We are all obsessed with weight and the idea of slimness, an obsession which is understandable as the media bombards us with messages that thin is beautiful and the only socially acceptable shape. Weight is a complicated issue. Many factors are involved, like individual metabolism and how much exercise we have. There is also the theory that, if you diet, the body automatically gives out less energy so the same weight is maintained.

However, if you are vegetarian and you are careful not to include large amounts of fats in your diet, you are unlikely to be overweight. It is only by eating more food than your body requires that you take in more calories than you use - thus leading to weight gain.

As 3,500 calories make up 450 g/1 lb of body weight, you need to cut them out over a period of 4-7 days in order to lose that amount of weight in a week. Aim always for a slow, gradual weight loss so cut, say, 500 calories per day. The easiest way is to reduce fat intake and cut alcohol out of your diet. Replace whole milk with skimmed milk and switch to low-fat cheeses and dressings. Cut out high fat foods like desserts, but do not cut out dairy products altogether, as they contain essential fatty acids, calcium, B_{12} and other minerals.

I believe that the key to achieving an ideal weight is to discover a new balance in your diet where you do not have to sacrifice food, you merely eat less of it and not so often and combine this with daily exercise. Your diet can still contain alcohol and dairy products, but instead of drinking a bottle of wine a day, drink only a glass.

When cutting down on your diet try to eat much more raw food and chew more slowly in order to extract maximum flavour and nutritional goodness.

Chilli beans ⑮ Ⓥ Ⓟ Ⓕ

As children become older, they become more adventurous in their tastes. This is a very good spicy dish, based on a Mexican original. Eat it with pitta bread or tortillas, and a crisp green salad (see page 137). Serves 4.

175 g/6 oz/1 cup dried red kidney beans,
pre-soaked (see page 51)
2 tablespoons olive oil
2 onions, chopped
5 garlic cloves, crushed
3 dried red chillies, broken up
2 red peppers, cored, seeded and chopped
1 can (400 g/14 oz) tomatoes
seasoning
2 tablespoons tomato purée/paste

Drain the beans, then bring to the boil in fresh water and boil fiercely for ten minutes. Throw away the water. Heat the olive oil. Add the onions, garlic, chillies and red peppers. Cook for a minute or two, then add the beans and tomatoes and cover with 2 cm/1 inch water. Simmer for 1 hour, then add the seasoning and tomato purée/paste. If the beans are too thick, add a drop more water.

Stir-fries ⑩ Ⓥ

These dishes are particularly popular with teenagers as they are fun to make and good to eat. Stir-frying also retains the maximum amount of nutrition in the food. Serves 2.

Variations

Substitute the carrots, broccoli and beansprouts with the following:
● *675 g/1½ lb trimmed French/snap beans. Blanch the beans (see page 53) then stir-fry for 2-3 minutes. Add 6 tablespoons dry sherry and 2 tablespoons soy sauce and cook for another minute.*
● *Thinly slice 225 g/8 oz tofu. Mix the ginger, soy sauce and rice wine together and marinate the tofu in it for 1 day. Roll the tofu in a little kuzu flour, then stir-fry until crisp. Use the marinade as a dipping sauce.*

1 tablespoon corn oil
4 garlic cloves, thinly sliced
15 g/½ oz root ginger, grated
2 baby carrots, julienned (see page 52)
2 broccoli stalks, peeled and julienned (see page 52)
1 tablespoon rice wine or dry sherry
2 tablespoons soy sauce
225 g/½ lb beansprouts, washed and drained

Heat the oil in a wok and briefly cook the garlic and ginger before adding the carrots and broccoli. Stir-fry until just softening, then add the remaining ingredients. Cook for another minute, then serve.

Kebabs

Kebabs are so quick and easy to make that even tired or impatient teenagers won't mind preparing them. Apart from the ingredients shown in the photograph, try a combination of smoked tofu, onion and mushrooms, or peppers, tomatoes and pumpkin. If you like, try marinating the tofu for an hour in lemon juice or flavoured vinegar.

*Ravenous teenagers, often impatient to eat,
will enjoy these tasty and healthy kebabs,
and might even be persuaded to make them as
they're so quick to put together. They're
served here with a simple diced tomato salad.*

Women

Women have to take special care of themselves during pregnancy and make sure they consume adequate levels of vitamins and minerals. Expectant mothers have expert nutritional advice available to them and vegetarian women are no longer frowned upon as being somehow irresponsible in their choice of diet. In fact, vegetarian expectant mothers have a plus factor in their diet. Folic acid is destroyed in cooking, so vegetarians who are more likely to eat raw foods, will be having plenty of it. Non-vegetarian mothers often lack folic acid and may suffer from anaemia. Vegetarian expectant mothers also eat more fibre. In addition, an interesting discovery is that vegetarian women who do not eat animal products have a higher proportion of polyunsaturated fat in their breast milk.

In the last six months of pregnancy, you will need more protein than in the earlier months (see page 25 for foods involving complete and complementary protein). If you are a vegan, one of the easiest and nicest protein foods to have daily is soya milk. Make sure you are eating plenty of foods rich in iron and calcium. Finally, check out your dietary needs with your doctor.

Soak up the sun (taking care not to get burnt) whenever you can, for vitamin D helps your body to use the calcium. If there is no sun, take cod liver oil daily and milk fortified with vitamin D.

Vitamin B_1 (thiamin) and B_{12} are other vitamins that you should take as supplements if you're vegan, although B_1 is found in grains, yeast extract, brazil nuts, peanuts and soya flour. B_{12} appears in tempeh and sea vegetables.

After your baby is born, continue with the diet described left, taking care to get the correct amounts of protein, calcium, iron, and vitamins D and B_{12}. But if you are on a well balanced, wholefood vegetarian diet, you should be in excellent health.

It is now believed that certain vitamin and mineral deficiencies in foods (most notably, vitamin B_6 and magnesium) may be in part responsible for PMT and PMS. Sufferers are advised by some associations to reduce consumption of foods high in sugar and salt, dairy products, tea and coffee, and to eat more fresh wholefoods. However, the relationship between diet and PMT/PMS is still unclear.

Like pregnant women, most people convalescing after an illness will be under the watchful eye of a doctor or have the benefit of a dietician's advice, but the most important point to remember is that, within their recommendations, you should eat and drink what you feel like. Do not be persuaded to consume something because someone has said it is good for you. Take liquid food which will slip down easily. Again, soya milk is marvellous as it can be strengthened with yeast powder and flavoured with carob, chocolate or fruit. But fresh milk shakes, if you like them, are good too. Once you can manage more, poached or coddled eggs on a fine bed of puréed potato or other vegetable, slips down a treat. You may even feel up to eating a baked potato with yoghurt and herb dressing.

But the invalid will know, and suggest, what he or she feels like eating. I am sure that, if we listen to our bodies, they are wiser than the self-conscious mind.

Walnut spread ⑤ Ⓥ Ⓕ

Rich in vitamin B₆, this spread can be eaten in sandwiches, on toast, or even as a pâté for a first course. Serves 4.

100 g/4 oz/1 cup crushed walnuts
50 g/2 oz miso
juice and zest of 1 lemon

Whiz the walnuts in a blender, then empty into a bowl with the rest of the ingredients. Mix to a paste and then transfer to a jar. Keep cool and use as needed.

Fondu ⑮ Ⓟ

This is a dish of melted cheese, traditionally eaten by scooping it up with cubes of bread or toast. The Swiss also drink hot tea while eating fondu as they maintain the hot liquid prevents the cheese coagulating in the stomach and becoming indigestible. This recipe makes 4 servings.

25 g/1 oz/2 tablespoons butter
25 g/1 oz/2 tablespoons flour
150 ml/5 fl oz/⅔ cup milk
150 ml/5 fl oz/⅔ cup single/light cream
seasoning to taste
175 g/6 oz/1½ cups Gruyère cheese, grated
100 g/4 oz/1 cup Cheddar cheese, grated
2 egg yolks

Make a sauce from the butter, flour and milk (see page 191). Add the cream, seasoning and cheeses. Stir until smooth. Remove from the heat and beat in the egg yolks. Eat while still hot.

Stir-fry broccoli and almonds ⑤ Ⓥ

This is a particularly valuable dish to eat during pregnancy as it is high in iron. Eat it with a pilaf or brown rice (see pages 170-173). Serves 2.

Variations

• *Add 100 g/4 oz beansprouts to the mixture.*

• *Blanch 675 g/1½ lb mange-tout/snow peas. Drain, then stir-fry for 2 minutes. Add 1 tablespoon soy sauce and cook for another half minute.*

450 g/1 lb broccoli
50 g/2 oz/½ cup flaked/slivered almonds, toasted (see page 56)
1 tablespoon corn oil
1 teaspoon sesame oil

Cut the broccoli florets from the stems. Peel the stems and slice finely. Heat both oils in a wok or frying pan and add the broccoli. Stir-fry for 2 minutes, then add the almonds. Fry for another minute.

Banana milkshake ③ Ⓟ

A natural source of goodness, being high in vitamin B₆. This is the perfect way to help build healthy teeth and bones. This recipe makes 2 servings.

1 ripe banana, peeled
225 ml/8 fl oz/1 cup soya milk
3 tablespoons plain yoghurt
1 teaspoon brewer's yeast powder

Chop the banana, then blend it with the milk and yoghurt to a smooth purée. Add the yeast and mix thoroughly.

Athletes

Most athletes will need to have extra protein in the diet for building up muscles in their training and for muscle repair when they are bruised or damaged (this will particularly apply to participants in 'contact' sports such as football and rugby). However, specific protein requirements should be discussed with the trainer or doctor for these will very much depend on the individual and the particular sport. Teenage athletes will automatically require more protein in their diet anyway.

It is misleading, however, to talk of protein as a thing apart. Although this is important, there should be more emphasis on consuming a larger amount of calories (or energy-producing foods) and it is best for the athlete to be having these in the form of unrefined carbohydrates, such as potatoes.

For athletes in training, protein *is* important and can be readily taken in the form of soya milk and soya products. Tofu is the most digestible of all foods and high quality soy sauce flavours it beautifully. Eat plenty of seeds - sunflower, linseed, sesame and pumpkin - and plenty of salads made up from sprouting seeds, alfalfa, lentils, mung beans, chick peas, lima beans and fenugreek. Stock up with cereal and grains, rice, barley, oats, millet and buckwheat to be eaten with cheese, eggs and fresh vegetables.

Many athletes suffer from pre-game nerves which can express themselves in forms of indigestion. It is best to eat a meal about three hours before the game and for that meal not to include any foods that are likely to make you feel uncomfortable - such as fatty, high-fibre or gassy foods.

Salsa romesco ⑩ Ⓥ Ⓕ

A piquant sauce that goes well with pasta or cauliflower. It can be used hot or cold and makes 2 servings.

300 ml/10 fl oz/1¼ cups olive oil
2 green peppers, cored, seeded and sliced
4 or 5 ripe tomatoes, peeled and chopped (see page 52)
3 garlic cloves, crushed
1 dried red chilli
20 hazelnuts, roasted (see page 56)
1 tablespoon wine vinegar
seasoning to taste

Heat the oil and cook the peppers, tomatoes and garlic with the chilli for 5 minutes. Grind the hazelnuts and add them to the sauce with the rest of the ingredients. Purée everything in a blender until smooth.

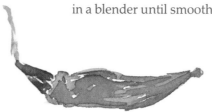

Carbohydrates are the new energy food for athletes - served here in the form of wholewheat pasta with Salsa romesco.

Millet, flageolet and chick pea pilaf ⑩ Ⓥ Ⓟ Ⓕ

A light and easily digestible dish that may be eaten hot or cold. Serves 4.

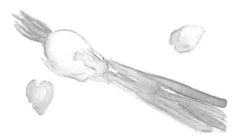

100 g/4 oz/½ cup millet, cooked (see page 50)
75 g/3 oz/½ cup chick peas, cooked (see page 51)
75 g/3 oz/½ cup flageolet beans, cooked (see page 51)
50g/2 oz/½ cup walnuts, broken and crushed
1 bunch spring onions/scallions, finely chopped
1 bunch watercress, finely chopped
2 tablespoons olive oil
juice and zest of 1 lemon
seasoning to taste

Mix all the ingredients together thoroughly. Eat cold with a crisp green salad.

Spinach and mushroom pâté ⑳ Ⓟ Ⓕ

Although it's now known that athletes require as much carbohydrate as protein, this protein-rich pâté will be very welcome as it is easily digestible. This recipe makes enough for 4.

450 g/1 lb spinach, washed
25 g/1 oz/2 tablespoons butter
100 g/¼ lb mushrooms, sliced
25 g/1 oz/2 tablespoons soya flour
2 eggs
seasoning to taste

Pre-heat the oven to 220°C/425°F/Gas mark 7. Cook the spinach with the butter and mushrooms in a covered pan for about 10 minutes, or until soft. Purée the mixture in a blender with the soya flour and eggs, then season. Pour into a buttered mould, place in a bain marie (see page 53) and bake for 30 minutes. Unmould while still warm.

Spring salad ⑩

You can win any race on this. The flavour of alfalfa is excellent, but sadly, often neglected. This recipe makes 4 servings.

4 celery stalks, chopped
5 tablespoons alfalfa
2 courgettes/zucchini, finely grated
1 bunch watercress, chopped
3 tablespoons plain yoghurt
lettuce leaves and watercress to garnish

Mix everything together thoroughly. Pile on to lettuce leaves and garnish with more sprigs of watercress.

The older vegetarian

As we get older, our energy requirements tend to decline. This is partly due to the fact that we shrink a little with age. But our consumption of food is directly related to our energy needs and whether we are still active or have become more sedentary. Unless a radical change has occurred, such as a grave illness or an accident, our dietary needs will stay basically unchanged.

But we should be circumspect over the amount of protein that is consumed. A diet which has too much protein when we are older can be harmful in that it places strain on the kidneys. It is also suspected that excess protein may be a factor in certain diseases such as osteoporosis.

Osteoporosis (porosity of the bones) is a common disease of old age, though it has in fact been known to begin as early as forty. The cause is not known, but is believed to be something to do with calcium deficiency. Calcium absorption tends to fall with age, so you may want to protect yourself by taking in more calcium in the form of skimmed milk, fortified soya milk and extra greens. Vitamin D aids calcium absorption, so make sure you are getting adequate supplies of this vitamin too - either from sunlight or from a supplement. In addition it is believed that vitamin D intake may well be a protection against another fairly common disease of old age, osteomalacia (softening of the bones).

Vegetarians tend to live long and have an excellent health record in old age. As always the message is to eat sensibly *for you*.

Steamed root vegetables ⑩

This is more interesting than it sounds, especially as it is topped with low-fat sour cream. It is an excellent source of vitamins and minerals, and makes 4 servings.

225 g/½ lb turnips
225 g/½ lb parsnips
225 g/½ lb celeriac
75 ml/3 fl oz/½ cup Smetana/low-fat sour cream
handful parsley, finely chopped

Scrub the vegetables and cut into 2-cm/1-inch chunks. Steam for 20 minutes. Mix the parsley with the Smetana/low fat sour cream, pour over the vegetables and serve.

Protein orange drink ⑤ P

This is an excellent pick-you-up if feeling tired or jaded. It is best drunk cold.

4 oranges
1 egg
1 tablespoon wheatgerm oil
1 tablespoon brewer's yeast

Squeeze the oranges and place the juice in a blender with the egg, oil and yeast. Blend thoroughly.

Menu-planning

Each day, when we choose what we eat, or plan the menus for the next few days, we perform a complicated balancing act between many demands, often of an opposing nature. Although we now have access to a wide range of imported foods which means we don't *have* to eat seasonally, it makes sense to choose the best fruit and vegetables on offer, and these will frequently be those growing locally.

However, we choose our meals for the day to refresh and sustain, and try to ensure they are nutritionally sound and appeal to our palate and our eye. It is short-sighted to underestimate the look of a dish. If we are put off by its appearance we are unlikely to taste it, and if we do, we will probably be prejudiced against it. Add to this the difficulty of catering for a family with perhaps a wide divergence of tastes, and the cook may be left quite bewildered.

As a general rule in meals of several dishes and courses, try to create a balance between raw and cooked, savoury and sweet, crunchy and soft, crisp and fluid. A cook will often do this automatically for it is the kind of mixture our bodies want, and consequently most of it will be nutritionally balanced too. If, in the course of a day we eat fresh fruit and vegetables, a grain dish (even if it is only wholewheat bread), and a dish made from dried legumes, we will be getting adequate nourishment, and can save cheese, eggs and other dairy products for a once- or twice-weekly indulgence.

In the winter, we need to eat a lot more carbohydrate to keep us warm, so it is wise to start the day with a good breakfast. Summer breakfasts are light to non-existent, and in my opinion, it would not hurt to fast for a whole day as long as plenty of liquids are taken (see page 14).

The winter and summer menu suggestions I give here (for a family of four) reflect these needs and eating patterns. I have planned the two weeks with a dinner party on Saturday night, a late brunch on Sunday morning, and supper in the evening. To be realistic, I have allowed for leftovers and the dishes one might make from them, for this food is so delicious that I'm sure the family will consume every crumb.

In planning these menus I have aimed for variety and ease; winter lunches consist of soups, and summer lunches consist of salads – but each one is different and they are simple to make, while being nutritionally sound. As most of us are busy and hardworking throughout the day, the main meal is often eaten in the evening. If you want a dessert I suggest you keep it simple; what could be better and healthier than fresh fruit? If you're still hungry, finish the meal with cheese – but I have not always suggested this if cheese has been used in one of the dishes.

The dinner party menus for Saturday, when we tend to have more time, are the most lavish meals, but the summer one is cold and can be prepared earlier in the day.

SUMMER	Breakfast	Lunch	Dinner
Monday	Fresh fruit juice Tea or coffee	Alfalfa sandwich made with wholewheat bread (*p.104*)	Eggs Florentine (*p.143*) Baked potatoes Fresh fruit
Tuesday	Honey and lemon drink	Green salad and cheese Wholewheat bread (*p.104*)	Cannelloni with mushrooms (*p.166*) Tomatoes with pesto (*p.120*) Skordalia (*p.188*) Fresh fruit
Wednesday	Yoghurt and honey Tea or coffee	Caesar salad (*p.118*) Wholewheat bread (*p.104*)	Gazpacho (*p.116*) Potato and mint tart (*p.177*) Broad beans in garlic (*p.132*) Fresh fruit
Thursday	Muesli (*p.97*) Tea or coffee	Greek salad (*p.122*) Wholewheat bread (*p.104*)	Chilled avocado and lemon soup (*p.116*) Italian pasta balls (*p.168*) Fresh garden peas Salsa romesco (*p.246*) Fresh fruit
Friday	Fresh fruit salad (*p.101*)	Tabbouleh and lettuce (*p.123*)	Fasoulia (*p.121*) Watercress and spring onion tart (*p.176*) Potato salad Fresh fruit
Saturday	High protein drink with fruit juice (*p.101*) Tea or coffee	Soupe au pistou (*p.117*)	*Dinner party menu* Chilled tomato and basil soup (*p.116*) served with Cheese brioche (*p.108*) Terrine verte (*p.163*) Salad Niçoise (*p.121*) Russian salad (*p.124*) Wild rice (cold) Cheese Glazed apple tart with Smetana (*p.204*)
Sunday	*Brunch* Gram flour crêpes with honey or fruit (*p.100*) Wholewheat muffins with herb butters (*pp.108 and 141*) Spanish omelette (*p.144*) Rosewater fruit salad (*p.205*) Buck's Fizz (Champagne and orange juice)		*Supper* Hummus and Tapenade with crudities (*pp.186 and 188*) Sweetcorn fritters (*p.137*) with Hot green tomato chutney and Gingered pickled onions (*pp.195 and 197*) Stuffed courgettes (*p.149*) Mixed green salad Potted cheese (*p.141*) Gooseberry fool (*p.205*)

	WINTER		
	Breakfast	**Lunch**	**Dinner**
Monday	Porridge with honey (*p.97*) Tea or coffee	Spinach and sage soup (*p.115*) Wholewheat bread (*p.104*) Slice of cheese	Cabbage and coriander pâté (*p.138*) Spinach quiche (*p.180*) Chicory gratin (*p.160*) Fresh fruit
Tuesday	Muesli with yoghurt (*pp.97 and 98*)	Onion soup (*p.113*) Wholewheat bread (*p.104*)	Celeriac remoulade (*p.124*) Tacos (*p.137*) Stuffed sweet potato (*p.150*) Cheese and fresh fruit
Wednesday	Porridge with dried fruit marinated in apple juice (*p.97*)	Garlic and potato soup (*p.112*) Wholewheat bread (*p.104*)	Sicilian orange salad (*p.120*) Cauliflower with tahini (*p.134*) Pakora (*p.136*) Cheese and fresh fruit
Thursday	Wholewheat toast with yeast extract or honey	Andalusian white bean soup (*p.114*) Wholewheat bread (*p.104*)	Greek salad (*p.122*) Okra, potato and ginger curry (*p.155*) Persian millet pilaf (*p.172*) Cheese and fresh fruit
Friday	Granola (*p.97*) High protein drink (*p.101*)	Curried cream of lentil soup (*p.114*) Wholewheat bread (*p.104*)	Avocado and quail's egg salad (*p.125*) Walnut and buckwheat croquettes (*p.167*) Parsnips in tomato sauce (*p.132*) Cheese and fresh fruit
Saturday	Toasted fruit loaf (*p.107*) Tea or coffee	Danish apple soup (*p.113*) Wholewheat bread (*p.104*)	*Dinner party menu* Walnut and cabbage moulds (*p.162*) Two artichoke pie (*p.182*) Gingered pumpkin (*p.135*) Buttered lettuce (*p.134*) Sprouted bean salad (*p.56*) Cheese Sussex pond pudding (*p.200*)
Sunday		*Brunch* Fresh fruit juice Corn muffins with apple jam or potted cheese (*pp.109 and 141*) Piperade (*p.144*) Wholewheat toast (*p.104*) Tea or coffee Black velvet (Champagne and Guinness/dark beer)	*Supper* Buckwheat pancakes stuffed with avocado, leek and feta (*pp.210 and 185*) Grilled mushrooms Baked apple with apricot purée (*p.201*)

Epilogue

'The time will come when men will look upon the murder of animals as they look upon the murder of men.' Leonardo da Vinci

If we can exist and enjoy life without the killing of other creatures, it seems unnecessarily inhumane to do so. Besides, the intensively factory-farmed animal leads a vile existence, often penned in a cramped stall unable to budge more than a few inches, existing on a rich protein and grain feed with added antibiotics and growth hormones which put on bulk but, because of lack of exercise, mostly as fat. If we indulge in the diet that this high-tech farming provides, not only do we connive in brutalizing the life of the animals, but we also harm our own bodies with a multiplicity of toxins.

I believe that good food - food that pleases the palate and the mind - should also be ethically good. What we place in our bodies should neither harm us, nor any other living creature of this planet on its journey from seed to table. Today there is a heightened ethical awareness of the inherent right to live of all creatures, a right which we must respect for our own good. This metaphysical view of the sacred nature of life has an ancient tradition manifest among nearly all our great philosophies and religions - from Plato and Socrates to Emerson, from Plutarch to Tolstoy, Emerson to Shaw, from Buddhist to Christian. Mahatma Gandhi best summed it up when he said, 'I do feel that spiritual progress does demand that at some stage we should cease to kill our fellow creatures for the satisfaction of our bodily wants.' There is, in my opinion, no reasoned argument which can stand up against such an attitude.

But the individual should take nothing on trust, not even the words above. Read up on the subject and look into your own feelings about life and animals. (Why is it that one can go 'Aah' over a picture of a child cuddling a lamb, and yet still like to eat lamb covered in mint sauce?) Explore your thoughts and your reactions over dry sow stalls, battery eggs, trout farms and slaughter houses. Consider how often the legal controls on 'humane' slaughtering are avoided, because the piece-work payment of the slaughtermen mounts up with the number of beasts killed so that they rarely get the legal eight seconds of electric stunning, but rather something like two or three seconds, leaving them conscious when the throat is cut. Is it true, as Dr Johnson said, 'that a man would rather kill a cow than not eat beef'? If you can eat the flesh of these dead animals, can you also face up to a visit to a slaughter house and view how it is done? If not, why not? And if we have progressed minimally in civilization since the eighteenth century, why is the size of the beast important? Why can some of us face shooting a pheasant, a hare or a deer, but not a cow? Why can we just about face eating the family's pet rabbit, but not the pet cat or dog?

All these shades of confusion upon the subject will be interpreted differently by each individual, and the conclusions we come to, and act upon, need not be final. We progress slowly, moving bit by bit. A final judgement spells out a closed mind. So let us be humane to ourselves as well as to every other living creature. Do not let us punish ourselves out of puritanical zeal, for in the concept of good food, there should also be sensual celebration. There is no need for ethically good food to be dull, bland and unappealing. There is every need for it to be the opposite - a feast of the mind and spirit, and of the infinite pleasures of the palate served with enormous elegance and style.

This book tells you, stage by stage, how, by changing the pattern of your dining table and the ingredients upon it, you can radically change your whole lifestyle and live with kindness, gentleness, health, and some semblance of consideration in this world.

Index

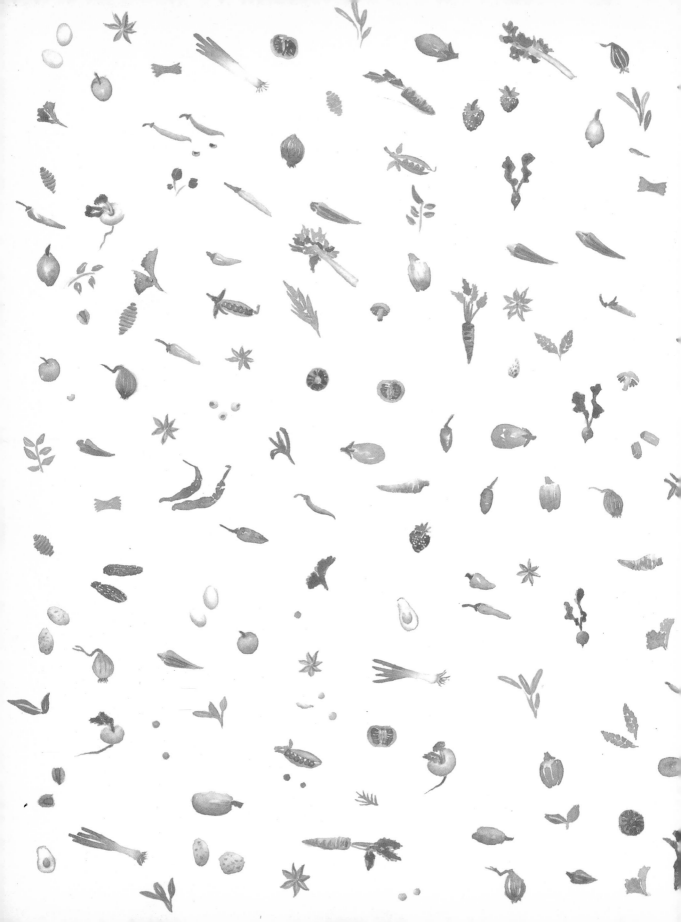